# BURNING DOWN THE HOUSE

## HOW GREED, DECEIT, AND BITTER REVENGE DESTROYED E. F. HUTTON

### James Sterngold

SUMMIT BOOKS

*New York    London    Toronto    Sydney    Tokyo    Singapore*

To Ellen

**Summit Books**
Simon & Schuster Building
Rockefeller Center
1230 Avenue of the Americas
New York, New York 10020

SUMMIT BOOKS and colophon are trademarks
of Simon & Schuster Inc.

Designed by Irving Perkins Associates
Manufactured in the United States of America

1   3   5   7   9   10   8   6   4   2

Library of Congress Cataloging in Publication Data

Sterngold, James.
Burning down the house : how greed, deceit, and bitter revenge
destroyed E. F. Hutton / James Sterngold.
p.   cm.
Includes index.
1. E. F. Hutton & Company—History.   2. Stockbrokers—United
States—History.   I. Title.
HG4928.5.S72   1990
364.1'63—dc20                                    90-43747
                                                  CIP

ISBN 0-671-70901-1

# ACKNOWLEDGMENTS

The destruction of E. F. Hutton left a remarkably bitter legacy of damaged egos and costly litigation. People were still exchanging venomous accusations years after the events took place. In trying to find my way in and then out of this captivating thicket of claims and counterclaims, I made what turned out to be a crucial decision: to obtain written records whenever possible. I pressed Hutton's former executives, brokers, customers, and consultants for every document they had to substantiate their stories. The response was a flood of confidential memos, financial reports, videotapes, legal papers, and consultants' analyses. It was an invaluable trove. The documents provided insights into both specific events and the fundamental veracity of my sources; they became a kind of touchstone. I want to begin by thanking these people for sharing the records and explaining their significance. They provided a remarkably vivid road map inside the unusual corporate mind of E.F. Hutton.

The hundreds of hours of personal interviews I conducted

were still essential for understanding the hows and whys of the Hutton drama. Only a handful refused to speak, and in many instances people agreed to meet on condition that they not be identified. But nearly all were generous with their time, in particular the key combatants, Robert M. Fomon and Robert P. Rittereiser. I enjoyed the additional benefit of having interviewed many of Hutton's key executives over a period of years. I also witnessed personally some of the unsettling conflicts. I want to thank the more than 100 people who shared their recollections, theories, emotions, and even their lies. They were all useful.

Of necessity, there remained a subjective element in reconstructing the events and conversations. I sought consensus where possible, returning to sources repeatedly to hammer out their differences. When they still disagreed, I relied on the documents, or sources whose veracity had been borne out in other instances. I decided early on, however, that it was the author's job not just to produce a mosaic of opinions, but to render judgments and state them. In a few instances I noted strong dissenting voices. I used peoples' own words, or drew on composite accounts of dialogue, tested against my knowledge of the way people spoke and acted. I also attributed motives, generally at the invitation of the people involved, to provide some understanding of why Hutton was robbed of its life.

The ultimate aim was to tell a story that reflected the real culture of Wall Street. This should not, in other words, be read as the tale of just one firm. The press's intensive focus on million-dollar investment bankers doing billion-dollar deals that characterized the 1980s, while entertaining, obscured many of the more commonplace excesses of this unusual industry. Big deals are not the everyday stuff of the brokerage industry. The kinds of events reported in this book are.

Many, many people helped in the task of writing this book, offering myriad forms of direct and indirect support. I do not want to save the most important one for last, however, and thus want to begin by thanking Ellen Rudolph, who offered unyielding affection, intelligence, and wit. She was a sharp editor, a relentless foe of the superfluous and hazy, and a source of laughter, a tonic that got me through many difficult days. She has always been a great wife and companion. Most of all, her clear-sighted sense of values was essential to this book—a story, after all, about the values by which people choose to live.

The editors at *The New York Times,* especially John Lee and Fred Andrews, were supportive and generous in providing me the time to complete the manuscript and in allowing me to do the initial exploring that made this book possible. John Motyka, from the *Times*'s Sunday Business Section, did a superlative job in editing the article in January 1988 that began this project. Greg Robb and Donna Anderson of the *Times* were, as ever, generous and cheerful in helping me research documents and articles.

James Silberman, editor in chief of Summit Books, and Dominick Anfuso, senior editor, may not appreciate how much their uncommon professionalism meant. I am grateful to them for their open minds. I also want to thank Dominick for his solid editing, good humor, and endless stream of ideas. Ileene Smith of Summit Books was, in her inimitable fashion, hopeful and tough-minded. She was a thoughtful and sobering critic and a good friend. My agent, Reid Boates, was an excellent editor and demonstrated persistence and patience in educating a publishing novice.

Not least, my friends were enormously supportive. They were ready to listen, encouraging, and a constant source of warmth during this process. To the Bellport crowd, my dining, traveling, fishing, and tennis companions, deepest thanks. I also want to express an especially warm acknowledgment of the support and trust of my family, where, after all, values begin: to my parents, Henry and Levona Sterngold, my sister, Nancy, and my brothers, Arthur and Paul.

At the Harvard Business School, Samuel L. Hayes III and Alfred D. Chandler, Jr., were helpful in explaining Wall Street history. I wish to thank Jane Steiner for her able research into Hutton's tax shelters. Rory Rothman generously provided important psychological insights. I also found a number of books and studies important during my research. Two amateur histories of E.F. Hutton, by early partners, provided helpful first-hand accounts of Edward F. Hutton. They were written by Theodore Lauer, who was present at the Western Union meeting in 1904, and Donald K. Phillips. Among the more helpful books I read were: *Heiress: The Rich Life of Marjorie Merriweather Post,* by William Wright; *Poor*

*Little Rich Girl: The Life and Legend of Barbara Hutton,* by C. David Heymann; *N.Y.S.E.: A History of the New York Stock Exchange 1935–1975,* by Robert Sobel; *The Go-Go Years,* by John Brooks; and *The Last Days of the Club,* by Chris Welles.

James Sterngold
Tokyo
July, 1990

# CONTENTS

# PREFACE

## THE MYTH OF WALL STREET AND THE MYTH OF E. F. HUTTON

Shortly after I began working on this book, I was contacted by a former E. F. Hutton broker who said he had some very important information but could not discuss it with me over the telephone. We arranged to meet a few days later.

He was a balding, friendly-looking man in a gray business suit and Brooks Brothers tie. After some nervous small talk, he began to relax and slowly got to the point. With his head tilted slightly to the side and both hands on the table, he looked straight at me and asked rhetorically: "How much do you think you know about Hutton's commodities department?" I said I was aware the department had a reputation for flouting the rules and then waited for his story. He shook his head at my ignorance and explained that the department had engaged in wide-scale money laundering, handling large amounts of cash from tax dodgers and organized crime figures to help them conceal its origin. This was not free-lancing by a couple of opportunists, he added. The criminal behavior was central to the division's operation. "You don't know who you're dealing with here," he said. "You have no idea what was going on at that place."

When I encouraged him to continue, his soft sell ended: How much was I willing to pay for the story? he asked. It was an awkward moment. I explained I could not buy information but probed for some alternative arrangement under which he might be willing to cooperate. He quickly lost interest. After a few more minutes, the fervor with which he had dangled out this enticing story cooled. Our meeting was coming to a close.

I sat there wondering how many more of these calls I'd be getting, when something even more unexpected, and revealing, happened. An emotional dam seemed to burst inside my would-be source, and the kindly man in the gray suit began to unleash a furious diatribe against the corrupted senior E. F. Hutton executives he felt had stolen the firm away from good people like himself.

The whole point, he argued, was that the 6,600-strong broker force *was* Hutton; they, not the top executives, were the engine behind this amazing money machine. The New York headquarters was made up of a bunch of hangers-on who handled the advertising and provided bookkeeping and other chores, in his view. The glory of E. F. Hutton, the secret to its aura were the 6,600 self-interested brokers—widely known as Wall Street's elite, the most productive sales force in the business—who were supposed to go out and broker anything they could—stocks, bonds, mortgages, tax shelters, even, I thought, allegations of felonies against their former colleagues. New York's job was to stay out of the way and make sure the paperwork got done. The real failure at Hutton, as he explained it, was that these headquarters minions came to believe it was their firm and used it for their own ends, destroying it. When we finally parted, I was left feeling slightly confused by his ambivalence and the vehement note on which he had closed. This soft-spoken, seemingly cautious man wanted me to see the unequaled greatness he was convinced Hutton had once achieved yet could not restrain his compulsion to bare the blackness in its soul. Hutton—and, one might add, Wall Street—had been great as long as it served him and then was deserving of its infamy when he felt it had failed him.

In various guises, that was an experience I would undergo repeatedly over the next year, through hundreds of interviews with people at every level of E. F. Hutton. Not once did I hear that the firm existed for its shareholders or its customers; it existed to serve the interests of whomever it was I was talking to. And that could only be done, they all maintained, by fighting off jealous rivals within the firm. No one spoke of competing with Merrill Lynch or Shearson Lehman—that was the easy part, almost a sideline. The real battles were over who would claim this juicy firm and all that went with it for themselves.

What these encounters continually demonstrated was that, underneath the complex financial mess that E. F. Hutton became, the collapse was a personal and ultimately, a moral affair. It was about the real Wall Street—not great takeover battles, but the everyday battles where individuals destroyed anyone in the way of their greed and ambition. In an odd way, the harshness of these conflicts was that much more sinister because it was on such a modest, human scale, not the high-wire of investment banking.

Of course, heightening the intensity of the Hutton drama was the time in which it was played out. Wall Street has never occupied so prominent a place in the public consciousness as it did during the 1980s. In spite of the wild financial ups and downs of those years, it would be wrong to call it a roller-coaster era, for as far as the level of intensity went on Wall Street, it was hell-for-leather from beginning to end. Never had so much money been made so easily, and nobody wanted to miss out on their share. Regulators cheered from the sidelines, while the public fed the fires of personal ambition with its unquenchable desire to be amazed by bigger deals and bigger fees. The media played an essential role, serving up a titillating series of larger-than-life demons and heroes to furnish the growing mythology. The press breathlessly handed Wall Street one of the few things its money could not buy: public recognition.

But one of the great ironies of Wall Street in the 1980s was that the industry that so vigorously demonstrated the impermanence of corporations also persuaded America that securities firms formed the permanent foundations of something called "the financial system." Wall Street argued that businesses were bundles of "assets" producing "cash flow." It only meant the markets were operating efficiently if those assets got reshuffled constantly through buyouts and takeovers. Preserving and nurturing the financial markets thus seemed more important than looking after the interests of the businesses being broken and remade. The press, accepting this notion, constantly probed for companies that were deemed to be mismanaged, top-heavy, or inefficient and thus deserving of some financial reengineering. Meanwhile, the suddenly huge securities houses that ran the chop shops, helped finance these deals, or peddled dreams of buyout wealth to the public went largely unexamined. None of the "discipline of the market" to which corporate America was subjected was meted out to securities houses. It was a blind spot for which many of Hutton's customers, employees, and shareholders would pay dearly.

In fact, no brokerage house took better advantage of that environment than E. F. Hutton—and particularly its shrewd chairman, Bob Fomon. Under Fomon's quirky leadership, Hutton became America's most well regarded brokerage house—largely through television advertisements, not conquests in the corporate takeover wars, innovations such as junk bonds, or deft investments. The compellingly arrogant line, "When E. F. Hutton talks, people listen," made all those other attributes unnecessary. Wall Street's aura of corporate solidity gave Hutton a sense of weightiness that could not be destroyed by any individual. So it seemed.

# HOSTAGE TO THE PAST

Pride and the quiet satisfaction of being proven right after years of frustration gave a spirited lift to Bob Rittereiser's loose gait in the cool morning air. A beefy man of slightly above average height with a round, friendly face, he walked across the dewy driveway of his Franklin Lakes, New Jersey, home and ducked into the waiting car, exchanging a cheerful greeting with the driver.

Ritt, as everyone knew him, peered at his watch; the car had arrived precisely on schedule, to the minute: 6:00 A.M. It was perfect—almost, Ritt thought to himself, too perfect: chauffeurs jumped for him; thousands of careers hung on his decisions; his salary had crossed that magic barrier, a million dollars a year. It was a lot to digest for a hardworking guy who grew up on the streets of Manhattan, the son of a truck driver. But Ritt caught himself, halting that painfully familiar sliver of self-doubt from intruding into this otherwise joyful morning. All of these trappings, he assured himself, were the sorts of things the president of E. F. Hutton & Company, a bastion of country club elegance and thoroughbred pride, ought to expect—even if it was only his second week on the job.

It was Friday, July 12, 1985, three golden days before Ritt's forty-seventh birthday. More important, it was two months since E. F. Hutton had scandalized Wall Street by pleading guilty to an astounding two thousand felony counts for defrauding its banks of several million dollars. Hutton had always been known as an arrogant firm that liked to make its own rules, but the contrast between its taut, patrician image and the blatant crookedness of the crime, a massive check kiting operation, was jarring. For decades a powerful mythology had surrounded Hutton as the home of Wall Street's shrewdest and classiest professionals. When Hutton talked people listened—the advertising line had been so successful because, to millions of investors, and the brokers at Hutton, it had seemed a simple statement of fact. That made it difficult for many to accept that the firm would try and pull off such a sleazy scam.

Of course, Ritt had an even better reason for persuading himself that, as Bob Fomon, the brokerage house's legendary chairman, had put it, the crime had been an aberration blown out of proportion by overzealous prosecutors. That old warhorse had had the sense to recruit Ritt to restore Hutton's good name. Fomon had made Ritt's lifelong dream come true; it was no time to doubt him.

Anyway, Ritt had been on Wall Street long enough to know that all brokerage houses played games with their bank accounts. If Hutton had gone just a little over the line, Ritt told himself, it only underscored the good news, that its brokers were more aggressive than their rivals. Give the eager bunch a leader with vision and a strong moral compass, Ritt believed, and you had the makings of a great firm. Where the prosecutors saw fraud, Ritt spotted opportunity. With that, Ritt had shaken hands with Fomon a few weeks earlier, taking over Hutton's presidency—without a contract or formal mandate from its board, just warm assurances from Fomon that he would have a free hand to work his magic.

As the dark gray Lincoln accelerated down his street in the hazy morning light, past the huge, gaudy new homes with their treeless lawns and diagonal wood siding or oversize columns— ready-made imitations of "old money"—the driver began reciting the stock trading results from Tokyo and London. It was just the sort of thing an important Wall Street executive needed to know. Ritt felt great.

Being a senior executive was itself nothing new to Ritt, who had been recruited from Merrill Lynch and Company. He was a down-to-earth man with an easy manner, whose broad black eyebrows worked their way like a hedgerow across his round, fleshy face. His salt-and-pepper hair was neatly held down with ointment, not brushed straight back in investment bankers' style, but with a small ledge across his broad forehead. Tiny flecks of dandruff tumbled to the shoulders of his expensive Paul Stuart suits.

Until a few months earlier, Ritt had been an executive vice-president at Merrill, the country's largest brokerage house and Hutton's keenest rival. He had, in fact, been in a three-man race for the firm's presidency. But it was a race he was clearly going to lose, a blow for this intensely competitive man. Losing did not bother him so much as the underlying message—for all his years of unstinting work, Ritt was regarded as a manager who could step in hastily and run a division or put out a fire, but who did not have the stuff to run the whole firm. He knew many of his colleagues found him likable but long-winded and limited. Those perceptions ate at him, burning deeper and deeper over the years, leaving a harsh residue. Finally he had fallen out of love with Merrill, the firm that had given him his first job.

Then came the seductive moment: Bob Fomon had asked him to breathe new life into the once great and now ailing Hutton. It was the ideal realization of his self-image as a tough, principled executive with a knack for taming the evil forces around him. In an important footnote to his Catholic upbringing, Ritt and his two brothers all intended to become cops; one actually did. Even after Ritt left an FBI training program for Merrill, he never lost sight of that mission. It took the Hutton presidency to bring him back to the boyhood ambition—not just of righting wrong, but of being seen putting the world in order.

On this July morning Ritt was traveling to the airport, where he would catch the shuttle to Washington for his first trip as Hutton's president. Breathing the incomparably fine oxygen of success, he turned first, as usual, to *The New York Times* sports pages, his great passion, then on to his beloved theater news. Casually he then flipped open *The Wall Street Journal*. He stopped cold after reading just a few paragraphs.

Bam! Instantly, like a jet's fuselage being ripped open, all the sweetness was sucked from the air. Ritt was in emotional free-fall as he pushed aside the poisonous newspaper article. His composure knocked askew, he reached over and rapped the driver on the shoulder, ordering the car to Manhattan, to Hutton's headquarters.

BATTERED BROKER: E. F. HUTTON APPEARS HEADED FOR LONG SIEGE IN BANK-DRAFT SCHEME, was the headline on the front-page article. E. F. Hutton was being held up not just as a national symbol of white-collar greed, but as a corporation with a dizzying array of problems that would clearly get worse before they got better.

There was something much worse in the article, though. Not only did the *Journal* question Fomon's credibility, which was already tattered—the article also suggested that Ritt was not up to the job of turning this sick brokerage house around. It was like telling a cop proudly directing traffic at the scene of an accident that he had no business being there. Ritt had been prepared for weeks if not months of negative publicity when he joined the firm. But he had never envisioned himself becoming the subject of such doubts, too. They were too much like the old doubts he thought he had left behind. A sickeningly familiar feeling began working its way over him: he was not a leader building this great brokerage house's bright future—he was a fireman again, bailing out someone else.

As his car probed the thickening early morning traffic for tiny openings, heading into the shadowy canyons of Wall Street, Ritt realized that the future he dreamed of shaping would be hostage to the past, his own and Hutton's.

Bob Fomon, a hard-drinking bachelor who carried a haughty air of authority and a haze of cigarette smoke everywhere with him, showed up, as usual, just after nine-thirty—leaving Ritt to wait and stew for more than two hours. Ritt strode into Fomon's office soon after the short, paunchy chairman, dapper in his European-cut, double-breasted suit, Bulgari watch, and short-kempt, paper-dry gray hair, limped in on his black-and-silver cane.

"What are you doing here?" Fomon said, a surprising curtness in his scratchy, small voice. The voice was one of Fomon's odder qualities, shrinking up when he'd been drinking, which was often, into almost a Truman Capote–like drawl. "I thought you had a meeting in Washington," Fomon added.

"Bob, I couldn't go to Washington when I read what was going on. Look, I'm just not sure we know what we're doing. We have to revisit our whole strategy and figure out what we're doing. Whatever we're doing now, it isn't working."

Ritt continued, long-winded as usual, rising to deliver what he considered an immutable truth. "Bob, there's no question there have been some permanent changes here. We can't just go back to business as usual. There are a lot of things that I'm going to have to change to reposition us."

Fomon, a laconic man with a wide, sensuous mouth, fine, chiseled nose, and broad forehead, looked thoroughly unenthusiastic. He stood silently for a moment as his secretary brought in his usual breakfast tray and set it on the nearly empty round table that served as his desk: four isosceles triangles of dry white-bread toast, a small crystal bowl of grape jam, and a cup of black coffee. The newspapers were set out, and Fomon read the headline and few paragraphs that had jolted Rittereiser.

Fomon's small, close-set eyes narrowed as he squinted through the smoke of a Winston and considered the unwelcome intrusion on his light morning schedule. He did not like being confronted. He did not like open bull sessions for resolving problems or coming up with strategies, and he most certainly did not like being told, even obliquely, that his public relations skills had failed. And goddamn it, Ritt or no Ritt, this was his firm; he did not like being told what he had to do.

Repositioning, Fomon thought, was this guy's code for "I need more control."

But there was, in fact, an edge of nervousness to the icy CEO exterior. Ritt had unwittingly found the chink in Fomon's seemingly impervious armor. More than anyone else at the firm, Fomon defined himself through Hutton and his position as its imperial overseer. He worried in his darker moments what else there was to the small man behind the small voice who had built his life around the elite Hutton image. For years now he had successfully concealed Hutton's shocking decline from the outside, and even from many inside the firm. Acknowledging that the firm needed more than a little fine-tuning, which Ritt was proposing, was an admission that in his fifteen years of iron-fisted rule Fomon had run Hutton onto the rocks. He immediately interpreted this as a challenge to his power, not as an attempt to get him focused on Hutton's real problems. The morning's message was not in the newspaper, Fomon thought, but in Ritt's reaction to it.

Ritt went on, tipping Fomon off to the dirty little corporate secrets he had been discovering. These were far more than the usual array of skeletons all large corporations have hidden in their closets; they were, taken together, unmistakable signs of a near collapse in management discipline.

• Within a week of the plea agreement in May, Ritt had been shocked to learn, Hutton had secretly suffered a potentially devastating liquidity crisis, a sure sign of the firm's fundamentally shaky financial foundation because of weak management.
• Because of an incredible series of blunders, Hutton was about to lose $50 million to a hotshot commodities trader in Houston—a year's worth of earnings for the firm up in smoke because of sheer management stupidity, if not corruption.
• A Hutton mortgage operation in Arkansas had turned sour in a ridiculously transparent scam that would cost Hutton more than $50 million in losses.

That was what two weeks' worth of getting acquainted with the firm had told Ritt. Other juicy tidbits lay in store, like the municipal bond fiasco that would cost more than $50 million, losses of more than $70 million from the sale of ill-conceived tax shelter investments, huge costs associated with the new headquarters building under construction, and personal use of corporate assets.

Hutton, like other retail brokerage houses catering to the small investor, had been protected for decades by a thick patina of myths about its supposed skills. Now it was all unraveling; just about every part of the firm was in deep, deep trouble. Ritt's excitement over the new job and eagerness to see Hutton as the answer to his dreams had made him happy to accept Fomon's previous assurances that each of these problems was isolated. This morning the bleak tone of the article and the self-questioning it forced on Ritt had sobered him. He did not need more information to get the full picture. There were no shades of gray, no extenuating circumstances. The level of malfeasance was blatant and massive. The great Hutton was a hoax kept alive by slick advertising, a public awed by Wall Street, lax regulators—and a wily chairman adept at manipulating images and people. Ritt felt Fomon had little choice but to listen to his new president, because Ritt was the key to saving the firm.

That was when Fomon did something Ritt had never seen before. His gray complexion slightly paler than usual, the chairman helped himself up with a little difficulty, paced a few times in silence, and limped out of the room.

Ritt stood with his hands in his pockets for a moment, at first confused, then felt the heat rise under his collar as he realized the meeting had just ended.

Had Ritt still harbored any doubts about the depth of the problems he faced, they were extinguished three days later, on his birthday. At a Manhattan hotel conference room that Monday afternoon, Ritt witnessed a full-scale rebellion by Hutton's brokers. In an incendiary two-hour session, Hutton's top brokers, branch managers, and regional executives—even some directors from the Hutton board—unleashed fusillade after fusillade of criticism over the way Hutton, and the scandal, were being managed.

At the moment the assault was about to reach its climax, when the brokers were going to demand Fomon's head, Fomon raised his scratchy voice, deftly turning the throng's ire toward one of his aides, a man despised by the brokers. With the rabble momentarily distracted, Fomon, pacing around the rim of the room, paced right out.

Ritt managed to take over the tumultuous meeting, and in a desperate bid to quell the storm, he offered some of the key brokers seats on Hutton's board so their voices would be heard. The shouts of insurrection quieted, but the savvier brokers realized that, with his well-timed exit, Fomon, not Ritt, had masterfully asserted control.

Now Ritt, too, was beginning to understand. Despite the seriousness of Hutton's problems and what many believed was the obvious softening of Fomon's mind due to alcohol and a stroke, his brinkmanship in the power game was uncanny. Fomon did not disappear to avoid confrontations; he fled to control them. This was not executive decision-making as described in the earnest management dot-to-dot manuals Ritt subscribed to. This was Wall Street in the raw. All of the supposed rules of organizational behavior were meaningless here.

The next morning Fomon summoned his new president and demanded to know why he had offered the brokers seats on the board, his board.

"That's not your fucking board to give away," Fomon snapped.

After a brief honeymoon, the gauntlet had been thrown down. The two men, slightly flushed as the tension built, had squared off. Each had fundamental decisions to make that would affect, perhaps dramatically, the courses of their lives. The fate of one of American capitalism's best-known success stories rested on two personal decisions, made in a sunny corner office overlooking the windblown swells of New York harbor.

Fomon had to decide what was more important, his personal prerogatives or E. F. Hutton & Company. In a huge miscalculation, Fomon believed he had hired a president who would miss the fact that the old chairman had laid waste to Hutton. Ritt had been hired not so much for his strengths, but for what Fomon took to be his blindness to the chairman's real agenda; Fomon wanted Ritt to tidy up the mess so that he could sell Hutton, cash in his chips, and be remembered as the firm's last chairman. Nobody would be permitted to succeed him. The ultimate expression of his power would be removing the throne. Anyone foolish enough to believe in saving the firm, and inheriting the throne, became Fomon's enemy.

Standing on the orange-and-blue Persian rug in the chairman's leafy aerie, near the small framed sign that read, "I am not asking you, I'm telling you," facing Fomon's spiteful anger, Ritt also had to choose. Right then and there. He couldn't launch into one of his recitations heavy with management buzz words or ask for more time to plan. The only way to demonstrate that Ritt had, indeed, overcome his gnawing personal doubts would have been to demand that he be given a free hand to institute radical reforms—or resign immediately. It would take an enormously self-confident man to issue that ultimatum. It would mean putting at risk the chance for which Ritt had waited a lifetime. But if Ritt's ability to change Hutton was left uncertain and he stayed anyway, he would be tarred by its inevitable collapse. He would become a victim of his own weakness.

The two men faced each other and the things they feared most. And then, in a moment, the battle was decided: Ritt made no demands. He tried to explain, to seek understanding. Fomon turned slowly, shuffled soundlessly toward the door, and left Ritt alone in the office.

# 2

## MARRYING WELL

The myth of E. F. Hutton & Company was born on April Fools' Day 1904.

Edward Francis Hutton, a short, wiry, dapper twenty-eight-year-old with a narrow face, longish nose, and burning ambition to reach the upper strata of society, gamely chose that spring day to open for business in an industry that barely existed, retail stock brokerage. Ed Hutton's personal and business backgrounds were not much more promising than his choice of starting dates. He had performed without distinction in two previous brokerage enterprises, known then as commission houses, and he did not hail from the kind of family that immediately linked him with a network of wealth. But the clever parvenu had devised a means to overcome those obstacles. He married well.

The Hutton family's origins were comfortable, but nowhere near the station to which Hutton, known as Ned or Ed, aspired. His father, James Laws Hutton, had left his family's farm in rural Ohio at age sixteen to seek a business career in New York. Edward was born in 1876, at 59 West Twenty-second Street in Manhattan. He

attended Public School 69 on West Fifty-fourth Street and ended
his education at Packer's Business College.

Edward Hutton moved to Wall Street quickly afterward, taking and losing two low-level jobs as a clerk at a mortgage company
and a trust company, which only whetted his entrepreneurial interests. In rapid succession he formed two tiny brokerage concerns
near the turn of the century, both of which held seats on what was
called the Consolidated Stock Exchange, a feisty competitor to the
New York Stock Exchange that dealt in odd lots, or small numbers
of shares. It was a suborder in the Wall Street hierarchy, easy to join
and distinguished by the fact that it was devoted principally to
smaller investors.

That was when Hutton created his first major break. He sought
the hand of Blanche Horton, the daughter of the wealthy Harry L.
Horton, proprietor of H. L. Horton & Company, a member of the
prestigious New York Stock Exchange.

There was, from her family's point of view, a problem. Harry
Horton objected to his daughter marrying a member of the inferior
Consolidated Exchange. But that was precisely the point: Hutton
had no intention of wallowing in this realm. He aimed to climb out
of the lower depths of the financial world and into the upstairs club,
with his father-in-law's aid. In short order Ed Hutton sold his Consolidated Exchange membership and won Miss Horton's hand, as
well as her father's blessing and financial backing. The couple married in 1902 and honeymooned in California.

Timing was on his side. The financial system was going
through an extraordinary period of ferment and growth that was
creating enormous new opportunities for brokers.

A second industrial revolution was under way, helped along by
a tremendous takeover boom. Around the turn of the century,
industrial enterprises, which had formerly been limited by modest-
size factories and mills and small distribution systems, began combining into corporations with nationwide reach. One advantage of
their new size was that they could achieve much greater economies
of scale. And their larger financial resources gave them the means to
make even greater investments to expand and improve their tech-
nology. Unlike the original industrial revolution, however, which
was led by industrial entrepreneurs, this upheaval was engineered
by men who controlled capital. It was a critical difference.

With the buffalo gone, the prairie dug up and planted, and the nation unified by railroad and telegraph lines, finance had become the new American frontier. Juggernauts such as U.S. Steel, Standard Oil, du Pont, National Biscuit, American Car & Foundry, and Borden's Condensed Milk were built through strings of mergers— under the aegis of Wall Street.

From 1895 to 1904 more than three thousand industrial companies were swallowed up. In 1899 alone there were $2.27 billion worth of takeovers and mergers, a huge number in those days. In 1897, when the takeover trend was just gaining momentum, there were eight industrial companies with market capitalizations of $50 million or more—a considerable valuation. In 1905 there were forty such companies.

The powerful financiers in New York were acting as matchmakers for these growing corporations and were financing the combinations through the stock market. The market was evolving into a center of economic power, speculation, and public fascination as the papers filled with news of the latest takeovers. High-rolling speculators such as Jesse Livermore and "Bet a Million" Gates became popular figures. The floor of the New York Stock Exchange was being transformed, like the baseball diamond, into a venue for a major national pastime.

Still, finding a niche in this bustling world was not easy, as Ed Hutton had already learned. Dominating Wall Street in those days were the towering figures of J. P. Morgan, architect of innumerable industrial powerhouses, including U. S. Steel; James Stillman, financier to the Rockefellers and chairman of the National City Bank, who helped build and then held directorships in more than fifty industrial and financial corporations; and the taciturn George F. Baker, known as the "Sphinx of Wall Street," a founder of the First National Bank of New York and creator of a railroad and insurance company empire.

These three men and others close to them created what came to be known as the Money Trust, a tentaclelike network that tied America's industrial and economic fortunes inextricably to Wall Street and the stock market. The wealth and influence condensed in those few hands was awesome, a fact that both frightened and tantalized the public.

One of the keys to Ed Hutton's success was that he seemed to recognize his limits. It was never his idea to engage in the substantive dealings of the financial power structure. Clearly he had neither the acumen nor the connections to compete with a Morgan, a Baker, or a Stillman. Hutton's brokerage house would not make or break companies; it would, instead, ride the coattails of those who did. Smaller investors who wanted to speculate on the machinations of the powerful empire builders needed to buy access to the exclusive stock exchange club. That would be E. F. Hutton & Company's targeted market. And Ed Hutton understood that what those investors often looked for was an image of savviness and wealth. Money sold money.

Hutton set off on his honeymoon with more than romance in mind. California, he found, while filling up with new wealth, had poor electronic links to the New York securities markets, since messages were sent across the nation by telegraph. California brokerage houses communicated with New York through a cumbersome relay system, from San Francisco to Denver to Chicago to New York. Since the securities orders and stock quotes were not the highest priorities on the wires, delays were common. It could take hours to get stock price information, order the purchase or sale of some stock in New York, and then receive a confirmation of the transaction back in California.

In a business where split-second timing can mean the difference between a profit and a loss, that was a crucial disadvantage. Hutton resolved to provide a swifter cross-continental service.

Immediately on his return he shared his idea with a friend, George A. E. Ellis, Jr. Just as Hutton selected his bride well, he chose his confidant with care; Ellis's father ran Ellis & Company, a prominent Wall Street bond house. He had another compelling credential: he was married to the heiress Florence Adams, daughter of the founder of the Adams Chicle Company, the prosperous chewing gum manufacturer.

Ellis visited California himself, was impressed, and announced that he would join the new venture. Two of Edward Hutton's brothers, William D. and Franklyn L., also became partners. Franklyn, in fact, would soon provide another important element for success. Bettering George Ellis, he married Edna Woolworth, the second daughter of F. W. Woolworth, founder of the five-and-dime empire and head of one of the wealthiest families in America. Just as speculators hoped that a propitious stock pick would win them the kind of fortune it might otherwise take a lifetime to assemble, the Hutton brothers had found a surefire way to charm their way into social rank and status through one matrimonial pick.

On October 12, 1903, the partners wrote a one-sentence letter addressed to "New York Stock Exch.":

"We beg to notify you that we have this day formed a copartnership under the firm name of E. F. Hutton & Company." After a six-month process of preparations and setting up correspondent relationships with other firms, the doors opened for business.

Ed Hutton quickly turned his attention to California and the technological problem of communicating between the coasts. Initially E. F. Hutton transacted its West Coast business through Logan and Bryan, a Chicago-based commodities trading house with telegraph connections. But Hutton's firm still suffered nagging delays. Seeking a solution, Ed Hutton made an appointment to meet the president of Western Union. It was to become a key moment in the young firm's lore.

Hutton said he was interested in leasing a private line to California. He was told, however, that wires were only available as far as Denver. The Western Union president added that his firm would not absorb the costs of stringing another wire for an unproven brokerage concern. The cocky young promoter did not hesitate. Ed Hutton asked one of his clerks to draw up a $50,000 check to finance construction of the line. It was a theatrical but impressive maneuver. The next day Hutton was told that Western Union would build the link. It was a business coup.

In December 1904 E. F. Hutton moved into quarters at the corner of Bush and Montgomery streets in San Francisco. Hutton opened its Los Angeles office at Fifth and Spring streets in 1909, and in the following years it added branches in Hollywood, Santa Monica, San Diego, and Los Angeles' Ambassador Hotel.

A natural disaster provided another opportunity for the scrappy young firm to establish its reliability to the moneyed set and add another chapter to the growing legend. On April 18, 1906, at 5:13 A.M., the great San Francisco earthquake leveled most of the city. According to the legend, Richard Mulcahy, manager of Hutton's San Francisco operations, arrived at his office to find the building in ruins. He started to sift through the rubble when, as the story goes, he found his books intact.

The resourceful Mulcahy rescued the account records, hired a fishing boat, and made his way across the San Francisco Bay to Oakland's Western Union office. Within twenty-four hours Hutton's clients were transacting their business again, ahead of many other firms. Whether myth or fact, the wealthy felt they had a friend in E. F. Hutton.

As the stock market began its first long rally in the mid-1920s, E. F. Hutton was ready to ride the crest. It opened seasonal offices in Palm Beach, Miami, and at resorts in California to follow the sun and its wealthy clientele. The offices at the Breakers and Royal Poinciana hotels in Palm Beach and at the Miami office at the Royal Palm Hotel were opened only January 1 to April 15, "the season." The office in the fashionable summer resort of Saratoga, New York, was open August 1 to September 1.

By 1924 the partnership had sixteen year-round branch offices—and all but two were in California. E. F. Hutton was evolving in a strangely decentralized fashion. The New York headquarters was not a profit source of any consequence. It serviced stock orders and kept the records. The firm's profits came from its far-flung branch offices.

But it was a remarkably successful formula. E. F. Hutton seemed to have ascended to an elite plane. It was small but had developed a special aura because of its top-drawer clientele. The brokerage business was decidedly uncomplicated in those days. A firm's principal asset was its seat on the stock exchange. Commission rates on stock trades were fixed at a high level, all but guaranteeing profits to firms that could generate a steady flow of orders. There were no options or futures or other complicated investment products. As long as Hutton could continue to attract business from its well-to-do customers, its profits would rise.

Socially the Huttons were also establishing themselves as among the more visible members of America's class of "super-rich," which added even more cachet to the firm.

Franklyn, remembered as an unpleasant man who would

eventually succumb to cirrhosis of the liver, had become notorious for his philandering and appeared regularly in gossip columns. When his wife, Edna, was found dead in a suite at the Plaza Hotel on May 2, 1917, reportedly from a severe ear infection, it was rumored that she had committed suicide because of Franklyn's refusal to break off an affair with a Swedish actress.

During the Roaring Twenties Ed Hutton would also plant his dandified image firmly in the American psyche. He was an energetic, lusty man, a heavy drinker and a snob, a "little bantam rooster," in the words of Robert Wigley, later an E. F. Hutton vice-chairman. Few saw Ed Hutton as much more than a lightweight with a powerful attachment to the good life. *Time* magazine described him as "an aggressive, dapper hustler." But that never seemed to hurt his brokerage house.

In 1918 Hutton's first wife, Blanche, had died of pneumonia. Two years later he outdid his first matrimonial success, and perhaps even Franklyn's, by marrying Marjorie Merriweather Post in one of the great social mergers of the time.

The alliance was to the daughter of Charles W. Post, an entrepreneur who built a vast fortune by capitalizing on a health-food craze and manufacturing Postum, a caffeine-free coffee substitute, and a breakfast cereal called Grape Nuts. Marrying into that kind of wealth rocketed Ed Hutton into a new social orbit. He became a limited partner in his brokerage firm and assumed the chairmanship of his father-in-law's business, the Postum Cereal Company. The position was titular rather than substantive. It was also not a great loss for E. F. Hutton & Company. Hutton never was, nor did he pretend to be, much of a manager.

E. F. Hutton won some of Postum's lucrative securities business, helping take Postum public in the mid-1920s, when it was going through a series of mergers from which it would emerge in 1929 as the General Foods Corporation. But for the most part E. F. Hutton & Company benefited just from an association with one of the most spectacular and visible life-styles of excess in the country.

Edward and Marjorie Hutton threw splashy parties at a three-floor, seventy-room Fifth Avenue apartment that included an indoor swimming pool, ballroom, gymnasium, bakery, and solarium. They spent winters at a 123-room Palm Beach mansion, Mar-a-Lago, one of the most sumptuous homes in America. Parked in the mansion's driveway was a fleet of Chryslers—Ed Hutton sat on the Chrysler board—one for the use of each guest. Their 350-foot, four-masted yacht, *Huzzar V*—later renamed *Sea Cloud*—was reputed to be the largest private sailing yacht in the world.

But for all its promise, the Hutton-Post union foundered when Ed Hutton's lusty impulses became unharnessed. Marjorie Hutton is said to have found Edward in bed with one of the maids at Mar-a-Lago, merely the most blatant of his trysts. He also began an affair with another woman who would later become his third wife. Finally Marjorie Hutton divorced Edward in 1935, for infidelity. Their only daughter, Nedenia, or just Dina, would later change her last name, when she became an actress, to Merrill—the name of E. F. Hutton & Company's keenest rival.

The firm that had withstood the San Francisco earthquake came through the Great Depression in better shape than most of its rivals, with an unbroken string of profitable years. One of its best clients in those years was J. Paul Getty, who provided a much-needed flow of commission revenue from his stock dealings. E. F. Hutton went to great lengths to finance Getty's stock-buying forays in the oil patch. Later, as a gesture of thanks, Getty would lend his image to the firm for a much publicized television advertisement, in which he praised his old friends for their fine service.

Once he had become a limited partner, Ed Hutton tried to fashion an image as a political thinker, but he met with considerably less success than he had in the business and social realms. He became an unabashed champion of the wealthy and their ways and fought against what he saw as government's antibusiness bias.

In one much-publicized and embarrassing incident, in November 1935 Hutton wrote an essay from his plantation in South Carolina encouraging industrialists to "gang up" on the Democratic-dominated Congress, form a single, powerful lobby, and fight President Franklin Roosevelt's interventionist economic policies in the utilities industry. General Foods, with which he was still associated at that time, immediately disavowed the position. And Ed Hutton soon recanted. But he continued to battle for many classic conservative causes, such as adding the words *under God* to the Pledge of Allegiance. In 1949 he financed the Freedoms Foundation to, as he wrote at the time, "block this avalanche of socialism in this country."

For all its success in simpler days, the postwar years were

tougher for Ed Hutton's brokerage house. The firm that had been the second most profitable on Wall Street in the early years of the Great Depression lapsed during the 1950s into complacency. The company was just not keeping up well with much faster paced markets. E. F. Hutton's partners were content to take their commissions out of the firm and put little back. The substance behind the Hutton facade, still highly prestigious, had eroded along with the firm's profits; Hutton barely broke even in 1961 and 1962. The partnership seemed to have run out of steam.

Ed Hutton himself died at the age of eighty-six in 1962. In his last years he kept an office at his old brokerage firm on lower Broadway but was removed from its affairs. He showed up most days impeccably clad in a double-breasted blue suit, his hair regally grayed. No one seemed to have ever recalled seeing him without a suit coat, as though Ed Hutton needed to look the part of an eminence even when none could see him.

Lunch at his club played the central role in his routine, his partners recalled. At all costs he hated waiting, along with everyone else, before beating his midday retreat. So, every day at noon, he would walk to the freight elevator for a prearranged rendezvous. Hutton would tap on the heavy metal doors twice with his Zippo cigarette lighter, and the operator would arrive. Alone, Ed Hutton would disappear.

CHAPTER

# 3

---

# AN INSECURE KING

Sir James Frazer opened his classic study of mythology, *The Golden Bough,* with the tale of a pagan king who ruled a land along Lake Nemi, near Rome. Frazer described the king as a grim silhouette, prowling at all hours with his sword drawn, lying in wait for would-be usurpers.

In this violent land, one took the throne only by murdering the incumbent, hence the king's constant vigil. The ruler was himself a murderer who was bound someday to suffer the same fate as his predecessor. A usurper had to prove himself, though, before he could mount a challenge; he had to steal a sprig from a golden bough in the tree the king was guarding. Once the test had been passed, the contest would begin, propelling the cycle of insecurity toward its violent, if temporary, conclusion.

By the time Ed Hutton died, the politics at his brokerage house had more in common with that ancient kingdom than a modern corporation. Companies are always battlegrounds, as executives vie for influence and power; and on Wall Street, where there are fewer bureaucratic impediments to raw displays of ego, rough personal clashes are the norm. But something different had been allowed to happen at E. F. Hutton. A destructive political dynamic was shaping the firm. The resolutions of Hutton's power struggles merely created a tense pattern of insecurities around the throne. It was a warped system that warped those at the top of it, a legacy E. F. Hutton would never shake.

The whispers of the coming clash started in 1960. Ruloff E. Cutten, the firm's managing partner, the equivalent of a chief executive, had ruled for twenty-two years. But his health was declining, and it was clear the throne would soon be up for grabs.

Increasingly absent from the office, Cutten left the running of Hutton to an ambitious younger partner, Sylvan C. Coleman. That seemed to give Coleman an edge in the jostling for succession. But when it came time to anoint a new managing partner, Cutten shunned Coleman and turned instead to Theodore Weicker, Jr. Coleman, however, was not about to give up so easily. The battle lines were drawn for the full partners' meeting, where a deciding vote would be taken.

Weicker was a wealthy, socially prominent man who had left Hutton some years earlier for a slot at a family-controlled company, the Squibb pharmaceutical concern. Cutten brought him back because he seemed to possess the right credentials—he was cut in a patrician mold, had experience, and his father, Theodore Weicker, Sr., had married into a great fortune.

More lay behind Cutten's choice, though. He consciously aimed to thwart Coleman, a pushy, bright, abrasive executive. With his lack of humor, irritating paranoia, and impatience, Coleman had not endeared himself with several of Hutton's senior partners. There was more: despite his efforts to conceal the fact, Coleman had been born a Jew.

Coleman recognized what a problem that could be in a business that, at the time, was ethnically segregated. After he graduated from the Harvard Business School in 1928, as Sylvan Cohn, he had adopted not just a Waspy new name but had become something of an anti-Semite; Coleman enforced a quota on the number of Jews he would hire for the research division he ran in New York, several former Hutton partners recalled, and was given to anti-

Semitic cracks. But that was not enough. Hutton was not a Jewish firm, and Cutten wanted to keep it that way. Having a few Jewish partners was one thing, having a Jew as the firm's leader was something else entirely.

Nonetheless, Weicker presented worse problems to a number of partners. First of all, he had no connection with the powerful West Coast contingent, which still held the biggest bloc of votes. In addition, Weicker was a gentleman businessman. At one time that might have been sufficient, but Wall Street was entering a booming era at a time when Hutton was, behind its still prestigious image, ailing financially. Weicker, in the view of many, seemed more interested in trips to Europe and his social activities than in working hard to restore the firm.

By contrast, Coleman had made his name building Hutton's stock research capabilities and its business with institutions, such as the Boston-based mutual fund companies. Coleman was also from the West Coast. He grew up in San Francisco and attended the University of California at Los Angeles before heading east.

Although its influence would be profound, the contest was brief. After a series of secret caucuses, the two dozen partners met in New York behind closed doors. Plotting in advance, Coleman had received the blessing of a group of senior partners. Weicker was conspicuously locked out of the partners' meeting, while a majority of his erstwhile colleagues voted against him. (So embarrassed were Hutton's internal historians that they ignored the succession battle in their official histories.)

Before long Coleman realized that he had achieved a curiously incomplete victory. It was the regional partners who held the real power, and in Coleman's coup, they had exercised it openly for the first time. E. F. Hutton had developed as a loosely knit confederation of regional powers. The regional vice-presidents operated like barons, lording over their domains much as they saw fit. By a sort of unwritten agreement, they looked to New York for services, such as the execution of trades on the floor of the stock exchange, and products, like new offerings of stock.

The barons paid what amounted to a "tax," in the form of part of the commissions that their brokers generated, for the right to wave the Hutton banner in their areas and for the other services New York provided. Hutton's cohesiveness thus depended on New

York's ability to keep the E. F. Hutton name well burnished. That was the source of the king's legitimacy. It was E. F. Hutton's glue.

Coleman was constantly looking over his shoulder for plotters, whom he imagined everywhere. Although he was regarded as intensely bright and good at his business, he was obsessed with keeping his chief lieutenants off guard, pitting them against each other in vicious and often useless contests. One top partner recalled Coleman's filching a memorandum and studying it for signs of disloyalty. Tom Lynch, a top financial executive, said Coleman constantly harangued him about what he thought was tampering with his personal accounts.

"Sylvan was not in a position to dictate in that firm," said one old partner involved in the coup. "It was a matter of playing games, not ruling by edict. He never had that kind of power."


Coleman focused quickly on E. F. Hutton's glaring weaknesses. Hutton was limping into what would later be dubbed the "go-go years," a wild era of speculative excess—just the sort of thing brokerage houses love. The Dow Jones Industrial Average would climb smartly, stock market trading volume would soar, the conglomerate-building craze would take hold in a hectic wave of corporate acquisitions. But Hutton still did business as it had for decades, cultivating rich customers through country club connections and executing their stock orders for a fee.

There were a range of new developments Hutton had missed. Investment banking—the business of underwriting securities for corporations and arranging corporate mergers and acquisitions—had enjoyed a burst of activity, while Hutton had almost no presence. Other retail firms had been expanding by hiring aggressive young brokers to chase newly wealthy and younger clients, while Hutton remained smaller and stuck with its older clientele. There was a lot of ground Hutton had to make up.

On the retail side, Coleman's smartest move was to permit a bright young broker, Arthur Goldberg, to create a new training program. A methodical, efficient, exacting administrator, Goldberg set up a branch staffed entirely by trainees that became the source for a steady flow of young talent. As was the case with most things at Hutton, it also made a political statement. The program produced a corps of brokers whose allegiance, for the first time, was primarily to New York rather than a regional fiefdom—a fact that won Goldberg few friends out west.

In another critical move, Coleman made Goldberg head of advertising. Goldberg recognized that E. F. Hutton's elite image was, in effect, an underutilized asset. Somehow the firm had to figure out how to mass-market its aura. With his prodding Hutton took the then revolutionary step of becoming the first Wall Street firm to undertake massive television advertising. (Another firm, Edwards & Hanley, had been first to use television but had not organized the kind of major campaigns Hutton, and eventually others, would.) The new advertising push was a smashing success. The Hutton mythology had entered the national arena.

Goldberg's training program also cultivated the next generation of managers. The most gifted trainee was a nervous and shy but enormously energetic young man with strawberry-blond hair named George L. Ball. Ball, an obsessive achiever, became Goldberg's protégé, following one step behind him up Hutton's retail hierarchy. Ball would also learn an important lesson from his mentor. Goldberg inspired with his intelligence, but not his charm, of which he possessed little. Ball saw that running a sales machine required a more outgoing, easy personality. He forced himself to change, developing a Dale Carnegie–like facility for motivating brokers with ebullient backslapping. He also learned quickly that nothing motivated a broker like money, and he saw rich financial inducements as a key to boosting sales.

In 1963 Coleman took his next important step, recruiting John S. R. Shad from Shearson, Hammill & Company, a second-tier brokerage concern, to build an investment banking department. In addition to trying to launch Hutton into this increasingly lucrative field, Coleman had a clear political motive: the move furthered New York's development into a profit center in its own right. It was one subtle way to loosen the grip that the regional barons had over him.

Shad, a man with a toothsome smile, a long, jowly face, and a gravelly voice, was a meticulous, hardworking investment banker who loved the nuts and bolts of corporate finance. He could be irritatingly pedantic. He was also arrogant and condescending toward those he considered inferior, which was most everyone. Shad was a weak administrator and cared little for the chores of running a department. But he loved doing deals. Although he turned some off with his impatience, he developed a small but loyal coterie that admired his drive and technical skills.

One of Shad's first tasks was to head to the Harvard Business School, from which he had graduated, to begin what would become an annual recruiting ritual. Shad was demanding of the applicants but, in that first year, found a young man whose hunger to succeed matched his own. He was a self-made former Harvard boxing champion named Frederick H. Joseph, whose short stature was easily outweighed by his ego and self-confidence.

Joseph grew up in a poor, working-class Jewish family in Boston. He had developed a zealous attachment to his self-image as a scrappy underdog and had fought his way up in the world. Now he was eager to do so again on Wall Street. He was bright and had an irrepressible desire to excel, to show those supposedly better just who was superior. Before long he became Shad's right hand.

Shad made another shrewd decision. It did not take him long to realize that an investment banking newcomer like Hutton stood little chance competing directly against the industry's heavyweights, such as Merrill Lynch, Morgan Stanley, and First Boston. The top firms made up what was known as "the bulge bracket," and between them they had a lock on most of the business of America's Fortune 500 companies.

Shad devised a second approach to the business that, he hoped, would bring in revenues quicker and produce strong long-term prospects. He would seek out smaller companies. The idea was to nurture these clients, helping them grow until they became powerful corporations. Since there was less competition in this area, Hutton could also charge higher fees.

The securities issued by these smaller corporations would have low credit ratings—later known in Wall Street argot as "junk" securities. As the name implied, it was not regarded as a terribly distinguished business, but Shad foresaw the potential of the neglected niche. He was willing to forsake prestige for profits. His lieutenant, Fred Joseph, embraced the strategy enthusiastically.


Although Coleman's steps helped, a powerful stock market rally did much more to revive Hutton's fortunes. The go-go years were a wonderful time to be in the brokerage business—not just because the market was booming, but because the media was developing a fascination for Wall Street. Mutual fund managers, such as Gerry Tsai, became overnight stars. Conglomerate builders, like Harold Geneen at ITT, were regarded as geniuses by many business reporters. The bull rally lifted Hutton out of its early 1960s doldrums. The firm's profits rose steadily from less than $1 million in 1962 to $9.3 million in 1967.

It was, in short, a business orgy in which Wall Street threw all caution to the wind. And then the inevitable happened. In 1968 the brokerage business was crippled by, of all things, a surfeit of business. Firms were choking on stock orders.

The Big Board experienced its first twenty-million share day on April 10, 1968. On June 13 a new record of 21.35 million shares was set. With commission rates fixed by the cartellike stock exchange, every additional share traded generated higher revenues.

The problem was that brokerage houses were ill equipped to deal with such volume. None were willing to turn away business, but their ability to process all those trades was collapsing. It was the most severe crisis Wall Street had faced since the crash in 1929.

The accounting for stock trades was still handled manually in those days. For every trade the selling customer had to deliver his stock certificate to his broker. That broker had to deliver the certificate to the buyer's broker. And then the certificate had to be assigned to the correct account. The payment for the purchase passed in the opposite direction. Much of this to-ing and fro-ing was recorded by hand, by a poorly paid and badly trained workforce.

Under the strain of record volume, numerous stock certificates failed to find their way along the chain during 1968, resulting in what were called "fails." The fails generally became the responsibility of the brokers involved. After a short while many prominent Wall Street firms were close to seeing their capital wiped out by the mounting tally of fails on which they would have to make good. The sums were mind-boggling. The total value of fails among Big Board members rocketed to $2.67 billion in April 1968, $3.47 billion in May, and $4.12 billion in December. That was easily more than the combined capital of all the New York Stock Exchange's member firms. The system was technically insolvent.

Like everyone else, E. F. Hutton was swamped. In July the value of its fails peaked at a level that, had the rules been applied, should have shut the firm down. It had failed to receive $61.6 million in stock for its customers' accounts, for which it was responsible. And it had failed to deliver $54.6 million in securities on behalf of its customers. The sum of its potential liabilities dwarfed its total equity capital at the time, less than $30 million. Hutton was one of the worst offenders on Wall Street. Its situation was critical.

During the crisis, the New York Stock Exchange and the Securities and Exchange Commission responded gingerly. Rules were ignored as the exchange sought to give its members time to dig themselves out from under the avalanche of paper.

At Hutton the problem was slowly cleaned up over the next year, but the mess had delivered a severe blow to the firm. Hutton's business was slipping, and morale among its brokers, confused by the depth of the problem, which they felt had nothing to do with them, was declining badly.

After the fact, the stock exchange instituted sanctions against only the worst offenders, whose recklessness could have caused their customers tens of millions of dollars in losses. Still, Hutton received a mere slap on the wrist. On August 26, 1969, Hutton was fined $10,000 and censured, a decidedly modest penalty given the risks it had created for its customers.

The fine was the least of Hutton's problems. The firm's earnings slipped to $7.3 million in 1968 and $1.3 million in 1969. Hutton scraped by with a $1 million profit in 1970, but that was done with smoke and mirrors. The firm that always boasted it had never suffered a losing year was, for the second time in a decade, on the ropes.

What might lie in store for any house unable to get its problems under control became clear when, for the first time, a major firm found itself teetering on the edge of chaos in 1970. Goodbody and Company, at the time the country's fifth-largest retail brokerage house, could not be extricated from its back office tangle and started to break down.

Wall Street, fearful that a failure of so large a firm might panic other brokerage house customers, secretly closed ranks. There was widespread fear that, if Goodbody collapsed, a devastating chain reaction would be set off. Wall Street's credibility with the public would be destroyed, and unquestionably, Congress would step in to impose heavy new regulation. After several weeks of intensive meetings, a special New York Stock Exchange crisis committee persuaded Merrill Lynch, Pierce, Fenner & Smith, the industry's largest house, to acquire Goodbody. The exchange's other members had to promise Merrill millions in aid to cover up Goodbody's losses.

Merrill turned to a thirty-two-year-old junior executive who had worked his way up Merrill's own back office to take control of the situation. It was a job that required not charisma, but steadiness and an understanding of thousands of mind-numbing details on how stock-processing systems worked. Their choice was a kid from the streets of New York with a powerful streak of loyalty and a willingness to put in long hours—Robert P. Rittereiser. Rittereiser's chief ally was a young accountant, Edward J. Lill. Working through the crisis together, the two would develop a lasting bond.

For Hutton, the crisis undermined what had been one of its greatest assets, self-confidence. A number of older Hutton partners, who were substantial shareholders in the firm, lost heart and sought to withdraw their capital. About $12 million to $15 million of Hutton's total capital of $60 million was threatening to walk out the door. Adding to the growing instability, another succession battle was looming. Coleman turned sixty-five, the mandatory retirement age, in 1970. The cycle of insecurity was about to play itself out again.

# 4

## THE DOUBLE
## DOUBLE CROSS

Bob Fomon watched impatiently as the room service waiter laid out breakfast in the sun-filled suite, already smoky after an hour of conversation. Then, with singular intensity, he focused again on John Shad, seated across from him in the cheerful room at the posh Boca Raton Hotel & Club, for the most important conversation of Fomon's career.

The Investment Banker Association's annual convention at Boca Raton happened to fall in mid-December every year, just as New York grew wintry, so it pulled in an appreciative and relaxed crowd. But Fomon, a driven executive, hated golf and had no time for lying in the sun. For the third morning in a row he was working at Shad, his means for entering Hutton's succession fray.

It was late 1969, and Fomon, forty-five, was head of corporate finance for E. F. Hutton on the West Coast. The title was overblown, since Hutton was a corporate finance lightweight on either coast, in spite of Shad's efforts, and Fomon was neither a particularly adept investment banker nor a skillful manager. But the designation had considerable meaning within his firm; it recognized that Fomon was a favorite with the West Coast powers, who had concocted the special position for a special salesman.

Fomon, in fact, possessed a remarkable knack for ingratiating himself with important people and letting them advance his interests. As a successful retail broker in Los Angeles earlier in his career, he had demonstrated little in the way of investment acumen; his genius was in selling himself to the country club set, which eagerly handed him their business. In many ways he was emulating Ed Hutton himself, relying heavily on image to win customers. Ed Hutton married well, and Bob Fomon befriended well.

Now, as a troubled E. F. Hutton entered a critical transition at the end of 1969, Fomon turned his powers of persuasion on Shad. He had no clear-cut plan for taking advantage of the situation, but he sensed an opening. If only he could get Shad to grab for the golden bough first and thus blow open the succession process.

"John, who else is there?" Fomon insisted at Boca Raton. "I can tell you, the West Coast would back you. I can promise the coast's votes. The firm needs you."

A key problem with the transition was that the incumbent, Sylvan Coleman, fought being deposed as mightily as that unhappy king at Lake Nemi. Being torn loose from Hutton was a kind of death for a man who had made such a large emotional investment in the firm. In public he professed fidelity to the mandatory retirement rule. In private, however, he began maneuvering in a last-ditch effort to stay on.

Technically the unloved old chairman could keep his job only if Hutton's partners voted an exception to the retirement rule, and that seemed unlikely; although many respected Coleman, the firm had clearly run out of steam under his rule, as demonstrated by its back office problems and threats by some partners to leave. But Coleman knew that if he could thwart a consensus developing on a successor, the door just might remain open.

Step one was undermining his hand-picked heir apparent, Keith S. Wellin. Although Coleman had named Wellin president three years earlier, Coleman now bad-mouthed him at every chance. And Coleman found a receptive audience in Hutton's senior ranks. Although handsome, able, rich, and outgoing, Wellin was regarded as too weak for the top job. He had performed well as a broker and a branch manager in Chicago, but under his presidency Hutton had struggled. Whether that was bad timing or a legitimate criticism, Coleman and some others held Wellin responsible.

Coleman and the others also resented how heavily Wellin relied on Arthur Goldberg. It was impossible to ask Wellin a question without being told, "Let me talk to Arthur and I'll get back to you." This dependence made Wellin look weak. It also made Goldberg appear a shoo-in for the presidency. For many partners that was unthinkable, even with the administrative skills Goldberg had demonstrated.

Coleman led the anti-Goldberg forces with spiteful vigor, systematically attacking him and just about everything he did before the other partners. Coleman had been personally angered by a series of small disputes with Golderg over retail sales policy and other matters. But most saw those squabbles as a smoke screen: Goldberg was Jewish, and that, once again, was the nub of the issue.

Some partners still felt a Jew was inappropriate as the leader of a brokerage house with the pedigree of E. F. Hutton & Company. Coleman, at least, had changed his name and adopted a visibly anti-Semitic bias. But what can you say about a guy named Goldberg?

For his part, Fomon had no ties or influence with Wellin and felt he could only lose if Wellin came to power. But Fomon could never make a run at the top job himself. He was still too young and too little known outside California. If the battle turned into a free-for-all, that would be a different matter. Shad was the key.

Getting to know Robert Michael Fomon was like reading an auto-biographical play by an author worried his audience might find him too subtle. He worked hard at the legend of Bob Fomon. A prominent investment banker recalled meeting him for the first time at a beachside cocktail party at Santa Barbara in the early 1960s. He was stunned to see Fomon, in a tuxedo and carrying a drink, stroll into the sea and take a swim. Others recalled the "cemetery story," in which Fomon delighted in loudly telling of the girlfriend he obliged when she pleaded to have sex in a grave-yard—after tying her up with dry-cleaning bags. In an interview with a fashion magazine he described women as objects of decoration better seen than heard, and he told a newspaper reporter that he preferred the company of models in their twenties—generally introduced to him by his son—because older women "had been around the block once or twice too many times." That was the Fomon touch.

He kept parrots and grew lovely flowers, signs that there was a soft side to his earthy machismo. He constantly wrecked his cars because of his heavy drinking, then showed up fresh at work in the morning—Fomon was immune from hangovers—laughing about the latest crash and insisting that he did not drive well because his mind was always on loftier subjects, like sex or closing a deal.

Fomon scripted his story with care to demonstrate that he was not bound by the standards that governed the merely common. Social conventions were props in his art, opportunities to shock; for instance, he loved telling the story of how he slept with a close friend's girl behind the friend's back, and then how the two men just laughed when Fomon was discovered. So much the better if his audiences were horrified. Fomon mastered the art of the outrageous, and he never lost his touch.

That style stood out in high relief on Wall Street. Although investment bankers are driven by whale-size egos and fight like terriers to be seen as uniquely fascinating personalities, they are also self-conscious about trying to project an image of professionalism. They are inhibited about their public behavior, and thus many envied the way Fomon could get away with the things they only dreamed of doing. Outwardly Fomon could make a show of good taste when necessary. But he loved the statement of defiance made by his antics and loved even more getting away with them.

Fomon had a provincial and rigorously religious upbringing that, he constantly told friends, scarred him for life. In short, it became another prop for him.

Fomon's mother died of cancer when he—the youngest of three boys—was just four. His father, a physician, used the opportunity to take his three sons from their home in Chicago and turn them over to his wife's sister, Marie Sherman, a spinster living in Appleton, Wisconsin. Her life revolved around the Catholic church, located a block away.

Fomon's father, Samuel, had been a brilliant medical student but was restless as a physician, shifting back and forth between a practice and teaching prep courses for the medical licensing exams. But his real love was plastic surgery, an interesting choice for a doctor described by his sons as a highly self-centered man who spent a lifetime hiding behind a thin facade of gregariousness. His specialty: remaking noses.

He was, his sons recalled, ruthlessly snobbish and insensitive. When the second son, also named Sam, went into medicine and specialized in pediatrics rather than surgery, his father reacted disdainfully. "My father thought that the only thing to be was a surgeon," Sam Fomon recalled. "He once told me, and I'll never forget it, that it would be raining quarters outside and all I'd get was nickels. He was trying to humiliate me."

He visited his sons twice a year—Christmas and summer vacation—and occasionally missed one trip. When he did show up he often argued with the boys' aunt over her expenditures.

"You could say he was an interesting person," Sam Fomon said of his father. "He was certainly not lovable, particularly in his family, and he was quite penurious. I was in high school before I realized that I had been rejected by my father. Once you realize that you've been rejected, you could deal with it. I analyzed it carefully."

Bob Fomon would remain disturbed for years by that gap in his life and would never let go of his bitter grudge against his father. "He was a mean bastard," Bob Fomon said. "I could have killed him at times. I was the only one who stood up to him."

In fact, Bob Fomon made a point of standing up to authority figures. He was thrown out of one Catholic high school, in Prairie du Chien, Wisconsin, for his pranks. Just before graduation he was tossed from a second high school. When his father insisted that he attend college in the East, somewhere near his brother, Sam, at Harvard, he signed up at the University of Southern California in Los Angeles.

Fomon dallied in a variety of subjects before ending up a fine arts major. He graduated, undistinguished, in 1947, then stayed on as a graduate student, still aimless, bouncing from one program to another. Finally, told by his father to take some practical steps toward a career, he enrolled at the USC law school. It took Fomon less than a year to lose interest in that, too. Finally, in 1951, he was informed he had to get a job.

If Fomon did not seem to have accomplished much in school, he had achieved something important in his personal life. He had found the first in a series of emotional replacements for his absent father. He developed a tight bond with George Davidson, an Episcopal priest in Los Angeles and an old family friend. Fomon had lived with the Davidsons for several years and adopted them as a surrogate family.

When Fomon was forced to hunt for a job, the relationship proved even more important. He had decided to try the brokerage business, partly because of what he found to be the attractive image of the stockbroker: moneyed, independent, and possessing a powerful secret—how to make money. Like his father, he took money to be the measure of a man, and Wall Street was where the money was. But with his unimpressive academic record and lack of a pedigree, Fomon's prospects were dim.

Both Merrill Lynch and Dean Witter, the first firms he approached to become a broker, rejected him. That was when the well-connected Davidson pulled some strings and won his young friend a position at the prestigious E. F. Hutton. Davidson, who had married into a steel fortune, became Fomon's first client and provided an entrée to wealthy circles.


Bob Fomon had obtained financial independence. The previously directionless young man found himself at Hutton. He blossomed.

Fomon exploited Davidson's (and others') social connections. People liked him, and they worked hard to see to it that he succeeded. Hutton became the fraternity he never joined in college, a religion to replace the Catholicism he had long since rejected. More than the wife and two children he soon left, it was his family. If he had been taught in church to look at the world as a struggle between good and evil, he now knew better. The world consisted of winners and losers in the Darwinian creed he adopted, and he would devote himself to winning at all costs.

Fomon quickly rose to prominence in the tight-knit Los Angeles financial community. He eventually became chairman of the Pacific Stock Exchange and joined the board of one of his most important clients, Pacific Southwest Airlines. He was regarded as having charisma.

He also became a leader of the Hutton clique. He was daring, gutsy, and fun. The office was full of adolescent challenges and shows of bravado, such as seeing how late one could stay out getting drunk and still show up sober in the morning. Few could outdo Bob Fomon. It was impossible for an executive to pass Fomon's open office door after five o'clock without his scratchy voice lassoing them in. They would be offered a drink from an ever-present bottle of Scotch. By six Fomon would make his way across the street from Hutton's Los Angeles office to the bar at the Pacific Stock Exchange with three or four cronies, where he would order round after round of what he called "traffic thinners"; that is, he'd keep everyone drinking until the downtown traffic had thinned.

That was just one example of how adept he was at the rituals of male bonding. His playing field was the bar. He talked the talk men frequently love to hear, speaking condescendingly and abusively of women, bragging of his infidelities or tales of business cunning. The key was exclusion. If you were in there with him, you were respected, a member. If you were out, you were laughable, a jerk.

There was a flip side to Fomon's impulsiveness, and it was the key to the success he would achieve. His outrageousness was a tool. In his manipulative hands, these twists became endearing or intimidating, as the situation required. He could melt the hardest of hearts with tales of his painful upbringing, or he could lash out with a Mephistophelian destructiveness. Behind his back, some began to call Fomon "the mongoose," because of his ability to destroy people with a single withering verbal blow.

Fomon's mechanism for winning others over was, if unoriginal, well tested—the confession. He loved creating opportunities to reveal his inadequacies and fears in intimate asides. Suddenly this tough figure would seem sensitive and soft inside, a creature that needed protection.

Late at night, after the bars had grown quiet, he would reach through the alcohol fog to one of his remaining partners and with startling frankness admit that, behind the facade, he hurt, and that his friends and his career were his only balm. He depicted his dedication to Hutton as a means of plugging a hole in his psyche caused by his twisted upbringing. Hutton meant everything to him because he had nothing else. He admitted to being totally unprepared for the responsibilities of marriage and having a family. When he left that union it only buttressed his image as a lonely figure with nothing but E. F. Hutton to lean on.

"You could not find a more loyal, warmer person who has friends more devoted," said Jim Lopp, one of Fomon's closest friends. "He can be so tough, but then melt you with one of his childlike grins. People worked hard because of how they felt about Bob."

It was, unquestionably, just as Fomon would have had it.

Fomon had insinuated himself into the Hutton power structure by developing another father-son relationship, this time with the respected head of Hutton's southern California region, Alec R. Jack. Jack, a Scotsman, was the most popular person in the region, and perhaps the firm. He was successful, he helped other brokers, he loved sports, and he loved the company of other men. Fomon's tight bond with Jack served a dual purpose: it helped Fomon's career, and Jack's stern gaze helped temper the wilder impulses that Fomon enjoyed venting.

Hutton's traditional career path would have meant waiting in line to become the regional baron. Fomon was too impatient for that, though, so the special position as head of corporate finance was created. Fomon, in short, had developed his own power base. The time to use it had arrived in 1969 with the succession battle brewing.


Shad presented Fomon his first opportunity to step out of California onto the national scene, so Fomon played his hand with care as the two chatted in their suite at Boca Raton. There was no great enthusiasm for the somewhat dour, detached Shad as a possible chairman of Hutton. Shad, in fact, had always expressed distaste for the chores of administration and management. But Shad believed himself better than most and was convinced that, at some point, others would recognize his genius. Shad's ambition and self-confidence made him putty in the hands of Fomon.

Shad approached Coleman when he returned to New York from Florida to test the waters. He was not about to start a war if the current chairman was opposed, given the political retribution that might bring down. But Coleman said he shared the misgivings about Wellin, and he encouraged Shad to mount a challenge. Coleman, of course, had his own agenda. He suggested that, together, they had a better chance of winning. Coleman said he would remain chairman, as a sort of peacemaker, while Shad would become president and chief executive. Politely, Shad deflected the idea. But the race was on.

Though a far from ideal candidate, Shad had some attractive qualities. He had grown up in California and, after joining the navy during World War II, had returned and graduated from USC in 1947. (Ironically he was in Fomon's class, but the two did not know each other.) Once on Wall Street he obtained a law degree by going to night school. Shad was a technician. He loved rolling up his sleeves and delving into the minutiae of difficult deals. It was one of his strengths and weaknesses. He would push his subordinates to prepare immense amounts of data for meetings, poring over it all with a fine-toothed comb. He developed a reputation for discovering the one figure out of a thousand that was wrong.

But he had little in the way of vision or leadership skills. He spent more time taking apart and analyzing unusual financing arrangements than articulating a view of where the business was heading. His ambitions had gotten the better of him, though. The prospect of running a prestigious firm like Hutton proved irresistible.

Shad initially explored several alternatives proposed by those who wanted to avoid open warfare. Wellin might become chairman and Shad president, a sort of unity slate. There was the possibility of the well-respected Al Jack, already sixty-four, becoming a transitional chairman, with Wellin vice-chairman and Shad president. But Al Jack refused, saying it was silly for someone his age to take the job. Wellin expressed no enthusiasm for a power-sharing arrangement, either.

It was clear that Shad would have to mount a direct challenge. But time was short. It was already January 1970, and the issue would be voted on at the firm's annual meeting, on February 11, 1970.

Step one was lining up votes. To run his campaign, Shad enlisted Fred Joseph and Irwin Schneiderman, a partner at the law firm of Cahill Gordon & Reindel. Immediately they began secretly to poll the partners.

Wellin learned of the challenge a few days later. He was in Washington when he received an unexpected call from Al Jack. Jack revealed that Shad had already contacted most partners. Jack then surprised him with a suggestion. "You know," Jack told him, "you ought to think about working with Bob Fomon. He's very popular on the West Coast." Wellin was noncommittal, but the seed of an idea had been planted. First he had to pull his own team together. Wellin sent out telegrams to all the firm's partners offering to pay their way to New York for the annual meeting if they would support him.

After intense politicking, Shad and Wellin emerged at something of a standoff, with about 35 percent of the votes each, according to their unofficial tallying. The swing vote, as it turned out, was California—the votes Fomon had secretly promised Shad. Shad had Fred Joseph call Fomon to deliver. It seemed to be the climactic moment. Fomon, as promised, said he had persuaded most of the key California partners to back Shad. In late January Shad's lawyers began collecting irrevocable proxies from the voting partners, the last detail to be sewn up.

Wellin would not give in so easily. Searching for an out, his lawyers went to the New York Stock Exchange, arguing that Shad had breached the rules on voting procedures by obtaining the irrevocable proxies. The Big Board demurred. The lawyers simply went around the block to the American Stock Exchange. With a little persuasion the Amex agreed with Wellin's contention that, indeed, the exchange rules prohibited the irrevocable proxies Shad had collected. Wellin had slipped out of the noose, temporarily. Shad would have to repeat the process, this time obtaining consent forms that were revocable, a key legal change. That gave Wellin a respite.

The process was repeated, with much the same results. Just a few days later it came down to the West Coast's delivering its swing vote again. Fred Joseph called Fomon. It was a Thursday.

Joseph got through to Fomon's office, but his secretary said Fomon was away and would not be available until Monday. Joseph grew insistent, but she repeated the message and would not disclose his whereabouts. Joseph was stunned and deeply suspicious.

In fact, he had good reason to be. Arthur Goldberg had persuaded Wellin that Al Jack and Bob Fomon were key to breaking the deadlock. The older partners would not resist Al Jack. And given some incentive, Fomon would stab Shad in the back for a shot at the brass ring, Goldberg argued. That would bring Wellin the essential West Coast bloc.

So at the last minute Wellin had gone on a clandestine mission to Los Angeles. Fomon was temporarily in the hospital after one of his innumerable auto accidents. As prearranged, Wellin visited him and made his pitch on Thursday, the day Joseph had tried to call.

"Bob, you and I both know that Shad is not the right person," Wellin began in what he expected to be a difficult task of persuasion. "We ought to fashion a deal that would be right for the firm.

"We need strong West Coast representation, given this firm's historic presence here. We also need a peacemaker at the top who can heal the wounds. You and I both know that nobody is more well respected than Al Jack. He's a prince, and I think everyone would accept him. I'm willing to wait my turn if we make him a transitional chairman. I also think there's a lot of respect for you among the younger people. Don't underestimate yourself. You should be president of E. F. Hutton."

Wellin was just warming up and had a lot more prepared, but he was stunned to find that he did not need it. Fomon bought in immediately. The meeting lasted all of five minutes. Jack would be chairman, Wellin vice-chairman, and Fomon president. Jack would retire after a year, and Wellin would succeed him, while Fomon would become CEO and president. Wellin also agreed that Arthur Goldberg would resign immediately, removing that irritant to the California partners. Fomon promised to deliver the West Coast votes for this slate.

Shad was out. It was a stunning double cross, and there was nothing Shad could do about it.

The deal—although no one else knew how it had been reached—was ratified at a bitter and unpleasant gathering on February 9 at Hutton's New York headquarters, on the forty-second floor of Chase Manhattan Plaza. After a day of maneuvering, the board members ended up in a conference room to complete the process. They went around the room, and each partner expressed support for the deal out of the hope that it would calm the firm's roiled waters and save Hutton. Then they got to Shad, who was still not ready to give up. Shad turned to Fomon.

"Well, Bob, what do you think?"

There was a brief pause. Fomon knew Shad expected him to back down when confronted so directly. He was embarrassed, but he blurted out, "What do you want me to say, that you should be president? I won't do that." The battle was over.

After Hutton announced its new executive lineup to a startled Wall Street the next day, the *Times* quoted a previously unknown Bob Fomon as saying that his meteoric rise came as "a surprise to me." Goldberg, whose resignation shocked many who knew of his skills, was quoted as saying he had contemplated leaving for some time.

There was a final act to this drama. As agreed, Fomon moved to New York and took up the presidency. He even shared a company apartment briefly with Keith Wellin before moving into the swanky United Nations Plaza. It appeared that all was going smoothly, and everyone waited for the second stage of the deal to play itself out when Coleman retired in September. But the mongoose struck first.

One night that summer Fomon asked Wellin, now vice-chairman, to dine with him at "21." Afterward they repaired to Fomon's favorite watering hole, an East Side bar called the Pear Tree, near the United Nations. As they drank late into the night, Fomon threw his last trump card on the table.

"Keith, I think we should delay the transition," he said.

"What do you mean?" asked a confused Wellin. "For how long?"

Fomon paused for a moment, then let Wellin have it. "Indefinitely."

Behind Wellin's back Fomon had already solicited the agreement of Jack and several other senior partners to deny Wellin the chairmanship that had been promised. Despite the deal that had been cut, people were no more enthusiastic for Wellin than they had been before.

Fomon had reneged again. Wellin became vice-chairman of nothing, with no duties and no chance of claiming the chairman's job. Fomon, meanwhile, took over as chief executive. Wellin quit in frustration, becoming president of the firm that would become Dean Witter Reynolds. Young Fred Joseph, bitter and disillusioned by Fomon's duplicity and the humiliating defeat of his mentor, Shad, stormed out, too.

Though successful, Fomon was shaken by the daunting responsibilities he had inherited. He was a stockbroker with a penchant for winning over influential people. Now he would be running a sprawling domain on the cusp of a financial and political crisis. Fomon realized that he could not afford to lose the Hutton managers who actually knew how to operate the firm. Quickly that fear turned into a strategy of conciliation. He named Shad vice-chairman and left him in charge of investment banking.

He also held on to the enthusiastic young retail expert, George Ball. Ball had backed Wellin and expected to be dealt with harshly. But Fomon, recognizing Ball's popularity among brokers, welcomed him into the fold. Three years later Ball would be named national retail sales manager.

Fomon also had to tackle the firm's desperate financial problems. Tom Lynch, the chief financial officer, delivered the sobering news that Hutton, at its rate of losses in late 1970—nearly $1 million a month—had only a few months before it would suffer a shortage of capital. And the older partners still wanted to withdraw their capital.

Pressed for action, Fomon unceremoniously laid off six hundred staff, nearly 20 percent of the firm. Hutton was not alone. Across Wall Street firms scrambled to reduce their overheads as volume in the stock market dried up. Fomon, however, showed none of the nostalgia that slowed some others. He was operating from his gut, not his heart.

Fomon also turned to some of Hutton's independently wealthy partners for help with capital. John R. Woods, a Hutton broker in St. Louis who inherited a fortune from his grandfather, a founder of the Ralston Purina Company, put up more than $3 million of his family's stock as collateral for a loan to Hutton. Fomon raised $10 million more from banks.

From the outside, E. F. Hutton appeared to be in reasonable shape. Fomon and his team knew the real story: Hutton was operating with an untested management, the wounds between Fomon and Shad threatened still to tear the firm apart, and the firm's capital position, in spite of the patch-up job performed by Fomon, was precarious.

## THE GOLDEN YEARS

The photograph showed Bob Fomon and John Shad beaming at each other, giddy as teenagers who know something others do not. *Finance* magazine, a Wall Street trade publication, featured the two seated together on the cover of its December 1972 issue, ignorant of the bad blood between them, veiled temporarily for the camera.

Not much had been altered between the two. But one thing had changed dramatically since Fomon's takeover. Through a combination of luck and toughness, E. F. Hutton was back on its feet. A stock market rally had saved the firm. The Dow Jones Industrial Average opened 1971 at 830. Fed by a wave of optimism about the economy, the average rose three months later to 917 as it closed in on what seemed the impossibly high 1000 mark. Volume jumped by more than a third from the previous year. Financial nourishment poured into a parched Wall Street and resuscitated E. F. Hutton.

Hutton rode the crest of the market rally with a flurry of new business. *Finance* magazine was merely picking up a growing view on Wall Street that Hutton was hot, and it declared Fomon and Shad "Investment Bankers of the Year." The cheerful cover photo was passed around Hutton to titters as everyone marveled at the uncharacteristic display of amity. But what Hutton's brokers and executives did take seriously was the recognition of the firm's momentum. The painful cuts Fomon had made were paying off.

The firm executed an average of 6,200 transactions a day in 1970, then 8,000 in 1971 and more than 10,000 in the first three months of 1972. With expenses reduced because of the massive layoffs, more of the revenues generated by that business flowed right to the bottom line. Profits jumped to $9.45 million in 1971 and then $10.9 million in 1972. Publications began falling over themselves to applaud Fomon's genius.

Like a mythic hero, Fomon had overcome severe tests before his magic was proved potent. Suddenly Fomon the duplicitous dark horse was revered. He had also surrounded himself with an aggressive and remarkably youthful team determined to show their mettle. Fomon was forty-seven; Shad forty-nine; Peter Detwiler, another vice-chairman and an investment banker, forty-four; George Ball, who quickly moved up to head the retail branch system, was thirty-four; and John Daly, head of syndication, was thirty-five.

Al Jack, now sixty-six, remained chairman, having been given an extension, at Fomon's urging, past the mandatory retirement age. But he was a distant figure, completely out of the decision-making loop. In fact, he still lived in Los Angeles and spent just a week or two a month in New York. His principal role was satisfying Fomon's need to have a father figure handy. As many of those around him knew, Jack's presence also moderated Fomon's wilder impulses, no small achievement.

Fomon's most impressive quality, though, was how he kept his management team motivated: he was an excellent listener. Fomon despised anything that smacked of methodical planning or management science. That stuff was for wimps. But he did encourage his executives with his attentiveness to their ideas. The energy they spun off electrified the whole firm.

On April 25, 1972, Fomon initiated the next step in solidifying Hutton's financial base. For the first time Hutton sold its stock to the public. A total of 1.245 million shares were offered at $23.50 each. The partnership era was over, but few were nostalgic; they were too rich for sentiment. Hutton's stock more than doubled in value because of the offering.

E. F. Hutton & Company had emerged as a big and solid member of the Wall Street community. It had $405 million in assets, 3,700 employees, 1,400 brokers, eighty-two offices spread out over twenty-one states, and 300,000 customers. That made it the eighth-ranking New York Stock Exchange member firm.

Fomon was on such a roll that even his timing for the public offering appeared to have been touched by genius (though he admitted privately it was pure luck). Weeks afterward the stock market began to weaken, along with Hutton's share price. In other words Hutton had sold its shares at the market peak, getting the best possible price. By the end of 1972 the market was in a nose-dive.

The entire country, in fact, was entering a troubled era. The Arab oil embargo would soon create an energy crisis. The dollar fell precipitously in value. Watergate entered the political lexicon as a synonym for scandal, and a president resigned for the first time in American history. The stock market, as usual, proved a barometer of the nation's sense of well-being—which was falling steadily. Hutton's stock tumbled to a low of $4 by 1974.

In 1973 and 1974 Wall Street entered its last serious slump for the next decade. With Darwinian ruthlessness, the decline finished off the last of the brokerage houses weakened by the turmoil of the 1960s.

The situation suggested caution. But Fomon, increasingly eager to demonstrate his intuitive skills, saw it as a chance to gamble. He spotted this as a good time to snap up other brokerage firms in distress at rock-bottom prices. And he had the cash after Hutton's public offering of shares. He would be able to expand Hutton's branch network sharply at little cost and pump out more products to a broader customer base. There was, of course, a huge risk: should the markets not recover later, the additional overhead would sink Hutton for good. But if things did turn around, Hutton would emerge as a powerful sales machine and advance even farther on its key rival, Merrill Lynch.

Fomon bet the firm on his hunch that the markets would improve. He acquired two regional brokerage firms, one in North

Carolina and another in Rochester, New York. With growing interest in Europe all across Wall Street, Fomon also took his first steps overseas. In 1973 he raided the European offices of Bache & Company, hiring away Giuseppe Tome, a flashy member of the jet set, and three of his colleagues. The theft of the four caused an uproar on Wall Street, where gentlemen were expected to refrain from such unseemly raiding. As much as anything else, Fomon was letting the reigning powers know what he thought of their rules. His defiance only added to his stature.

Tome became "president" of Hutton's new international division, a tiny group of offices in posh European quarters. Their business was not high finance, but, as Fomon and several other executives at that time admitted, handling hot money being spirited out of European countries to evade taxes or flee other restrictions. (It was a thinly disguised secret within Hutton that the European offices had their own set of peculiar rules designed to evade a range of international currency and tax rules. Fomon acknowledged that suitcases of cash were flown back and forth, at least in part to help the European brokers get around local tax laws.)

But the dapper Tome meant much more to Fomon than a boost in commission revenues. He provided an entrée to the world of European aristocracy, something that Fomon, now growing comfortable in the role of a corporate CEO, craved. Fomon, indeed, was changing as Hutton's fortunes improved. As he saw it, any fat cat could live on Fifth Avenue and dine at "21." Only the select could move in Tome's elite European circles. He was determined to show that, like the Hutton myth he embraced, he was a cut above.

Tome introduced the parvenu to his friends, and the cocky midwesterner who despised his homely roots reveled in it. With his excessive drinking and crudeness when he was drunk, Fomon was never accepted in these circles. But as chief executive of the great Hutton he could afford to have his company throw one hell of a party, and it did.

In no time Fomon was beating a path to 29 Via San Marco, Milan, where he bought custom-made double-breasted suits from Tome's tailor, Ferdinando Careceni. He began to go on shooting trips in Europe—not hunting, "shooting," as he began to insist. He hired a Spanish nobleman as a broker to gain entrée to another flashy social circle. And he had Hutton open an investment banking office in Paris, in spite of the fact that the expensive location produced almost no business; the Eurobond market, the source of most investment banking opportunities, was solidly based in London, not Paris. It was not very chic, though, to fly to London for the weekend. Fomon had Hutton maintain an apartment in Paris, which he used frequently; it was overseen, as Fomon admitted, by one of his old girlfriends from California.

The buttoned-down world of Wall Street looked dull by comparison. Fomon delivered that message in every way he could, even in the way he furnished his office. Resting on a floor of dimpled black Italian rubber was a dense row of ficus trees. He kept a huge macaw named Alexander. The bird would snap Brazil nuts in its viselike beak, a somewhat disconcerting spectacle for visitors, but a suitable metaphor for the image Fomon wanted to project.

Fomon took his expansionary gamble a step farther in 1974. Du Pont Walston, the second-largest brokerage house in the country, had run into serious trouble. Tied to the prominent du Pont family, the firm had never fully recovered from Wall Street's back office mess of the 1960s. After it had teetered on the brink of collapse, the New York Stock Exchange devised a rescue plan that involved the legendary Texas billionaire, H. Ross Perot, "saving" the firm by injecting capital and installing new management.

Once he had been lured in, Perot, who controlled EDS, the huge data-processing concern, invested close to $100 million in du Pont Walston and a sister company, du Pont Glore Forgan. Perot's plan was to use them as vehicles for selling data-processing services to Wall Street. But it did not take this Wall Street outsider long to figure out why Wall Street's insiders had been unwilling to touch du Pont Walston. It was beyond repair, and within a few years Perot was waving a white flag. By early 1974 du Pont Walston was hemorrhaging capital.

The New York Stock Exchange was still determined to avoid a collapse. Du Pont's 138 branch offices were second only to Merrill Lynch's 261. A failure could easily cause a panic that would take even healthy firms under. In desperation the exchange decided the only hope was to sell off du Pont's assets, principally its branch offices, bit by bit, sort of like Sears announcing it was auctioning off its stores one at a time. Of course the real point of the liquidation was not to find takers for the assets, but to pawn off its (as yet) undetermined liabilities.

The jarring news of the sale made the front page of *The New York Times* on January 22, 1974. "At the very least," wrote the *Times*'s Vartanig G. Vartan, "this represents a psychological blow to an industry that has been battered by a bear market, congressional pressures for reform, rising costs, and plummeting morale."

Making matters worse, the response to the auction was tepid. Taking on any of du Pont Walston's branches was like buying an overheated nuclear reactor, because of the uncertain state of their financial liabilities. So nearly everyone on Wall Street battened down the hatches. Paine Webber announced that it was backing out of a deal to acquire ten branches. Bache had already pulled out of negotiations for fourteen.

As the crisis deepened, Ross Perot turned to an old friend for help. He called John Shad. Several years earlier Perot had secretly tried to recruit Shad to run du Pont Walston. Shad turned the offer down after deciding that the situation was hopeless.

Ironically, just a year earlier du Pont Walston had sued Hutton for swiping all the brokers in its Palm Beach office. Now du Pont was on its knees asking that Hutton take the rest of its branches at a fire sale price. Shad introduced Perot to Fomon and George Ball. Smiling cover photos aside, Fomon quickly cut Shad out of any further discussions, in yet another humiliation to Hutton's head of investment banking.

The two sides met at the Waldorf-Astoria and discussed du Pont's prospects. Fomon listened to the pitch, went back to his office, and told his executives he would not touch the dying firm. But cherry picking was another matter. Du Pont had an extensive branch network in several regions where Hutton was weak, such as the Southeast. Fomon was interested in grabbing a handful of top, strategically located branches if they shook loose. Originally du Pont wanted any buyer to take some of the bad with the good. Now it could not afford to be so choosy. Hutton grabbed fourteen choice branches in the Southeast and New England. It was an act of faith, a seat-of-the-pants decision.

Almost instantly Hutton's reputation soared. Fomon's courage had captivated an otherwise nervous industry. E. F. Hutton became the first real challenger to Merrill Lynch's dominance of the retail brokerage business in the postwar era. By the end of 1974 Hutton had more than two thousand brokers in 128 offices. The E. F. Hutton Group Inc. was formed as a holding company for the burgeoning brokerage house, in anticipation that it would buy or develop new financial businesses.

In the very difficult markets of 1974, Hutton earned $5.7 million. By the end of 1975 its net profits exploded to $20.1 million. Hutton's confidential internal records demonstrated the improvement even more clearly. The brokerage house's retail operating profits—before taxes and certain expenses—totaled $33.5 million in 1974; in 1975 they reached $62.8 million.

The press embraced this risk-taking star with unusual energy. E. F. HUTTON SHOWING WALL STREET HOW TO SCRAMBLE, read the headline on a laudatory article in *The New York Times* on September 3, 1974. "Some Wall Street executives call their competitors at E. F. Hutton Group Inc. 'aggressive.' One says Hutton is 'ruthlessly aggressive,' " the article began.

A major article also appeared in *Institutional Investor* magazine. Setting the tone, the cover depicted Bob Fomon as a buccaneer. "Almost while no one was looking," the article gushed, "Hutton has surged into second place among U.S. brokers—and very probably leads the pack when it comes to sheer aggressiveness."

The article claimed that "Fomon and the top executives who work for him have suddenly become known as the toughest guys on the Street." In what seemed a flippant aside, Fomon described his strategy as nothing more than being "opportunistic." Forget long-range planning. Fomon's strategy: waiting for opportunities and then seizing them. In typical Fomon fashion, he was being bluntly honest. He followed no design, just intuition. In a relatively uncomplicated world, that was good enough.

Fomon's stature only rose farther when Hutton pulled off another recruiting coup by raiding Merrill Lynch's Southfield, Michigan, office and snaring its four top brokers. Outraged at this breach of etiquette, Merrill filed an antitrust suit. The action was unsuccessful for Merrill while burnishing the Hutton myth further. It was like free advertising.

Fomon's second marriage in 1975 secured his position above

the merely mortal. He wed Sharon Kay Ritchie, a former Miss America introduced to him by one of his Hutton cronies. With his European-cut suits, glamorous wife, late-night drinking sessions, and arrogance toward the rest of Wall Street, Bob Fomon embodied everything a Hutton broker wanted to be.

Hutton's structure was simple in those days. On the one side was the retail business, which consisted largely of the branch office system. Each office, filled with brokers, had a branch manager, and each geographic region was headed by a regional vice-president. These barons reported to George Ball, who had emerged as a tireless motivator. The retail division was an efficient, massive system for distributing products, in this case financial products, collecting commissions for each sale.

The wholesale, or investment banking, division in New York had two purposes. One was to generate its own revenues by providing services to corporations. It charged fees for underwriting stocks and bonds or arranging mergers and other transactions. In addition, one of its key functions was to "manufacture" financial products for the distribution system to sell. As in any business, Hutton earned more if it distributed products it manufactured itself, since it did not have to pay any middlemen. Fomon and Shad had been honored by *Finance* magazine because Hutton had started to develop a reputation for underwriting hot stocks—shares issued by smaller companies that would generate good profits quickly.

As the 1970s progressed, Fomon began to put his personal stamp on this corporate structure. Nowhere was this more evident than in John Shad's investment banking department. Despite a decade of work, Hutton remained an investment banking laggard under Shad. Shad had developed a reasonable, although far from impressive, stable of medium-size clients, often issuing what would later be described as junk securities. But there was little momentum. Shad was doing deals one by one rather than envisioning the market as a patchwork of relationships that he could build on and enhance. He did not know how to lift Hutton out of the lower tiers of the business.

Fomon was ruthless in his denunciations of Shad's failures. He did not just tell Shad of his disappointment, he humiliated his investment banking chief publicly at every chance.

In fact, Shad developed a habit of avoiding Hutton's executive dining room because of the blasts Fomon would often level at him there. It was a shocking spectacle. When Shad did make the mistake of showing up, Fomon would generally start up slowly, taking potshots at Shad for his dinky clients and the complicated but unglamorous deals he pursued—sometimes by shouting insults across the room. The momentum would then carry Fomon into prolonged, highly personal attacks. Many executives recalled observing the painful exercise as Shad barely lifted his face from his plate.

"This is a first-class house," Fomon would snap. "This is the best you can do?"

The companies were often interesting, but modest-size, at times ailing, and less than prestigious. Caesar's World, Color Tile, Ramada Inns, American Beauty Macaroni, and Western Union were among Shad's corporate customers.

Fomon, who regarded himself as a master deal maker, felt free to meddle behind the scenes. He did some of his own recruiting, developing a cadre of investment bankers who were loyal to the CEO. He told people which deals to do and how to do them. And, most important, he controlled compensation. It was a telling fact that the department in which Fomon had the greatest involvement performed the poorest. As long as Fomon relied on image, Hutton worked fine. But when he actually applied his capricious hand, the results were disappointing.

From 1975 on an effort was made to ease Shad out. There were no prospects on Wall Street; it was clear he enjoyed a title and position at Hutton that nobody else on Wall Street would have offered. So Hutton officials tried to help him win a position in Washington. Shad was a staunch Republican and at one point came close to being appointed head of the Overseas Private Investment Corporation, a government body that insures foreign investments by American companies. That eventually fell through. Hutton's investment banking operations were stuck in a rut.

The retail system was a different matter. Retail was Hutton's strength, the area where the firm was in the top tier.

Heading Fomon's retail team was George Ball, an exuberant

Hutton cheerleader. Where he had once suffered from a nagging stammer, tutoring and practice had turned Ball into an able public speaker. Fomon had become inaccessible to most brokers, but nearly anyone in the Hutton army could pick up the phone and call "George," as all knew him. No broker would have dared phone Fomon, and none would have had the courage to address him as "Bob."

Where Fomon was brooding, Ball was effusive. Fomon used language with care and spoke in short, precise sentences. He rarely wrote or read memos. Ball, one of the most prolific memo writers in Wall Street history, rambled, often inventing words. Ball's secretaries would often titter among themselves over what they dubbed the "Ballisms"—invented words he sprinkled throughout his little missives to the field.

Ball also had a prodigious appetite for the figures and details Fomon abhorred. A branch did not change a light bulb without his noticing. He knew how much every office earned in commissions, who their best brokers were, how much interest income they brought in. When he visited branches he studied beforehand— literally—the birth dates, anniversaries, names of wives, and alma maters of the branch manager and his top brokers.

Every month Ball went through an elaborate ritual of ranking every branch and region. He sent out dozens of cases of champagne to the winners. When he traveled Ball had his mail shipped to him in heavy bundles nearly every day. He did not want to fall even a day or two behind. The retail system was becoming, slowly, Ball's personal domain.

Fomon knew this but did not object. And for good reason: it was not much of a secret inside Hutton's headquarters that Fomon loathed the crass retail trade, which he saw as filled with earnest, half-smart men from the provinces who captained their high school football teams, attended forgettable local colleges, married prom queens, and aspired to little more than honored places on the entertainment committees of their local country clubs.

What was an executive who wore Careceni suits going to think of a guy who spent his day calling up doctors and lawyers, pleading with them to buy some schlocky stock or tax shelter?

Fomon regarded Hutton's retail customers as sheep waiting to be sheared, and he often said so. He harbored no illusions about the quality of the firm's products. It was the same junk the other firms sold. In fact, by the mid-1970s there was almost nothing to distinguish the products sold by the major brokerage houses. Hutton's brokers just sold more of it than the others.

Customers buy image, Fomon knew, so he worked hard to maintain the marketability of the Hutton name. The Hutton myth was the firm's most effective sales weapon. Ball was Fomon's emissary to those who actually believed the myth.

Fomon described Ball's approach as "the kiss-ass theory," but he respected the results. Fomon genuinely liked Ball because of Ball's effusive demonstrations of loyalty and because, when they spoke behind closed doors, Ball demonstrated just as cynical an attitude toward the brokers and customers. As with all of Fomon's tight emotional relationships, this one slowly began to take on the character of a father-son bond; this time Fomon was the father figure, and he loved it. Ball used his brilliant salesmanship to encourage that view.

Gestures aside, Ball was developing the only real power base at Hutton other than Fomon's. He cultivated the sales force to build allegiances. And he used a tool that Hutton's brokers were sure to understand: money.

Ball recruited heavily from other firms, using promises of big bonuses and huge commission rates as lures. Ball cut special deals with dozens of brokers. He went around branch managers and regional executives to establish personal arrangements. Ball's methods began to have a profound impact on how Hutton's retail system operated by encouraging brokers to bargain constantly for better terms with him.

The ultimate expression of this system was a smooth Texan named Don Sanders.

Sanders was by far Hutton's most productive broker. He was a lithe, trim, attractive, silver-maned Houstonian with a silver tongue and a bloodhound's nose for money. He owned a stake in the Astros baseball team and swung in Houston's toniest circles. He always sounded measured and confident.

Sanders started with Hutton in 1960 and by the mid-1970s had become an institution, spinning out millions of dollars in commissions. Sanders also became the broker for a number of Hutton's top executives, creating huge potential conflicts of interest within the firm. He grew extremely close to Hutton's other supersalesman: George Ball. The two spoke several times a day, shared ideas, discussed strategy, played tennis together.

Of all the special deals Ball cut, Sanders had the best. Eventually a separate subbranch was created in Houston just for Sanders and his partner, John Mundy. (Sanders specialized in stock dealings and Mundy in commodities. They had a partnership that gave Sanders 70 percent and Mundy 30 percent of their operation's profits.) The purpose of this unprecedented subbranch was clear— it allowed Sanders to bypass Hutton's bureaucracy whenever it got in his way. When the designation "N53," the code for Sanders's Houston office, showed up on a document, no questions were asked.

One of Hutton's outside lawyers, Bill Campbell, was amazed by the setup when he stumbled on it, calling it "an aberration in the Hutton system."

"It is Sanders's personal office and because of his power he is able to control and override the system," Campbell wrote in a confidential memo.

When applied to the whole branch system, Ball's techniques for winning hearts added hugely to Hutton's overhead. Enough special deals meant Hutton was paying millions of dollars a year more for brokers than anyone else on Wall Street. It created a coddled, spoiled cadre of brokers who racked up heavy expenses. More important, it left the brokers beholden to Ball.

Unquestionably the most important event on Wall Street during the 1970s and the greatest challenge to retail brokerage houses was May Day. On May 1, 1975, stock commissions were freed for the first time, under congressional pressure. Fixed commissions were dead. A rush of competition immediately sent commission levels spiraling downward—from 20 percent to 60 percent lower. It was a traumatic event for an industry that had been used to focusing only on revenues, not expenses.

Although it would take years for the full effects of this change to be manifested, it radically altered the economics of Wall Street. The simple truth was that fixed commissions had subsidized brokerage houses. They had never needed to make sure each account paid its way. They had never needed to restrain staff growth as long as the market was strong. They had not needed to diversify into new products, develop new sources of revenue, or streamline bloated operations to keep up their profits. After May Day firms were faced with a choice: they had to slash expenses and become more productive, or they had to find new, high-margin products to pump through the sales force. Fomon decided to look for the fancy new products. Believing his aggressive sales force could market anything, Fomon pursued the strategy of making Hutton a financial "supermarket," selling all sorts of investment products in the search of increased profit margins.

This pressure would produce Fomon's last business coup. In 1975 he lured away the three top public finance executives of industry leader Blythe Eastman Dillon. The group included Richard S. Locke, W. James Lopp II, and Scott Pierce. Their specialty was underwriting tax-exempt bond issues by state and local governments, a high-profit product that, up to that time, Hutton had all but ignored.

Jim Lopp, a slightly bulge-eyed dandy, was the salesman in the group. Dick Locke was more of a technician. He knew the nuts and bolts of putting the deals together and administering the department. And Scott Pierce was expert at distributing the securities.

There was a silent partner, too. Lopp relied heavily on an Omaha-based lawyer named Bob Kutak. A former Senate aide and then a partner in the law firm of Kutak Rock & Campbell, Kutak gave substance to Lopp's ideas. Many regarded him as the real brains of the team, since Lopp impressed few with his technical abilities.

The new municipal finance team was a natural fit with Hutton. The tax-exempt status of municipal bonds made them attractive to wealthy individuals—something Hutton had in large supply.

As a result of the hirings, Hutton rose from the distant reaches of the public finance business to rank in the top five by the early 1980s. Hutton's public finance team started landing the kinds of major deals that had eluded its corporate finance department.

Fomon's next step to produce new products came in 1978. Hutton bought a life insurance company so that it could manufacture and sell its own insurancelike products, such as annuities. The next year Hutton Life introduced "CompleteLife," the first universal life insurance product. It was one of the most successful life insurance products ever sold.

In another important step, Hutton added tax shelters to its list of financial products. Tax shelters, sometimes called direct investments, are organized to raise capital for businesses favored by the tax code, such as real estate and oil and gas exploration. The point is to create a vehicle for passing those tax benefits directly to investors, giving them substantial write-offs or deductions as well as capital gains.

The shelters also stand out in that they generate the largest commissions and fees of any investment product. An investor has to pay fees to the organizers of the tax shelter, fees to its managers, and fees to the broker who sells it. As much as 20 percent and more of the sum a customer sinks into a tax shelter is skimmed off in this way. Also there is little if any secondary market for the tax shelters, should an investor want out before maturity.

In other words, tax shelters are by far the worst investment products Wall Street has perpetrated on the public, and government regulators have largely been asleep in policing the systematic abuses that have taken place in the business. But given the hefty commissions they paid, tax shelters were ideal products for Hutton's confident dream merchants. Hutton quickly became the hottest peddler of tax shelters in the business.

Hutton took in $13.8 million in revenues from tax shelters sales in 1978, its start-up year. The figure reached $39.4 million in 1980 and $73 million in 1982.

Hutton's bottom line continued its upward course, too, reaching $28 million in 1978, $37.3 million in 1980, and a stunning $82.6 million in 1981.

"I cannot describe to you how great it felt to be at Hutton then," said Dale Frey, the Denver-based head of Hutton's mountain region.

"We loved coming in to work every day; you were playing for the Yankees," said Bruce Tuthill, a Boston-based broker who was one of Hutton's biggest producers. "Those were the greatest days in our lives."

Given the payout structure Ball created, it was easy to understand why the brokers would carry such fond memories. But every share of stock, or bond, or tax shelter that Hutton's salesmen sold cost the firm significantly more every year. Hutton was like a racing car that, as it accelerates down the track, halves its gas mileage for every five-miles-per-hour gain in speed. With the firm lapping its rivals and having a ball doing so, not many were willing to challenge the engineers of the success. It was too exhilarating.

Nonetheless, the evidence was there: Hutton's pretax margin—the ratio of its pretax profits to revenues, a standard measure of profitability—plunged from a vigorous 17.3 percent in 1975 to a lethargic 9.1 percent in 1979. That was considerably below the average profitability for the brokerage industry.

But who wanted to be so gloomy? Fomon took his board of directors to lavish meetings on the French Riviera. Ball feted the firm's top brokers at America's most expensive resorts. The only one who seemed to reflect on his good fortune and find it a bit unreal was Bob Fomon. "Everything in the world can be borne," Fomon wrote, quoting Goethe, in the firm's 1979 annual report, "except for a series of beautiful days."

CHAPTER

# 6

CUT LOOSE

The Brook Club had become a symbol to Bob Fomon. European aristocracy occupied him some of the time, but he needed something to do with himself back home. He had selected New York's WASP establishment as appropriately snobby to satisfy his self-image. He hired several useless brokers at Hutton who did little more than provide an entrée to this society. He had gone out and bought an old Hamptons home and constructed "the most beautiful garden in the Hamptons," as he loudly advertised. But the Brook, a men's club and old Manhattan society fixture, required more than money. Finally he persuaded a senior investment banker at Morgan Stanley to sponsor him for membership.

But something funny happened. Fomon was not the sort of social climber who would parrot the social circle he had targeted for entry. He was not about to show any more reverence toward the Brook than any other establishment institution. Fomon would saunter in after work for what, in the Los Angeles days, he would have called "traffic thinners." Since he always craved an audience, he would try to gather a group around him at the bar to swap tales of bravado. But it was not like the old days. Fomon's crudeness looked even rougher in the staid confines of the club. After a couple of hours he would often end up clinging to the bar with one hand, waving a cigarette with the other, while regaling anyone who would listen with his flippant remarks and off-color stories. Some remember it as a pathetic spectacle.

By the late 1970s something indeed seemed to have changed. Fomon was losing his razor-sharp edge. People whom he had once charmed with his wild antics he now disgusted. He was losing his audience. He was also losing his wife, Sharon Kay Ritchie, in just as visible and humiliating a fashion. A fellow Brook Club member recalled the sad sight of Sharon sitting in Fomon's limousine at the curb in front of the club, waiting in vain as Fomon stalled at the bar. She occasionally stopped a club member she knew and asked them to remind Fomon she was ready to go home.

Jarring as the changes might have seemed, it was really the same old Fomon. The adjustment in his personality was almost microscopic. He was like an aging slugger who loses just a split second in his timing; instead of knocking fastballs over the fence, he was looking silly thrashing at the air. Fomon had become so used to walking close to the line of propriety that losing just a bit of his self-control pushed him over. The bitterness concealed in his sarcasm slipped out a bit more, making him mean. His drinking, which once transformed his hostility into shrewd repartee, now made him gratuitously abusive.

It seemed powerfully symbolic that the 1980s also began with the death of the one man who had the ability to keep Fomon's wilder compulsions in check: Al Jack died on December 16, 1980. Fomon took the news harder than the death of his own father six years earlier. Fomon's notions of right and wrong had been defined by what would please or displease the well-liked old man. When Jack finally left the firm in 1978, Fomon lost that touchstone. When Jack died, Fomon was cut loose from his anchor.

One thing, however, had changed dramatically: Wall Street was once again in turmoil as the new decade opened. The markets had grown edgier, much faster paced and more dangerous as, first, inflation rates soared into double digits and then Federal Reserve chairman Paul Volcker took a historic gamble of trying to tame the price spiral by spiking interest rates to unprecedented heights. The markets had been transformed into far larger and far more turbulent waters where only the most skilled navigators could survive. Fomon had never faced such a test. Meanwhile the effects of May Day were still being felt, with retail brokerage firms under continuing pressure to reduce expenses.

To maintain their market shares, Wall Street firms commenced a period of breakneck expansion that, in hindsight, was one of the most ill-considered and poorly executed transformations any major industry has undergone. The staffs of the major firms grew geometrically—including Hutton's. Wall Street executives had no previous experience managing such growth. Hutton, with George Ball pushing, tried to keep up.

The first step for Hutton was to build, once and for all, a real investment banking department to take advantage of the explosive growth of this business. A golden opportunity presented itself in 1980. Finally John Shad had gotten his shot at Washington. He had been a strong backer and fund-raiser for Ronald Reagan. After the election he had been rewarded with the chairmanship of the Securities and Exchange Commission. That gave Fomon a relatively clean slate.

Fomon toyed with the notion of buying an established investment banking firm. It was certainly a faster way to obtain a foothold in the business than building, at which he had already failed. He made an appointment and met with the head of Dillon, Read & Company, a prestigious investment banking firm that had remained small as its competitors expanded more aggressively. It might have been a splendid match if the courtship had been handled well. Fomon wasted little time.

"We'd like to buy you," he rasped at John Birkelund of Dillon.

Offended by the crudeness of the pass, Birkelund ended the meeting five minutes later, and the subject was never touched on again.

Hutton's declining profitability and Fomon's moodiness only put more pressure on George Ball. Ever the loyal soldier, Ball still professed fealty to the king, but it was difficult for him to conceal his frustration, particularly with his own inability to get the firm's flagging fortunes back on track.

Ball's old tactics for winning over the retail sales force were, in fact, coming back to haunt him. By protecting Fomon and covering up for him, he had helped foster the chairman's irresponsibility. By pushing growth at the expense of cost control and strong management, he had created an unwieldy machine that would not respond to gentle prodding.

As these strains began to destabilize Hutton, the stage was set for the first serious political confrontation in a decade. Fomon was losing his legitimacy. If Ball could find a short-term means of significantly boosting Hutton's profits and margins, the rest just might fall in place. But he had to get earnings up, somehow.

Donald H. Kasle, an executive vice-president at the First National Bank of Kansas City, got right to the point. His letter, dated April Fools' Day 1980, was addressed to William T. Sullivan, E. F. Hutton's "money mobilizer."

"As I am sure you are aware from having seen the January and February account analyses," Kasle wrote testily, "we have had a loss for both of the first two months of this year."

Something was funny in the way Hutton was using its account at Kasle's bank: banks are supposed to make money from their client accounts, but Hutton was making money from the First National Bank.

Sullivan operated the intricate system by which Hutton's many branch offices transferred their daily revenues to the home office. When Sullivan left for a better-paying job in May 1980, Tom Morley inherited the job.

The cash concentration system was extremely complex in practice, but simple in concept. Ideally the system would have the income from Hutton's branches deposited every day first in local banks and then transferred to regional bank accounts. Once concentrated at the regional level, the sums would be passed on to New York in the form of another check. The aim was to move the money to headquarters as swiftly as possible, rather than allowing it to linger in accounts where it could not be put to corporate uses. Every day the money sat in a provincial bank account it made money for the bank, not Hutton.

The complexities developed because of the antiquated system for clearing checks. When a check is deposited into an account, it must be passed to the bank on which it is drawn, or to a clearing house operation where the bank maintains an account, to collect the money. That series of laterals, known as clearing, takes time. When the banks are in the same city, checks can clear in the same day. When the banks are in different cities, or at opposite ends of the country, the process can take several days. It is a quirky system full of regional differences that can create further delays.

When there is a lag between the time money is deducted from one account and credited to another, the money can end up temporarily in the hands of one of the banks involved in the transfer process. And banks put every cent they have to work all the time, by lending it and earning interest. Thus the banks enjoy some interest income from funds that are in transit. In other words, the banks enjoy the float.

Sullivan had designed a complicated system that took into account the delays in the check clearing system and attempted to compensate for them. The system's aim was to put all of Hutton's money to work at all times and thus reduce the float that the banks enjoyed at Hutton's expense.

The key to Hutton's method was what appeared, on the surface, to be a form of overdrafting. Introduced to regional officers at a meeting in Kansas City in May 1978, the system permitted the branches to write checks—quite legitimately—for sums larger than the collected balances in their accounts. The checks looked like overdrafts, since they were drawn against uncollected funds, or funds deposited in the form of checks that themselves had not cleared yet. But they were designed merely to reduce float going to banks.

If Hutton would normally have lost $100 in interest income from the three days it took for a large deposit to clear, for instance, Hutton would overdraw against uncollected funds in its account by a sum calculated to generate about $100 in interest for Hutton. Banks had to be compensated for the services they were providing, so the system, as designed, was supposed to take away only the excessive float enjoyed by the banks.

Nobody would win, nobody would lose. It was all completely legal. If checks were written for sums larger than Hutton's account balances, the overdraft would be covered in a day or two with the deposit of a new Hutton check from another bank. Complex but strict formulas—written into what was called a drawdown sheet—

told the branch office cashiers just how much they could overdraft in this manner.

But by 1980 the cash concentration system had become more than an obscure sidelight to the brokerage business. With double-digit inflation, interest rates had risen to punishingly high levels. Hutton, like every brokerage house, borrowed hundreds of millions of dollars a day from its banks to meet normal operating expenses. The interest it had to pay on those borrowings was also shooting upward, eating into its profits.

One way to reduce the borrowing was to find a means of boosting the firm's cash bank balances. The more money in its bank accounts, the less debt Hutton would have to take on to fuel its operations. That might save tens of millions of dollars a year. It was a critical point; if Hutton could not increase productivity or cut expenses in Ball's overpaid retail branch system, then it could try to make up for the problem through its banking practices.

This is where an interesting twist developed in the cash concentration system. The system was designed to push Hutton's many bank accounts just up to the edge of propriety. But a number of people at Hutton, who had always been encouraged by Hutton's culture to see themselves as smarter and more aggressive than others, began to realize the benefits of stepping just a little bit over. If it was legitimate to create a small overdraft to recapture float lost to the banks, why not write larger checks against uncollected balances to actually create float for Hutton and inflate its bank balances? Why not pass multiple checks from one Hutton bank account to another, with escalating sums—something known as a pinwheel—to try to create more clearing lags, and more float, for Hutton's own benefit? With interest rates at more than 20 percent, the check clearing system suddenly looked like a world of opportunity.

Such abuses would clearly violate Hutton's guidelines, if not the law. But Ball's team knew that they had to squeeze as much profit from the retail network as they could. And, as Sanders's special subbranch made clear, strict adherence to the rules was largely for those who did not know better. Besides, if the banks were too stupid to realize what was happening, it was hard to feel sorry for them. In the con man's vernacular, Hutton began kiting checks. If some bankers, like Kasle, caught on, Hutton could refund what it had taken. If a bank did not notice, Hutton was the better for it.

In 1980—the first year that these systematic abuses of the system went into overdrive—Hutton slashed its bank borrowings to $192 million a day from $383 million the year earlier. At an average borrowing rate of 14 percent, that meant Hutton saved $27 million in interest payments—equal to a third of its total profits for the year. That was a massive benefit. And as interest costs fell, Hutton's net interest profits soared. The firm earned $26.5 million in net interest income in 1977. That jumped to $50.1 million in 1979 and $95.9 million in 1980.

This was no fluke. Playing with the float in Hutton's dozens of banks accounts across the country was the brokerage firm's single most profitable "product," ahead of tax shelters. In other words, selling stocks and bonds and tax shelters to its customers had become a sideline. The core business was losing money. It was like a gardening store discovering that it was earning more from over-charging customers on their sales tax than from selling begonias.

In 1980 George Ball began a wholesale push for more interest income. Within a year a third of Hutton's branches were engaged in at least one of the two abusive practices, direct overdrafting or pinwheeling. Ball exhorted his troops to use overdrafting to boost their income, while leaving the precise method vague. Questions were referred to the "money mobilizer."

When the regional operations official who had been overdrafting the account of a Washington, D.C., branch moved to the Bethesda, Maryland, office, the secret went with him, and another branch began to steal free loans from its bank. His successor at the regional job later moved to Louisville, and that branch suddenly began to see its interest income from overdrafting swell. Word was spreading mouth to mouth.


A sharp accountant could easily spot the potential for abuse in Hutton's cash concentration system. Indeed, one had. Just three weeks before Kasle's letter arrived, a group of auditors from Hutton's outside accounting firm, Arthur Andersen & Company, pointed out quite plainly the risks Hutton faced with its overdrafting.

It was a chilling meeting. The accountants pulled out a recent newspaper article reporting that a corporation, TI Industries, had been indicted on felony charges for an overdrafting practice hauntingly similar to Hutton's. Accountants are, by their nature, rarely so bold as to suggest that a client—in this case one of the most respected brokerage houses in the country—is committing a felony.

The Hutton officials, led by the firm's top lawyer, Tom Rae, scoffed at the warning. The banks were aware of the overdrafting practice, Rae explained, and hence approved. Besides, he added, Hutton had the money ultimately to make good on these overdrafts.

The auditors were still uncomfortable and did something even rarer for their breed: they asked if Rae would provide a written legal opinion confirming that view. It was a direct challenge, as loud a warning as an accountant will usually sound. Rae refused.


Kasle was forced to write to Hutton again four weeks after his first letter, on April 29, 1980, sending yet another warning to Hutton's executives that something was amiss.

"As you are aware, the month of March reflected a $109,435 deficient balance which E. F. Hutton had with us," it began. "Once again, the problem came about because of a too rapid drawdown of funds with the float amount being greater than the ledger balance."

The bank was losing more than $1,200 a month to Hutton.

What Kasle did not know was that he had lots of company. Bank officers from around the country were sending similarly sharp letters to Tom Morley. Neither Morley nor the people he reported to—Norm Epstein, head of operations and his direct boss, or Tom Lynch, the chief financial officer—nor anyone in the controller's office tried to stop it.

With his voracious appetite for numbers, Ball had observed with precision just which branches were raking in large amounts of interest income by playing the float. In an effort to spread the word, he asked Hutton's financial staff to analyze two particularly egregious abusers of the cash concentration system, the Casper, Wyoming, and Washington, D.C., offices. In March 1980, for instance, the small Casper office earned more than $30,000 in net interest income; Washington earned $82,500.

"Both offices have one thing in common," wrote Tom Lillis, Hutton's assistant controller, in response to Ball's inquiry. "They overdraft substantially through Bill Sullivan in New York. At 20 percent interest, it is a very profitable product for the branches." Once again, the "overdrafting" per se was not illegal. But the flow of letters from Kasle and others made it clear that the practice went over the line.

Hutton was not alone in trying to boost interest profits, of course. Every major brokerage house sought to take advantage of the high interest rates, employing a range of techniques, such as "remote disbursement"—sending customers' checks from distant banks to win a few extra days of float. A judge ordered Merrill Lynch to pay damages to its New York customers because the firm was purposely sending them checks drawn on a California bank. But nobody was as systematic about using the overdrafting technique as Hutton.

In October 1980 Ball had a four-page memo sent to all branch managers explaining Hutton's growing reliance on interest income and suggesting several tricks for boosting it. Besides the easy ones—mailing checks to customers late and remote disbursement—the memo stated that "the lion's share of the interest profit generated in this category is due to the float earned on . . . overdrafting the branch's bank account."


Ball was walking on thin ice, but he had the luxury of knowing that Fomon would leave the retail operation alone. Ball could build his power base in peace. Hutton's other executives were not so lucky.

In one instance Fomon overrode his trading chief, a streetwise manager named Jim Gahan, and threw Hutton's weight behind a high-risk venture called Trading Company of the West. The event would have reverberations throughout Hutton.

It was an investment vehicle run by William A. Lupien, a close friend of Fomon's from California (who would, several years later, help introduce Fomon to Bob Rittereiser). The new venture planned to trade mortgage and other government securities in an effort to create short-term tax losses and long-term capital gains for wealthy investors. To get started, Trading Company of the West collected a total of $31.7 million in capital from Hutton customers.

What angered Gahan was that he had been trying to steer Hutton into the burgeoning mortgage securities business. So why give it away to an outsider when it could be done in-house? Gahan also had little confidence in Lupien and said so. Fomon, once such a good listener, ignored Gahan.

A year later Trading Company of the West had traded away an astounding 84 percent of its capital, leaving a number of Hutton customers fleeced and Gahan fuming.

Later, after Shad withdrew for his departure to Washington, Hutton's corporate finance department made a pitch for a more organized strategy. Paul Bagley, who had been the department's administrator, appeared before Fomon to propose that Hutton pursue the "junk" business more aggressively.

"We're a first-class company, and we don't deal in junk," Fomon said, ignoring the fact that most of the department's revenues came from just that source. Fomon thus had Hutton miss one of the most powerful trends to reshape the financial system in this century.

The culture would next manifest itself in Jim Lopp's public finance department. The department spent months during 1980 trying to win the public finance business of the U.S. Steel Corporation. Under the federal tax laws, industrial corporations were able to issue tax-exempt bonds to finance pollution control investments. Hutton wanted to win a piece of the business with an innovative security.

Hutton had been working on a new kind of tax-exempt bond whose interest rate would float. Previously, tax-exempt bonds were sold with a fixed interest rate, which would be paid until the bonds matured. But with interest rates growing more volatile, investors grew leery of holding these securities, whose value rose and fell unpredictably. In a floating-rate bond, the interest rate might swing up and down, but the bond's principal value would remain relatively constant.

U.S. Steel issued a challenge: complete a floating-rate bond issue, it told Hutton, or we will go back to our traditional investment bank, Morgan Stanley, for a fixed-rate bond issue. Jim Lopp pursued the deal and, to Fomon's delight, succeeded by getting around a host of thorny technical problems. Hutton underwrote two lucrative floating-rate bond issues for U.S. Steel, peddling the securities to its customers by telling them they were buying a bond that would always be worth close to what they paid for it, even as interest rates moved. That safety factor made it a big hit. In effect, Hutton provided a guarantee that it would always be prepared to pay an investor one hundred cents on a dollar for these bonds, which came to be known as "upper floaters."

Fomon ignored warnings from Dick Locke, another public finance executive, that the short-term gains might be overridden by some long-term problems. What happened, Locke asked, if the credit ratings of the bond issuers were lowered? The prices of the bonds would fall, of course. But Hutton had provided an implicit guarantee to buyers that the price would not drop. Who would pay the difference if that happened? Fomon pushed such concerns aside. Get business, whatever the cost, was the message Fomon delivered.

Between June 1980 and June 1981, Hutton underwrote slightly more than $500 million worth of the tax-exempt bonds for other clients as well, including the National Steel Corporation and the Cleveland Electric Illuminating Company, collecting $12 million in fees in the process.

This "whatever it takes" culture seeped into every part of Hutton. Vice-chairman Peter Detwiler arranged to hire prostitutes for a senior government figure in Trinidad and Tobago to help out a client, Tesoro Petroleum, ignoring the damaging effect this could have on Hutton's image if it ever leaked out (which it eventually would in a lawsuit). Detwiler later sent Tesoro a $3,100 bill for "professional services."

In another instance, a senior public finance official had submitted an expense statement on September 18, 1981, seeking reimbursement for $2,539.31 in "entertainment" costs. On the back of the expense statement he wrote that he had taken out a group of South Carolina state legislators and state lawyers in pursuit of business. But Hutton's internal auditors checked each bill with American Express and discovered that the receipts had been doctored.

In a memo written on October 28, 1981, a Hutton accountant outlined the fraud. The memo ended up on the desk of Dick Locke, the administrative head of the public finance department. He discovered that the receipts had been changed to cover up the fact that the investment banker had entertained the state officials at a brothel (not uncommon in the public finance business). Locke followed with a short note to Hutton's accounting department. "Tom Rae [Hutton's top lawyer] and I have agreed to pay this and drop the matter. If you have any questions please call me. [signed] R. Locke."

The incident set an extraordinary example as word spread around Hutton about the executives' tolerance.

While the other guys may have been having fun, Fomon, who had always pursued this side of the game with zest, lost his energy for tomcatting around 1980. He knew morale was slipping, and he also knew that he did not have the stomach—or the basic skills—for managing a turnaround. He felt sorrier and sorrier for himself, leaning more and more on Ball.

Fomon had generally kept work and women separate in the previous decade. Starting in 1980, however, he began combining business and pleasure, finding girlfriends within the firm or, once he found them, placing them in comfortable jobs at Hutton. And these would be no former Miss Americas. Fomon pursued far easier game. The aim was not wowing his audiences, but finding women whose adulation would be won easily and kept without a great deal of effort.

Fomon's first such paramour was Robin Davis, a young woman in her twenties. Not long after their relationship began, she moved into his Fifth Avenue apartment and was given a remarkable job at Hutton—over the strenuous objections of several jealous executives—as head of advertising, a job for which she had no formal training.

At Davis's insistence, Fomon fired Benton & Bowles, Hutton's longtime advertising agency and the creator of the "When E. F. Hutton Talks, People Listen" campaign. Fomon agreed that Hutton would do its advertising in-house, under Davis's (and his own) watchful eye.

Next, Fomon began an affair with a vixenish young Hutton secretary, Pam O'Neill—who worked for Ball. Fomon saw that she was taken care of, too. She was given one of Hutton's many company apartments to live in, on Hanover Square near Wall Street. She paid about half the monthly maintenance cost and a fraction of the apartment's rental value.

But there was a pathetic edge to these affairs. Fomon was losing the confidence of the executives who had once enjoyed drinking late with him and laughing at his biting asides. Outwardly an appearance of reverence was maintained; Hutton's officials took the occasion of Fomon's tenth anniversary as CEO in 1980 to buy him a pair of valuable Purdey shotguns, which cost the firm $15,-000. And, of course, no one objected when Fomon asked Hutton to pick up the tab for his European shooting holidays. One such trip, an expedition to France in early 1981, cost Hutton $74,600. Tom Lynch approved the expense in a memo dated January 23, 1981.

Hutton was starting to run out of control. The mounting pressure took an ever greater toll on Fomon, who vented his frustration with spiteful attacks against those he felt had crossed him.

One such target was Giuseppe Tome, the Switzerland-based head of Hutton's "international" operations. First, Fomon fired Tome in 1979—the only time anyone in the firm could recall him actually firing someone himself. Fomon acted, he recalled, after learning that Tome kept his household staff on Hutton's payroll and forced some of his brokers to kick back part of their bonuses. It was also after Tome had begun to snub Fomon and let him know that his crowd found the Hutton CEO boorish. That was enough. Fomon called Tome to New York, met him in the office on a Saturday, and dismissed him.

But the mongoose was not through yet. He sought to destroy Tome for his efforts to belittle Fomon. Fomon would not put up with that humiliation.

Fomon learned later that Tome had been trading in the American stock market with inside information about pending takeovers. That was not terribly rare, but Tome operated on a larger scale than most. Tome was close to the Bronfman family, which controlled Joseph E. Seagram & Company, the huge spirits company. When Tome learned that Seagram planned a takeover bid for St. Joe Minerals, a major resources concern, in March 1981, he secretly acquired thousands of shares in the target. St. Joe's stock price rocketed when the hostile raid was announced, and Tome earned $3.5 million—all of it illegal.

Fomon's relationship with John Shad, his former head of corporate finance, had cooled years earlier. But this was a special occasion. Shad, now the chairman of the Securities and Exchange Commission, was surprised to receive a call from his former rival one afternoon. There was little in the way of pleasantries. Fomon tipped Shad off to Tome's trading. Tome, still living overseas, was subsequently indicted for insider trading and became a fugitive. It was the largest insider trading case ever mounted by the government up to that time—and a forewarning of the lengths that Fomon would go to exact revenge.

The letters kept arriving on Tom Morley's desk.

"In seven out of twelve months during 1980, average float exceeded the average ledger balance in the account," the National Bank of Detroit wrote in an angry letter dated March 11, 1981. "This situation is totally unacceptable and cannot be allowed to continue."

Later Ball sent around another internal memo. It noted that a particular Hutton branch had been earning a consistent $30,000 per month "just from overdrafting of the bank account."

It went on, "At the beginning of March 1981, the branch manager changed cashiers, and for the months of March and April 1981 the same branch earned less than $10,000 per month by overdrafting the bank account.

"A good branch cashier is worth as much as an A.E.," or account executive, the memo concluded.

The National City Bank in Cleveland wrote in August 1981. "As you can see," the bank told Morley, "our bank got pretty well clobbered due to the transfer of uncollected funds."

Chemical Bank in New York City complained in a November 1981 letter that "certain of the accounts have run substantial uncollected or overdraft balances."

The flood of letters did nothing to discourage Hutton. In fact, it was quite clear to Ball, as his memos showed, that the need for overdrafting was growing as Hutton's real financial condition deteriorated. That's when a subtle change took place in the tone of Ball's memos—they began to show the building tension. No longer exuberant, witty, and positive, they now revealed an uncharacteristic worrying.

In August 1981 Ball circulated a memo warning that "interest levels are a two-edged lord [sic]; they can go down as well as up. When they do, the impact on the bottom line of many branches will be a grave one."

In a strikingly candid October memo, Ball noted, "Without gigantic interest profits, the bottom line would have been a dismal one, as I know you are aware."

And in his regular "Region of the Month" memo shortly afterward, Ball acknowledged, "In many respects our reported financial results were, I believe, better than our actual performance," because interest profits covered up for the weakening retail operation. The expense problem was getting worse.

At the same time, overdrafting was generating so much income that branch managers and regional executives began to brawl over who would claim the spoils. As tempers flared, Ball was called in to intermediate what had become a top issue for Hutton, since it affected the personal bonuses of branch managers and the regional barons. For weeks memo after memo was circulated. Solomon-like, Ball spread the money evenly among the branch managers and regional barons, not wanting to upset any members of his constituency.


In early December Hutton's Batavia, New York, branch wrote an $8 million check against its account at the Genesee Country Bank, in LeRoy, New York, near Rochester. There was not $8 million in the account, just another check that had been deposited but had not cleared. That check was drawn on a Hutton account at the United Penn Bank in Wilkes-Barre, Pennsylvania. The check was covered by the deposit of another check that would not clear for several days.

Worried United Penn Bank and Genesee Country Bank officials swapped phone calls and discovered that Hutton was playing the same game with both of them. In fact, a total of $22 million in checks had been shuffled around in this way, a dangerously large sum for such small banks. They were infuriated that Hutton would try and sting them in this way, and they decided to blow the whistle.

On December 18 an angry United Penn official contacted the

Federal Deposit Insurance Corporation, the federal agency that insures bank deposits and regulates banks, and explained that the bank was being ripped off in an obviously coordinated fashion by Hutton.

On December 29 Genesee Country Bank contacted the New York State Banking Department. At least twenty-five chains, or pinwheels, had developed at Hutton, with as many as thirteen branches in each. United Penn Bank and Genesee Country Bank were just small links in these nationwide networks, but they were the first to go to the authorities.

In January 1982 Gerald B. Korn, a Federal Deposit Insurance Corporation examiner, began looking into Hutton's banking practices. Korn wrote an extraordinary single-spaced, two-page memo leveling the strongest charges ever made against such a huge financial institution. "At first glance it could appear that Hutton was 'playing the float,'" he observed, "but further investigation revealed evidence of an apparent deliberate kiting operation almost 'textbook' in form."

Korn added ominously, "In view of the nature of this operation and the involvement of various interstate branch offices of Hutton, the shift of funds appears to be directed from a central source."

Four days later two Hutton officials met with a senior vice-president at the United Penn Bank. Told plainly that Hutton had been caught red-handed, one of the Hutton officials, Paul Bentz, offered to pay United Penn Bank $5,000 to drop the matter. It was too late.

Donald J. Kavanaugh, the deputy superintendent and chief examiner of the New York State Banking Department, called Bob Ross, Hutton's cashier, in early February. Ross passed the call like a hot potato to Hutton's deputy general counsel, Loren Schechter. An appointment was set up for February 10, 1982, a Tuesday, at ten A.M.

From the meeting's first moment, something seemed horribly wrong. Instead of being shown to some bureaucrat's cubicle for what they supposed would be a routine discussion, the Hutton officials were led to the department's imposing boardroom. Then they were confronted by a phalanx of senior examiners and lawyers from both the state and the Federal Reserve.

Schechter, a hulking, voluble man with a staccato laugh and a mop of salt-and-pepper hair, waited tensely for a bombshell. The deputy general counsel of the New York Federal Reserve Bank asked if he had heard of the Genesee Country Bank in LeRoy, New York. And then: "Did you know that E. F. Hutton bounced $22 million in checks there?"

"First of all, I've never even heard of LeRoy," Schechter replied. "Why is this important?"

Ernest Patrikis, the fed lawyer, said that an investigation had shown the checks to be part of a pinwheel.

"What's a pinwheel?" Schechter asked, still in the dark.

"That's when you move money for no other purpose than to create float," Patrikis replied, instantly ending the game and crushing any hopes Ball and Fomon had for a short-term fix to Hutton's deep problems.

# A REAL WRENCH

"It is with enormous regret that I am tendering my resignation from Hutton. By any measure, my association with the firm has been an incredibly fine experience, and I will always treasure it. In particular, leaving a great friend, and a fine mentor, and a superb leader like Bob Fomon is a real wrench for me.

"However, I have been offered the opportunity to head Prudential Capital and Investment Services Inc., a company which includes Prudential Capital Corp., Bache, and other units.

"The chance to be chief executive of a group of major financial services firms, and to help shape them, is simply too magnetic to pass up. It will give me a chance to build something new.

"I hope and trust that the environment, attitude and esprit that has made Hutton so successful will burn brightly for many years. To each of you, my very best wishes for continued business and personal success. There are none better.

"With thanks and [garbled], George Ball."

Ball delivered the message to all Hutton employees on Monday morning, July 19, 1982. It was just the blackest of a number of dark clouds gathering over the firm. Ball's resignation came days after Hutton reported that in the first half of 1982 it had earned a paltry $6 million before taxes, a 90 percent decline from the year earlier and a sure sign of Ball's inability to deal with Hutton's growing expense burden. The firm's profitability was less than half of the industry average.

But that was the least of the problems, as only a few knew. Ball's abrupt departure came two months after David Dart Queen, the United States attorney in Scranton, Pennsylvania, sent grand jury subpoenas to Fomon and two other Hutton officials as part of a massive investigation of the bank overdrafting.

In addition, Hutton's public finance department had just decided, secretly, to halt underwriting upper floater bonds after realizing that the securities were bound to cause Hutton tens of millions of dollars in losses.

Ball had one other problem: as he had told a number of friends, including Hutton colleagues Tom Lynch and Scott Pierce, he had political ambitions in his home state of New Jersey. At times he hinted that he might run for governor, at others he suggested that he wanted some sort of high appointive position. Either way he needed a spotless business record. Hutton, however, was almost beyond help. The tantalizing alternative was to ride into Prudential-Bache on a white horse and deal with problems not of his own making. He could only look good. It was no coincidence, as he made clear to his friends, that Prudential Insurance, based in Newark, New Jersey, was one of the largest employers in the state and a major political influence.

"George Ball is resigning from Hutton to become the head of Prudential Capital and Investment Services Inc.," Fomon, too wounded to speak, wrote in his follow-up message to the firm that Monday. "George has been a good friend of all of us. We will miss him, and wish him well.

"I will assume the position of president. Our new divisional alignment, although not in any way designed for this purpose, will make my taking over the responsibilities of the president work well.

"I am sorry to see George leave, as I know most of you are, but know that Hutton has a wealth of talent that will let us continue forward and even more successfully in the future.

"Robert Fomon."

. . .

That day proved the most traumatic in the careers of nearly all of Hutton's twelve thousand employees. But no more than for Fomon. Ball's departure was a deliberate slap at Fomon and his monopoly of the real power at Hutton, a deliberate assault against the father by his son, with the ultimate weapon, abandonment. Fomon had made it clear that he was not prepared to cede any of his titles or power to Ball. Worse, Ball had plenty of company. The heads of trading, institutional sales, and research and asset management all quit around the same time. For the first time since Fomon had taken over in the turmoil of 1970, his management team was breaking apart.

Ball's defection hurt the worst. Fomon wandered the firm that day in something close to a trance. He had spent his life trying to overcome his father's rejection and now faced this, from the man he had groomed, he thought, like a son.

That evening, Norm Epstein, head of operations, Scott Pierce, and Jim Lopp shared their dismay with their stricken chief over a bottle of Scotch Fomon kept handy in his office. Fomon, drunk and nearly in tears, surprised his lieutenants. He spoke glowingly of Ball. He refused to admit that this imagined son-figure had been disloyal. It suggested that he might not have been an ideal father, and that was too much.

"He's always been so loyal," Fomon said. "He understands the retail business better than anyone on the Street. Goddamn, he understands that business."

"Bob," Epstein finally said, "you better wake up. He's going to hit us. If we don't get ourselves pulled together in a hurry, you wait and see what he does to us."

Epstein was right. It was Ball, after all, who had made an art of paying huge bonuses to swipe brokers from other brokerage houses. In short order, Greg Smith, head of the equity department and a close friend of Ball's, was lured to Bache. Ball recruited Hutton's chief economist, its top stock strategist, and a handful of stock analysts. He tried, but failed, to entice Don Sanders, Hutton's top broker, based in Houston. Loren Schechter, the deputy counsel, later jumped ship.

In fact, Ball began a huge bidding war among retail brokerage houses. He threw hundreds of thousands of dollars at brokers to try to lure them away, which prompted even higher counterbids by the other firms. For two years Wall Street's pay scale for retail brokers was thrown out of whack by the war Ball started.

Belatedly the vengeful side of Bob Fomon came to life. Two weeks after Ball quit he spoke at a dinner in Denver where the region's best brokers were being rewarded—something he would never have gone to before. Fomon presented a dismaying contrast to the man who, so many times before, had walked along the edge of propriety by telling his off-color jokes while remaining generally impressive. That evening, what Hutton's top brokers saw was an angry drunk. His odd voice slurred and his balance unsure, Fomon delivered a biting, humiliating diatribe against the impudent Ball. The vitriol embarrassed the brokers, unused to seeing their chief executive so out of control.

Fomon was no longer a distant eminence. After willingly giving up so much operating authority to his understudy, he was back in the saddle.

It was a frightening prospect. His closest remaining aide was Tom Lynch, the chief financial officer, a man never known as a hands-on manager or as someone having any real influence over Fomon. And Hutton's board of directors, in theory the guardian of the stockholders' interests, had been hand-crafted by Fomon to follow his lead blindly. The board was a grouping of sycophants.

Of the twenty-one E. F. Hutton Group directors, eighteen were insiders. In other words, the career paths and incomes of the vast majority of directors were directly controlled by Fomon. It was not a good bet that they would be willing to stand up and say no to him.

None of the three independent directors Fomon placed on his board were remotely up to the task of exercising any real oversight. Edward C. Cazier, Jr., was a close friend from Fomon's brief stint at law school and Fomon's personal lawyer. His law firm received hundreds of thousands of dollars a year in business from Hutton, a dependency that, in the eyes of many, made him one of the biggest yes-men on the board.

Warren A. Law was a Harvard Business School professor, whose annual income came largely from the many board seats he held. Law was Hutton's first outside director, joining the firm in 1974, and though he knew the board was powerless to challenge the CEO, he never raised his voice to express his skepticism.

And there was Dina Merrill, the actress and daughter of Edward F. Hutton. She was the keeper of the flame, the direct link to the firm's legendary past. But she was unschooled in the financial esoterica of a brokerage firm. There was no way to resist Fomon.

Fomon was taking charge at a time when the securities world was still in a state of flux. By mid-1982 Hutton was triple its size in the mid-1970s, a vastly more complex machine. Ten years earlier Hutton was trying to take flight at Kitty Hawk; now it was on a launch pad at Cape Canaveral, with all the danger that entailed.

Several crosscurrents were shaping the new Wall Street. The most important was simply its growth, a change whose effects could hardly be overstated. Money market funds had exploded in popularity, draining hundreds of billions of dollars from passbook savings accounts and funneling it to brokerage accounts. The brokerage firms then devised numerous new products to try to lock up that huge inflow of capital. Firms that had to deal with a few thousand employees were now managing well over ten thousand and many billions of dollars in transactions a day.

Much had changed in the way a retail broker operated, too. At one time a stockbroker was known as a "customers' man." The name expressed the ideal that the broker did nothing but look out for his clients' interests. Brokers often did their own research on stocks rather than being served up prerecorded messages from analysts at headquarters. The customers' man measured himself by his customers' profits.

By the 1980s this ideal was a quaint memory. Brokers were measured by production, how much they sold, not by the quality of what they sold or how their customers fared. None of the major firms rewarded brokers whose customers' investments performed well. The major firms provided almost identical services and identical products. Brokers were trained at mass marketing, not custom service. Brokers became, as the industry called them, "asset gatherers" for their brokerage houses, not professionals offering a specialized service.

Still, the marketing pitch remained old-fashioned. Advertising was used to overlay these nearly indistinguishable sales machines with facades that seemed to differ from house to house. In the public eye, Hutton held on to much of its prestige. "We are individual, not mass marketers," Bob Fomon wrote, quite disingenuously, in one annual report. That was a difficult claim to make for a firm that had 6,600 brokers in 413 branch offices and 16,800 employees.

Like a Sears or a K mart, a brokerage house had to keep pumping products through its sales systems in high volume. Wall Streeters have an expression for this: "stuffing paper." Adding to the pressures toward uniformity and volume production was competition. Other types of financial institutions began to eye the securities industry covetously. Management experts persuaded legions of executives to believe in something called synergy. In other words, related financial services concerns, if merged, would increase their sales because of a cross-fertilization of ideas and a wider product line for customers—or so the argument went.

The pressures for change burst out in 1981. Bache & Company, foundering throughout the 1970s, found itself the subject of a hostile takeover bid by the Belzberg family of Canada. Bache found a white knight, the huge Prudential Insurance.

In rapid succession, American Express acquired Shearson, Sears bought Dean Witter Reynolds, and Philipp Brothers, a secretive international commodities dealer of vast wealth, bought Salomon Brothers, the elite bond firm. Equitable Life Assurance would later buy Donaldson, Lufkin & Jenrette, and General Electric would grab Kidder, Peabody & Company. And then Primerica acquired Smith Barney.

Within a few years the only remaining independent, full-service retail brokerage firms were Merrill Lynch (still Wall Street's largest), Hutton, and Paine Webber. Merrill was of ample size and had a strategy. Fomon was being left behind.


Ball had taken some tentative steps toward trying to prepare Hutton for this new world, but they were too few and too late. Just three weeks before he quit, he had assembled his managers at Scanticon, a corporate retreat in Princeton, New Jersey, where he launched the most sweeping reorganization in Hutton's history.

Before, Hutton's feudal barons had reported directly to Fomon, even if Ball gave them their operating instructions. Ball tried to rationalize the reporting system, creating ten division

heads who would report to him, the president. Thus the reorganization expanded Ball's role beyond the retail division. He was
grooming himself for broader responsibilities.

This was the "divisional alignment" Fomon had referred to in
his message announcing Ball's departure. But now that Ball was
gone, there was one glaring problem: the retail operation was
completely headless.

Ball had spent months designing the new organization so that
he could broaden his influence without loosening his grip over his
personal power base, retail. Thus Ball chose as head of the division
someone who would still have to rely heavily on him to run the
sprawling retail network. Scott Pierce was Ball's tool.

The decision shocked the whole firm, but two people in particular: Pierce and Jerry Miller. Miller, who had followed one step
behind Ball up the retail hierarchy, had longed for the retail job
and believed he had been prepared for it. But Ball made him head
of Hutton's equity division, a business he knew little about.

Pierce had initially been confused when Ball broached the
idea. He had always worked in public finance, never retail. He also
acknowledged that he did not have the personality for the job. It
required someone who was outgoing, smooth, good with a crowd,
and a strong leader. Pierce was an earnest, often reticent, hesitant
man who wrestled at length over tough decisions, eventually giving him ulcers.

There was another important factor, even if it went unstated.
Pierce's sister, Barbara, was married to then Vice President
George Bush. Pierce's connection with the White House had never
been explicitly tapped, but Hutton officials found opportunities to
let it drop in conversations when it seemed it might help.

"Scottie, I'm going to be there right behind you to help until
you develop your own feel for it," Ball had promised a reluctant
Pierce. Eventually, Ball said, he would end up as chairman when
Fomon left, while Pierce would become president and CEO. "It
appealed to my ego," Pierce conceded.

Three weeks later George Ball had cleared out his desk. The
man who could only do the job with Ball's backing had been suck-
ered. Fomon, terrified that further changes could begin a process
he would not be able to control, refused suggestions that Pierce
and Miller switch jobs. Hutton's management was in disarray just

as all the problems created in previous years began bobbing to the surface.

In April 1982 the worst fears of the public finance department were realized. The credit rating services lowered their rating of National Steel, an issuer of upper floaters. Hutton's brokers argued fiercely that the firm had to stand by its guarantee on the value of the bonds or they would lose customers. Ball had agreed. Immediately the customers sold back $20 million of the $52 million in National Steel bonds Hutton had underwritten. Hutton was stuck holding the low-quality bonds, whose real value was significantly below the prices the firm had paid. The firm had just taken its first multimillion-dollar loss of the 1980s.

The decision had also set a terrible precedent: Hutton's shareholders, not the brokers or officials themselves, would pay for the shortsighted mistakes that the firm's officials had made. The brokers would not have to return the commissions they earned selling all of those bonds.

The next year the rating agencies twice lowered the credit classification of U.S. Steel, another issuer of upper floaters. Again Hutton bought bonds back from its customers at the artificially inflated level of par, to spare its brokers any loss of commissions. The losses from the upper floaters were now running in the tens of millions of dollars—a year's worth of earnings.

It also became apparent that Hutton's headlong rush into tax shelters had produced a string of disasters, a string of lawsuits, and growing anger among Hutton's brokers. They were losing customers—and their own money, since they had also invested in these poorly conceived deals.

Oil prices were falling. Hence, oil drilling activity was declining, hurting all the energy deals Hutton had marketed. And real estate prices started heading south in the Southwest, taking with them a number of Hutton tax shelter programs.

Hutton's lawyers were starting to examine some of the deals the firm had greedily peddled and were shaking their heads in disgust at what they found. Names like Anadarko, Gulfstream, Lovelady, and American Completion were the sources of enormously expensive headaches around the firm. Tens of millions of dollars of losses clearly stood in the offing. Kutak, Rock & Campbell, Hutton's key outside law firm in handling the tax shelters, was starting to warn of massive losses and massive litigation.

Hutton's internal procedures for vetting the shelters, known as due diligence, were ridiculously weak. Numerous deals got through that consultants would later declare poorly structured or outright rip-offs. By then, of course, it was too late.

There had been one clear warning. Simpson, Thacher & Bartlett, the prominent Manhattan law firm, worked as counsel on one of Hutton's early tax shelter deals. It stood to earn a steady stream of fees if Hutton continued the relationship, so there was plenty of incentive for the lawyers to minimize the potential problems and focus on the pluses.

But the deal proved jarring for the lawyers because of its riskiness and the huge fees being taken. So disturbed were the Simpson, Thacher lawyers that they took the extraordinary step of arguing that their firm should reject any further work with Hutton in the area. After a lengthy debate, the partners agreed. Hutton simply found a new law firm.

Hutton brokers would sell more than $8 billion of these investments. A review of these tax shelters indicates that approximately $3 billion of that was lost or produced returns significantly below what had been projected. Hutton, of course, focused on the short term. So what if its customers were fleeced. Any losses would be paid out of the shareholders' pockets.

Every department at the firm would start demonstrating the same short-term orientation at this time, including the commodities department.

Arnold H. Phelan, known as a prankster with a wild temper and an offbeat sense of humor, ran Hutton's commodities department as a demiempire. Phelan was a former lawyer who was now an aggressive generator of income for the firm. Thus there was no alarm when Phelan went to Loren Schechter in early 1982 to ask about the propriety of handling a major new account he had just swiped from Merrill Lynch.

The account would be handled through a Hutton branch in Lugano, Switzerland, Phelan explained, but would involve large cash deposits being made in New York. The account holder was an Italian, Franco Della Torre.

Given no further information, Schechter told him that that would be permissible, as long as any deposit of more than $10,000 in cash was properly reported to the government—under the terms of a law intended to halt money laundering. Ball was also contacted, and he approved.

Della Torre did indeed make large cash deposits. Between April 27 and September 27, 1982, he deposited $15.5 million in the form of small bills stuffed into gym bags, received personally by Phelan.

Then, on October, 5, 1982, Schechter heard from Hutton's head of security, Bill Condon. He reported that an agent from the FBI had just called, explaining that Della Torre was connected with a Mafia crime family and that his account was being used to launder drug money.

In fact, Della Torre was a kingpin in what was later called the Pizza Connection, one of the largest Mafia heroin distribution enterprises the government had ever uncovered. The great E. F. Hutton & Company was laundering drug profits.

When Arnie Phelan was informed of the FBI queries, Della Torre was told that the feds were on to him. The account was closed, Della Torre disappeared, and the feds, after two years of painstaking detective work, were thrown off the trail. They were furious—particularly when they discovered that Phelan had accepted a gold Cartier watch from Della Torre for his special handling of the account. (The watch was said to have been returned later.)

Fomon, meanwhile, had his hands full trying to wrestle with the expense monster Ball had left behind. Hutton's confidential internal records showed that the operating profit of the brokerage subsidiary, E. F. Hutton & Company, peaked in 1980 at $79.2 million. The unit's operating profit then slid to $74.8 million in 1981 and $68 million in 1982.

Those internal records showed something else strange going on. In late February 1982 Hutton's lawyers had ordered the overdrafting stopped in response to the secret meeting with the state banking regulators and then the subpoenas. The huge amounts of interest the firm had been generating since late 1979 dried up. Not only was Hutton facing a criminal investigation, but it had just lost a major source of earnings.

A perceptive stock analyst at Jessup & Lamont Securities wrote a detailed report on Hutton in which he struggled with this odd fact. He calculated what he described as Hutton's "system float," or the sums Hutton kept on deposit with its various banks. The sum, he found, had plummeted to $112 million in the first nine months of 1982, from $405 million in the first nine months of 1981—completely counter to the trend at other brokerage houses. He had no idea of the importance of what he'd stumbled onto.

"While I have had several meetings with management on this point, no clear understanding has emerged as of this writing," the analyst reported.


The deterioration grew so alarming and Fomon's self-confidence was shrinking so quickly that he allowed himself to be persuaded to do something that was, for him, shocking: he hired the equivalent of a corporate psychoanalyst—a consulting firm. He chose Arnold Detri Associates, which spent months examining Hutton.

In a nine-page report filled with pithy observations, the consultants concluded that Hutton had completely lost track of which businesses made money and which businesses lost money, noting that revenues had more than tripled from 1977 to 1981, but operating profits of Hutton's core business, without the interest earnings, had declined from $7 million to $6.3 million. Expenses were eating up the rest.

The analysis also made clear that Hutton's growth in revenues had come largely through adding new offices, not making branches more productive. But that could not be maintained because Hutton had opened branches in virtually all regions of the country.

The most penetrating observations were on the ethos Fomon had created. "A number of managers lack either the skills or capabilities to manage effectively within the current scope and complexity of the firm's activities. The organization structure has evolved far more slowly than the size and complexity of the firm."

Sobering as the report was, Fomon knew something that the consultants did not—the government's criminal investigation was moving ahead with dangerous speed, despite the tough tactics taken by Hutton's lawyers. Huge numbers of Hutton documents had been subpoenaed by the Pennsylvania grand jury.

It was worrisome, but Fomon had been given one assurance by his lawyers: there was no smoking gun, only complex, vague, and circumstantial evidence. At least Fomon had that to comfort him, or so he thought.

"Our banking activities during the last six months have been no different than our banking activities off and on for the last five years. Additionally, I believe those activities are encouraged by the firm and are in fact identical to what the firm practices on a national basis. Specifically, we will from time to time draw down not only deposits plus anticipated deposits, but also bogus deposits."

Perry H. Bacon, manager of a Washington, D.C., Hutton branch, was an angry man. He had been caught red-handed ripping off a local bank through egregious overdrafting. That had prompted a bitter memo in March 1982 from Steve Bralove, manager of another Washington, D.C., office and an intracompany rival. Bralove complained that Bacon's excessive overdrafting had cost him the bank's trust account business. Bacon decided to fire back with his own broadside on April 23, 1982. It was the most important memo written in E. F. Hutton's history.

"Those bogus deposits create a reduction in our net capital ratio requirement which allows the firm to deploy capital elsewhere," Bacon wrote. "Furthermore, we (as a firm) learned to use the float because it is exactly what the banks do to us. I know of at least a dozen managers at E. F. Hutton—managers who along with Bill Sullivan and Tom Morley taught me the system—who do precisely the same thing."

Bacon conceded, "The obvious drawback to the system is that it can cost the bank money." But, he added in a contradictory afterthought, "our objective is not to steal money from the banks. Whatever the bank may have lost, we have enjoyed a greater profit due to the spread float.

"By the way," Bacon went on, "Tom Morley believes that within 2–3 years the entire system will be automated and all domestic checks will clear in one day. Therefore, as Tom stated in our New York BOM [branch office manager] meeting, the time to take advantage of the system is now."

The plain-looking document sat in a closed file for nearly three years.

# RUNNING
# OUT OF CONTROL

After a boozy dinner at a Mexican restaurant with his son and a flock of dazzling models—with whom he had entertained himself by exchanging sexual gossip—Fomon had wandered to his Fifth Avenue home on this warm summer evening. It was August 9, 1983, and Fomon, rejected by many of his old drinking cronies, increasingly went out with his son and his son's friends, who were far more easily impressed by his CEO's title. That night he fumbled out of his clothes, then decided to go to the bathroom to get some medicine for a cold sore. Feeling his way through the dark room, he swung his leg under the heavy wooden bed frame, where it became wedged, and then stumbled to the side. Fomon's leg snapped, then twisted unnaturally, knocking him out cold.

After what seemed like ages, he came to, his leg shattered and aching madly. Fomon became panicky as he struggled to remain conscious through the excruciating pain. He managed to crawl across his bedroom floor to a telephone. Fomon called his ex-wife, Sharon Kay Ritchie, with whom he had remained close despite their messy divorce.

"Sharon, I think I broke my leg," Fomon struggled to say. It was the middle of the night.

"Bob, you don't 'think' your leg is broken," she told him, not pleased at having been woken up at that late hour and believing he had, as usual, just been drinking too much. "It is or it isn't. Go back to sleep and see how it feels in the morning. Now get some sleep." She hung up.

Fomon tried his current girlfriend, Pam O'Neill. She was too far away to come herself, so Fomon asked her to contact Redington Jahncke, a Hutton broker who lived nearby—and who was married to Robin Davis, Fomon's previous girlfriend.

By morning Fomon was in the hospital and being prepared for hours of delicate surgery to realign the ruined bone. A steel rod had to be drilled into place. Later he would need more surgery. The bones just would not knit properly.

Around Hutton, Fomon's history of womanly exploits encouraged gossip that he had injured himself while engaged in an acrobatic sexual maneuver with some limber-limbed minx. There was also speculation that he must have been stoned on drugs, since a number of the young people he hung out with were believed to be drug users and Fomon was certainly not one to say no to a good time.

At one time that would have been the source of pride around Hutton. Now it only made Fomon seem ridiculous, an old man who had nearly killed himself trying to have sex with some kid. The Dorian Gray–like blessing that had once kept Fomon unusually vigorous and handsome had suddenly turned into Dorian Gray's curse of unnaturally swift aging.

The heavy smoking and drinking seemed to be catching up with him—just as the decadence was catching up with Hutton. Fomon's mind was slower. His hair was grayer. His confidence wavered. He grew more arbitrary. His squeaky voice shrank up even more.

Now that the firm was effectively headless, the once subtle jostling between Hutton's ruling barons was breaking out into increasingly vicious battles for position.

A Denver newspaper carried a brief item saying that Dale Frey, Hutton's powerful mountain region head, was about to move to Hutton's New York headquarters for an important new job, left unnamed, but implied.

Clarence G. Catallo, Jr., a senior executive in the midwest region, also lobbied for the top job. Jerry Miller, running the equity division, still harbored hopes that he would be named president and lord over the retail system. Norm Epstein was yet another contender. And Perry Bacon, the aggressive Washington branch office manager, had believed the coddling noises he'd heard about bringing him to New York sometime for a "very important job."

Fomon discussed with his cronies, particularly Dick Jones, an old friend from Los Angeles, the possibility of recruiting someone from outside the firm to replace Ball. One name kept popping up—Bob Rittereiser, a senior executive at Merrill Lynch and a friend of Jones's. Rittereiser's brother, Fred, a former police detective who had moved to Wall Street to work with Bill Lupien—of Trading Company of the West fame—would act as an ongoing intermediary between Fomon and Bob Rittereiser.

Fomon had a better idea. Ailing though he might be, he shrewdly chose Scott Pierce as president of E. F. Hutton & Company, the brokerage subsidiary. Tom Lynch was appointed president of the holding company, E. F. Hutton Group.

The news drew gasps of disbelief and anger. Few recognized, though, how cleverly Fomon had reasserted his control. The holding company's president was a finance man who was used to following orders, and the president of the brokerage unit was a mild-mannered newcomer to the retail business with no independent power base and no interest in challenging the old chairman. Not least, he was the brother-in-law of Vice President Bush, which could only boost Hutton's public image.

Fomon had surrounded himself with a protective ring of competent but unthreatening managers. True, he had alienated a number of would-be usurpers, but he correctly anticipated that none would quit and give up their ambitions of grabbing the brass ring at Hutton. Most important, Fomon had placed the sprig of golden bough in hands so weak that it was as though it had not been plucked at all.

For the first time, preserving his position had clearly taken primacy for Fomon over restoring Hutton's tattered operations. Fomon felt threatened, and he demonstrated that holding on to power was more important than protecting the firm. What would that mean in practice? Two deals in particular would provide an answer.

. . .

"Dear Art," Tom Lynch began, "I am writing this letter to record
our agreement on your employment as President of E. F. Hutton
Mortgage Corporation."

The letter to Art Mueller was dated January 31, 1983. According to the terms Lynch outlined, Mueller—who pronounced his
name Miller—was guaranteed a minimum income of $180,000 for
the year. Mueller would receive 8 percent of the annual profits of
the new unit he would head, the E. F. Hutton Mortgage Corporation.

"We are looking forward to a pleasant and profitable association," Lynch, who became the new unit's chairman, wrote in concluding the agreement.

The letter culminated a long campaign by Mueller. Over a
period of months he had been trying to persuade Hutton's corporate finance division to start up a business buying and selling mortgages, largely second mortgages. Demand from thrift institutions
for these high-paying loans appeared to be growing, so Hutton
could rake in commissions for acting as an intermediary.

Hutton's risk, in theory, would be limited. The Hutton mortgage company would buy mortgages from mortgage companies
that originated the loans. Hutton's account executives would then
sell bundles of these mortgages, charging substantial markups.

Originally there had been resistance to the idea. The concern
was that Hutton simply did not possess the expertise to oversee a
business that serviced these mortgages—receiving the monthly
payments from the individual homeowners and passing them to
the holders of the mortgages, while maintaining records of the
transactions. Mueller also wanted to operate out of Little Rock,
Arkansas, which Lynch and others feared was too far away for
them to oversee.

Mueller came back six weeks later and said Hutton could do
the business without servicing the mortgages. This time, the pitch
worked.

Like many decisions at Hutton, this one was tangled in a political thicket. Robert M. Adams, a senior vice-president in Hutton's
corporate finance department, was responsible for most of Hutton's dealings with thrifts. His antagonist was William T. Dunn, an

executive vice-president and head of Hutton's bond department.

The two had been engaged in a vicious turf war. Dunn's sales-men and traders conducted a modest business buying and selling mortgage-backed securities issued by government agencies, such as the Government National Mortgage Association, known as Gin-nie Mae. They did not want to share that business—which was just starting to mushroom into a major profit source at several other securities houses—with Adams or anyone else.

Meanwhile Adams was trying to cultivate his own mortgage business to tap his contacts with the thrift industry. Rather than combine the efforts into a cooperative venture, as most other Wall Street firms had done, the Hutton managers battled jealously. Much of the fighting was over who would receive the commissions on sales of mortgage-backed securities.

The result was chaos. Adams had developed an excellent busi-ness in converting mutual savings and loans to stock ownership, giving Hutton a potentially huge lead over its competitors in build-ing a mortgage business. But the infighting crippled the firm.

Now Adams was taking the initiative. He had secretly encour-aged the formation of the new mortgage corporation in Little Rock—he was one of its original three directors, with Lynch and Mueller. By operating so far from New York, Adams figured, Dunn would not be able to control his business. It was a bad sign to be born under.

The year 1983 would also prove to be a busy one for Jim Lopp's investment banking division. In August 1983 Hutton closed on its largest investment banking deal of the year, and Lopp, one of Fomon's closest friends, who had been named head of investment banking in the wake of John Shad's departure, hailed the deal as a sign of his department's comeback.

The Mercury Savings Association and Ben Milam Savings and Loan, two Texas thrift institutions bought earlier that year by John Baylor ("J. B.") Haralson, had acquired the mortgage banking units of Orbanco, an Oregon bank holding company, and Baldwin-United, a large insurance company. Hutton acted as the adviser in the deal.

Haralson's thrifts paid slightly more than $100 million for the companies. More important, the thrifts paid Hutton a $5.835 million fee—the largest fee Lopp's department brought in for the year. The deal, however, had some unusual features.

For starters there was Haralson's partner, a Houston real estate speculator, rancher, and high-stakes wheeler-dealer named George Aubin. Aubin's relationships with the thrifts was kept deliberately fuzzy and distant, but it was clear to many at Hutton that he was the real brains behind the operation. Haralson was regarded as a front.

Aubin controlled personally a multimillion-dollar securities trading account the thrifts maintained at Hutton's Houston office. His broker: Don Sanders. Aubin also lavished hugely expensive gifts, such as jewels, furs, and cars, on a key officer of the thrifts, Caren Grant, giving him further influence over their affairs. Aubin described himself as a consultant to the thrifts and denied that Haralson was a front.

With big fees to be earned, Jim Lopp's corporate finance department was not going to let a little charade get in the way—even if there was good reason for Aubin to remain in the background.

Aubin, in fact, was well known to the Texas thrift and banking regulators. The regulators believed Aubin was behind the failure of several banks in the state during the 1970s and did not want him in either the banking or thrift businesses. After a series of financial setbacks, Aubin had filed for personal bankruptcy in 1979 and was involved in the costly failure of a company called Mortgage America—which provided loans for mobile home purchases—that nearly caused Hutton $4 million in losses.

On top of that, on August 5, 1981, Hutton's Commodity Credit Committee voted to refuse to do business with Aubin. But there was an overriding consideration: Don Sanders was Aubin's broker and wanted the business. Sanders had worked with Aubin since 1972 and had even invested in several of Aubin's bank deals.

It was Sanders who had subsequently introduced Aubin to the corporate finance department. (Sanders would personally collect $750,000 of Hutton's fee for the acquisition of the mortgage companies by the thrifts.) With Sanders pushing for the deal, Hutton just took elaborate precautions to conceal Aubin's role—particularly since both of the sellers of the mortgage companies had explicitly refused to do business with Aubin. No problem. Hutton passed itself off as the buyer of the mortgage companies. After two very difficult closings, Hutton simply on-sold the companies to Aubin's thrifts.

The result: both Orbanco and Baldwin-United sued Hutton when they learned the truth. There were expensive out-of-court settlements that cost Hutton—certainly not Sanders—hundreds of thousands of dollars.

There was an even more peculiar twist. Hutton had stopped doing business with Aubin several years earlier when an account in the name of his wife, Cameron, sustained heavy losses and developed a negative net worth of $850,000. The losses came from commodities trading, a passion of Aubin's. Aubin walked away from the debt, and Hutton refused to do business with him until he repaid it.

So Hutton added an extra $850,000 to the investment banking fees charged Mercury Savings and Ben Milam Savings for the acquisition of the mortgage companies. The money was then used to pay off Aubin's old debt. In other words the two thrifts, supposedly owned by J. B. Haralson, paid a debt owed personally by Aubin. Even by Texas standards that was a remarkable show of generosity.

Aubin then reactivated his old trading accounts with Don Sanders. That is when the story got even more interesting.

By mid-1984 Aubin was trading heavily in commodities again, mostly Treasury bond options and futures. He also dealt in stocks, accumulating large positions in, among other companies, E. F. Hutton. He operated through a string of eleven accounts, in the name of two ranching and real estate companies he controlled, Wichita Land & Cattle and Sigma Capital.

Sanders and his partner, John I. Mundy, were delighted to have Aubin back. It was easy to see why: Aubin's trading generated huge commissions. He was on a wild speculative spree, the kind that brokerage houses are supposed to halt because of the risks involved. But not at Hutton. Not with Sanders involved.

There was little notice in New York when Art Mueller signed an agreement on December 13, 1983, with the First American Mortgage Company, or Famco. Operated principally out of Maryland, Famco had second-mortgage origination offices across the South.

Mueller saw the company as a good source of new mortgages to pump through the Hutton system. Within months Hutton became Famco's principal customer.

These were no ordinary mortgages, though. The loans carried usurious interest rates, as much as 18 percent. In addition, the up-front points could rise to as much as 30 percent of the value of the mortgage. These extraordinary costs meant that the borrowers were paying in some instances 100 percent and more in interest. Only a certain kind of borrower would accept such terms: they were desperate, unsophisticated, and unable to borrow at more reasonable terms. This was just a form of loan sharking.

If desperation forced people to borrow at those rates, why would a thrift buy such a risky mortgage? Often because they were also desperate. A number of ailing thrifts were eager to buy loans paying high interest rates, despite the high risks, to try to bolster their sagging returns. Hutton, the first-class firm, had thus become an intermediary in what was by far the riskiest and most unethical end of the financial spectrum.

In New York Hutton's management paid almost no attention to the satellite in Little Rock. It was making money, so Lynch left it alone. Thus, neither did New York notice a letter that Mueller sent to the chairman of Famco on August 15, 1984.

As part of its agreement with Hutton, Famco was obliged to provide a regular flow of information, including annual statements of Famco's financial condition and statements detailing how many of the mortgages were delinquent. Since Hutton had not permitted Mueller to service mortgages, Famco was supposed to be handling those chores, for a fee.

But Famco failed to produce any of the required information—which should have set off an alarm that something was amiss. Indeed, Famco was covering up a rising tide of bad loans. Instead of reporting to Hutton that a certain borrower had stopped making payments—an admission that would have harmed Famco's credibility as a source of quality mortgages—Famco was using the proceeds of new loans to cover overdue payments on old loans. It was a classic Ponzi scheme.

All the signs of the fraud were there. But Mueller told Famco, in effect, not to worry about it. In a neat, five-point letter, Mueller noted that Famco had not complied with the terms of the 1983

agreement, but that Hutton would waive receipt of the account-
ings. The concessions plainly recognized that Famco was in chaos.
Famco's fraud had been discovered—yet Hutton did nothing to
upset the flow of business. Hutton kept buying the Famco mortgages at the rate of $10 million a month.

"Hutton further acknowledges that the Servicing Agreement
is not now in default and waives any right to claim a default under
the Servicing Agreement," Mueller wrote. "If I can be of further
assistance to you, please feel free to call me."

In November 1984 a Hutton accountant flew to Little Rock for
the first inspection of the mortgage unit's books and records. Neither Lynch nor Adams nor anyone else at Hutton had looked at the
documentation providing details on the sorts of mortgages Famco
was selling. The accountant immediately discovered the depth of
the mess. He returned a few weeks later sounding like an astronaut
who had just visited a distant planet. Lynch and the controller
could not believe the unearthly financial tales he related—and he
had yet to uncover the Ponzi scheme Famco was operating.

"This is the foreclosure business," one accountant yelled at
Tom Lynch, the ostensible chairman of the Hutton unit. "We are
in the fucking foreclosure business. Where is the oversight at this
company? Who is minding the store?"

# 9

## UP THE CREEK

Scott Pierce was panicky. He was struggling to deal with George Ball's legacy, the huge expense problems of the retail system, but he was feeling swamped. Profits were down and were destined to decline further. The productivity of Hutton's fabled sales force was tumbling sharply—from $587,000 per account executive in the second quarter of 1983 to $374,000 in the second quarter of 1984.

"Bob, we have to take some steps to get this under control," Pierce pleaded with Fomon. "It is getting worse."

Fomon had little interest in tackling such thorny problems. He had, in fact, developed an unusual habit. When he heard something he did not like, such as what poor shape the business was in, he would get up and limp out of the room. He rarely joined a management meeting at its beginning. Instead he would wander Hutton's executive floor, popping into meetings as he liked. As soon as tough issues came up, the graying old wraith would just float out the exit, the only evidence he had been there a curl of smoke and a dirty ashtray. The message his disappearing acts sent were, "It's your problem, you figure it out. I'm the chairman, so don't bother me with details." It was a shrewd way of evading responsibility.

Pierce brought in yet another outside consultant. Handy Associates, hired initially to study Hutton's compensation system, wrote in a lengthy report that Hutton was riven by ponderous political divisions, that the regional barons focused on their own domains at the expense of the firm, that there was a widespread sense of drift, and that there was no hint Fomon had a real strategy or that he did any formal business planning. The study joined the growing pile in a file drawer.

But Fomon could not ignore all the warnings flooding in. He listened to a few friends, in particular Dick Jones, an old drinking buddy from California.

"Bob, with your leg, the problems at the firm, and everything else, you aren't going to last unless you get involved again," Jones told Fomon. "I hate to say this, because I know the company means so much to you, but you're going to lose your job."

Fomon was silent, but he did not disappear. Jones had said the one thing that could move him into action.

With Jones and a few other friends pushing, 1984 was the year Bob Fomon was going to become responsible again. Almost. He looked over the firm's gloomy results and decided that a grand gesture was what Hutton needed. The master manipulator of symbols responded with a campaign of symbols. Fomon decided Hutton needed a new headquarters.

A "search" was supposedly conducted, but it miraculously came up with the results that Fomon wanted. He did not want to move into "used" space, he wanted a new building. CBS, which occupied one of the most striking and well-known skyscrapers in midtown, was constructing a new office tower next door to its Avenue of the Americas landmark. It was across from the Museum of Modern Art and a few doors down from the "21" Club. The address reeked of the kind of class Fomon still imagined the Hutton name exuded.

Fomon's enthusiasm could not have come at a better time for CBS. It was spring 1984, a dark time for the giant media company and its embattled chairman, Tom Wyman. CBS was suffering from an earnings slump and internecine political warfare. The new office tower had originally been intended for CBS's own use, but the company's ills had forced Wyman to put it out for lease. But to his dismay, the potential tenants had been dropping out one by one, spooked by the high rent. Everyone, that is, but Fomon. Bob Fomon had to have that prestigious finger in the New York skyline for E. F. Hutton.

Wyman had secretly decided to accept a modest rent just to get the structure occupied, but that did not prove necessary. Fomon's offers strayed into the stratosphere. When E. F. Hutton finally signed the lease agreement on May 2, 1984, Wyman and his lieutenants practically leapt for joy.

"Is this renegotiable, or is there some way they can back out?" Wyman asked his lawyers. He was assured the deal was solid.

Fomon was consumed by his new project. As he limped excitedly across the dimpled black rubber floor of his old office, he delved into the minutest details of lighting, bathroom fixtures, and the size of individual offices. He wrestled over the right sort of china, silverware, and linen for the huge executive dining room. He sweated with his art consultant over acquisitions.

The building, a granite-clad, pink-hued structure that looked like a cross between a Moorish castle and a set from *Star Trek*, extended the width of the block between Fifty-second and Fifty-third streets. The original address was 40 West 53rd Street, but Fomon felt Fifty-second Street—the address of "21"—carried more status. So he had the address changed to 31 West 52nd Street. A wartime general was busy redecorating his bunker as the rumble of artillery shells grew closer.

The ploy did not fool Hutton's accountants, who were as stunned as Tom Wyman at what Fomon was doing. Rich Carbone, the deputy controller, calculated that the $53-a-square-foot rent would add from $48 million to $56 million a year to Hutton's expenses for more than a decade—and it would not own the building, but just rent it. Hutton was tying up 10 percent of its capital in an asset that produced no return. The capital became, in a Wall Street term of art, illiquid.

Carbone and other executives demanded that Hutton sublease at least half of the building's thirty-two floors. Fomon finally appeared to relent. Hutton went to the city government and negotiated to develop a smaller office tower in the less fashionable neighborhood of Brooklyn Heights, at much lower cost. It would house Hutton's back office, computer operations, and training facilities. In August 1984 the city's Public Development Corporation forwarded an agreement that provided substantial tax subsidies to develop the Brooklyn site.

But each of Hutton's departmental fiefdoms persuaded Fomon that it was unfair for them to be exiled to Brooklyn. Weeks later the Brooklyn deal was abandoned. (The site and tax deal were later taken up by Morgan Stanley, which built the operations complex Hutton passed up.)

Carbone, an owlish, blunt man with a taste for salty language, expressed his outrage by clipping a magazine cartoon. Two campers with a canoe stand at the foot of what is labeled "Shit Creek." Carbone had penned in at the head of the creek a towering Hutton World Headquarters.

"I don't think we should go up there," one camper says to the other, "especially without a paddle!"

Tom Lynch showed the clipping to Fomon during a meeting in the chairman's office with Carbone. Fomon took one look and, without uttering a word, picked up his cane and strolled right out of the room.


In addition to the problems on the retail side, the investment banking business was also in trouble. Detri Associates, the consulting firm, was called in to do a study and reported widespread unrest, a lack of direction, and a growing lack of trust in the highly politicized department. The consultants tiptoed around another major problem: Jim Lopp's womanizing.

Trying to be discreet, the consultants wrote that Lopp, one of Fomon's closest friends, seemed "preoccupied," but they discussed the real problem openly with several Hutton officials. It was Pam Zilly, an attractive young investment banker who had been spending inordinate amounts of time with Lopp and was visibly intimate with him. A Hutton internal auditor began a secret file called the "Lopp-Zilly Connection," recording the couple's joint travels at company expense.

Fomon set the example at Hutton, so few were outraged that Lopp would be fooling around with a young woman who worked for him. However, office gossip increasingly focused on the perceived favoritism Lopp showed Zilly, in the form of what were rumored to be large bonuses and choice assignments.

"The visibility of their affair was total," said Paul Bagley, who was the department's administrator. "It was very obvious. It had a very damaging effect on morale. But morale was already bad because of the other problems." (Jim Lopp denied that he had had an affair with Zilly. Zilly said she had no comment.)

Rumors of affairs were far from the only problem. Low morale and poor management caused a heavy outflow of talent from the corporate finance department during 1984. The backbone of the department, three dozen professionals, quit. Jim Lopp had gutted Hutton's investment banking capability.

Seemingly in response to the immense pressure the firm was under, Fomon's health took a sudden turn for the worse. He suffered a strokelike attack on September 11, 1984, that left him incapacitated for several weeks. He kept it a secret, but the deterioration was so pronounced that it hardly mattered. Fomon's closest friends, Lopp and Dick Jones, had already begun a campaign to get him help.

First they wanted Fomon to hire an executive assistant to organize his schedule and, most important, shield him. Jay Moorhead was the choice. Moorhead was ambitious, bright, and politically well connected. After a year and a half with George Bush's presidential campaign, he rode the vice-president's coattails into the White House, where he worked for Pendleton James, President Reagan's personnel director.

In 1983 Moorhead became a Washington-based aide to Peter Ueberroth, head of the Los Angeles Olympics, and then planned to open his own public relations concern in Washington. But before he could make the move, Penn James, a friend of Jim Lopp's, connected Moorhead up with Fomon.

Moorhead had grown friendly with Ueberroth during the Olympics, and they had agreed to talk before moving to other jobs. So the night before his first interview with Fomon, Moorhead rang up Ueberroth's Los Angeles office.

"I know," Ueberroth said when Moorhead told him of the appointment. "I'm also meeting with Fomon. I think they're going to ask me to join the board."

Ueberroth was part two of the plan to get Fomon help. The Hutton board was widely understood to be a rubber stamp that never challenged the chairman. The aim was to give that supposedly supreme body some backbone. For his part, Fomon saw it largely as a public relations move. The firm needed a bright new face to show the world.

Ueberroth was a clever businessman with a commanding air and a powerful desire to make money. He looked the part of the wealthy California entrepreneur; he was tall, boyishly handsome, perpetually tanned, and trim, with a once broken nose angled sharply to the left beneath a pair of serene blue eyes. He had established himself by building a travel business, then became a national celebrity through the Olympics—he was named *Time* magazine's Man of the Year in 1984.

That wave of popularity swept him into the office of commissioner of baseball and E. F. Hutton's boardroom. Fomon, as usual, had cut a special deal with his new man. He agreed to pay Ueberroth $100,000 a year, more than double what any other director was paid. Ueberroth also lived rent free in one of Hutton's midtown apartments—widely known as the Fifth Avenue bordello because of their convenience for trysts—until he found his own home in the city.

Secretly Fomon had also made another offer to Ueberroth. He'd suggested that Ueberroth succeed him as chairman, especially if, as Fomon feared, he died suddenly before retiring. Obligingly, Ueberroth negotiated a contract with Major League Baseball that permitted him to become a nonexecutive corporate chairman outside the commissioner's office.

Despite the generous treatment, Ueberroth was appalled by what he found at Hutton. He sat on several real boards, Coca-Cola and Transamerica, so he knew how they were supposed to operate. Hutton was a joke.

"It would be an overstatement to state that it was a zoo," Ueberroth said of Hutton's board, "but not a wild overstatement. It was filled with all these people from all over the country who had some high-sounding titles, but in effect they were brokers. And each one had a private deal with Fomon."

Ueberroth was not so dismayed that he was willing to pass up the $100,000 or the prospect of leading Hutton someday. He rarely showed up for meetings but willingly lent his name to the enterprise.

The two recruits took some of the heat off Fomon and helped firm up his power. Moorhead would be his eyes and ears within the company, and Ueberroth would be his man on the board.

There was one last piece to the new strategy. Dick Jones pushed Fomon to bring in a chief operating officer to finally replace Ball. And he had a candidate for the job: Bob Rittereiser, the executive vice-president at Merrill Lynch. Ritt, as he was known, was no Wall Street star. He was regarded as an able and affable administrator, a technocrat. Eventually a dinner was set up, and Fomon came away impressed. Rittereiser seemed to understand the business, and he seemed unthreatening. He did not discuss power or politics; he talked about planning, organization, structure—all the stuff Fomon abhorred but knew to be the mark of a good staff man.

Rittereiser made it clear that he was not happy at Merrill Lynch, where he was losing a three-man race to become president. But by the end of the meal Ritt told Fomon that, nonetheless, he could not commit to anything yet. Ritt was still clinging, completely unrealistically, to the hope that he might be offered the prize at Merrill.

Discouraged by Fomon's refusal to really shake things up, a number of Hutton executives and Detri Associates broached another potential solution to the chronic thinness of Hutton's management ranks: selling Hutton or buying another firm. It was the first time this had been seriously considered.

"If firm does acquisition, sole purpose would be to acquire a complete, effective management team that, in short period, could take over running of firm," read the notes from a meeting between Fomon and his advisers.

The first lead came from Henry Boettinger, a former senior executive at AT&T and now a consultant. Boettinger had helped Hutton land the corporate finance business of Denver-based U.S. West, one of the Baby Bells. Eventually Boettinger interested Jack MacAllister, chairman of U.S. West, in the idea of expanding into financial services.

MacAllister already knew Hutton's Denver-based regional vice-president, Dale Frey. So Frey became the go-between. He invited Fomon for what was ostensibly a social visit to his home, which included a dinner with MacAllister. The results were positive enough that Fomon authorized further meetings, held in London, New York, and Denver. With no clear decision having been made to sell Hutton, the discussions never got to specifics.

It was the first time Fomon acknowledged that his troubles had grown too dire to fix himself. The truth was, as much as Fomon tried to take the offensive, he increasingly found himself just fighting off problems. Hutton had no offensive plan.

On Friday, November 9, 1984, Moorhead took a break from moving into the lower Manhattan apartment Hutton was providing and went to see Fomon. He did not begin work until the following Monday, but, hoping to start off on the right foot, he asked if there was anything he could do. Fomon said yes. He asked Moorhead if, from his Washington days, he knew the attorney general, William French Smith. Moorhead said he knew Smith's wife well.

"That's perfect," Fomon said. "See if you can set up a lunch, a social lunch, sometime soon in Washington."

Those were Fomon's first instructions to his new assistant.

When Moorhead asked why, Fomon took him into his office and closed the door. He explained that Hutton was being investigated by a grand jury in Scranton, Pennsylvania. The firm was trying to make some submissions, but the grand jury's term was about to expire. Fomon did not go into details other than to say the government was pursuing Hutton for technical violations of some obscure banking laws.

He gave no hint of the fact that he was, in fact, terrified that the firm and some officials might be indicted. On April 20, 1984, Al Murray, the assistant U.S. attorney in Scranton pursuing the case, had sent target letters to E. F. Hutton Group, E. F. Hutton & Company, Tom Lynch, William Sullivan (who was no longer with the firm), Tom Morley, Mike Castellano, Hutton's controller, Art Jensen, a regional operations official, and Norm Epstein, the head of operations. All were warned that they might be indicted on felony charges.

Fomon faced a grave challenge. All of Hutton's senior officials knew about so much corruption within the firm that, should one of them start to spill his guts, Fomon feared he would not be able to control the situation. Worried that the normal legal channels were not working for him, he thus decided to try to fix the case from the top. It was a sign of his nervousness and of how closely he was following the case.

Fomon ended the discussion by telling Moorhead not to mention the "F" matter, as it was known within Hutton, in his invitation to Smith.

(Smith had announced in January 1984 that he wanted to resign. President Reagan nominated Edwin Meese III as his replacement. But Meese immediately became embroiled in a bitter confirmation battle. Until Meese was confirmed in early 1985, Smith retained the job.)

The four met for lunch the next week, Thursday, November 15, at Washington's posh Jockey Club. It began as a pleasant social encounter, with Fomon at his charming best. They discussed mutual friends in California and the attorney general's desire to return to his home state. The table was cleared, dessert was served, and they chatted a bit longer when Smith delivered the ultimate line for a Washington insider—he had to get to the White House for an important meeting. That was Fomon's cue.

"I don't know if you're aware of it, but a grand jury in Pennsylvania is investigating E. F. Hutton," Fomon began.

"I was not aware of it," Smith replied, recoiling slightly from what already sounded fishy.

"Well, there's been a grand jury investigation for two years. It's about to close, and the firm has been trying to submit some materials, and the U.S. attorney there is not allowing our lawyers the time they need," Fomon said. "I'd just like someone to look into this to make sure the firm can present its evidence."

The air became leaden. Smith had been caught off balance by Fomon's blatant attempt to influence the grand jury's proceedings. "I'm not sure, but . . . well, we'll see," Smith mumbled.

He then hurried off. Fomon sat back down and had coffee with Moorhead and Mrs. Smith, awkwardly trying to make small talk as the lunch wound to a close.

Several embarrassing phone calls between Moorhead and some angry top Justice Department lawyers followed, in which they thrashed him for trying to go through a back channel. Anyway, Smith had made it clear he would not get involved.

Nonetheless, a couple of days later Hutton's lawyers were told that the grand jury's term was being extended. All the government lawyers denied that Fomon's approach to Smith had anything to do with the decision. They argued that the prosecutors never intended for the case to go to court, where proving such an abstruse financial crime would have been difficult at best. They needed to bluff Hutton into a plea, and they required more time for that.

The problems were mounting so fast, however, that Fomon could hardly keep track.

By late 1984 George Aubin had become the single most important customer of E. F. Hutton. For starters his monthly commissions and margin payments shot up from $100,000 a month—already exceptionally high—to $254,704 in June. In October the monthly costs exploded to $1.2 million, then $1.8 million in December. The eleven accounts in which he traded were bringing Don Sanders more commissions in a month than five average brokers earned from all their accounts in a year. It was an insane level of trading.

Aubin had also brought another very substantial piece of investment banking business to Lopp's corporate finance department. Less than two years after acquiring Mercury Savings and Ben Milam Savings, and then the two mortgage companies, J. B. Haralson was selling the whole lot. On Aubin's say-so, Hutton was hired to line up a buyer.

Aubin and Haralson were not exactly volunteering to sell the thrifts, however; they were being thrown out of the business by the Texas State savings and loan commissioner. Because of numerous breaches of the banking laws and a fear that Aubin was pulling the strings behind the scenes, the state had forced Haralson to unload the thrifts. The papers, completed on September 25, 1984, also demanded, "Mercury shall, as soon as practicable, terminate all business relationships it has with Aubin."

Haralson and Aubin had called in Paul Yang, the Hutton investment banker who handled the acquisition of the mortgage companies in 1983. "For reasons not fully known to me, J. B. Haralson has apparently decided to comply with the demand of federal and state of Texas' regulators that he ceases [sic] to continue in the thrift and mortgage banking businesses," Yang wrote to his boss, Jim Lopp.

He added, "It is no secret that J. B. Haralson and his associates do not enjoy a particularly fine reputation in this marketplace," indicating that more lawsuits were likely if Hutton took the assignment of selling the thrifts. Lopp decided to move ahead anyway.

Aubin's wild trading continued unabated. He was engaging in spectacularly reckless bets on the direction of interest rates by playing the Treasury bond futures and options markets. If interest rates fell and bond prices rose, he would make a killing. If interest rates rose instead, he stood to take a shellacking. Which is just what happened.

In late 1984 the market turned against him viciously. By the end of December the net worth of Aubin's accounts was minus $10 million. He would either have to sell out his positions and accept the losses or put up more capital to meet his huge margin requirements. That would slow his frenzied trading and thus reduce the astronomical flow of commissions to Sanders and Mundy.

Hutton's officials came up with a better alternative. It was, in effect, a check kiting arrangement Hutton perpetrated against itself.

The key was what are known as prepayments. Normally a customer has up to five days to pay for certain securities purchases. The customer must also wait five days from the time of a sale to receive the proceeds. In the kiting arrangement, Hutton paid Aubin for the sales of stock from one account to another immediately, often the same day. But it allowed him to wait up to two weeks to pay for purchases. This was a radical departure from industry practice.

The result of this legerdemain was that Aubin was illegally given an extended loan of millions of dollars. He used that money to meet the margin calls on his Treasury bond futures positions. As he kept trading, his commission and margin interest payments soared to $4 million in January 1985 and $5.2 million in February. His losses, meanwhile, kept growing.

Now, however, Hutton faced more than the risk of losing money, a lot of money, if Aubin suddenly found himself unable to continue his game of musical chairs. The firm was deliberately and systematically skirting a series of important margin rules. Hutton was filing false records with regulators as it lied to cover up the kiting scheme. It was failing to supervise its employees properly. The records suggest that a number of Hutton executives may have been participating in a violation of some basic market laws. The company was risking its most precious asset—its ability to stay in business—for Sanders's hot customer.

On February 12, 1985, three years and two days after Hutton first learned that the government was investigating the overdrafting scheme, Tom Curnin of Cahill Gordon dictated a cover letter to a batch of documents Hutton was handing over to the grand jury.

"The document dated April 23, 1982, from Mr. Bacon to Mr. Bralove was produced to us late yesterday afternoon by counsel for Mr. Bralove," wrote Curnin, the firm's top lawyer in the matter, a hint of apology in his choice of words since the memo should have been produced years before.

Bacon's smoking gun had just been handed to the prosecutors.

When Al Murray, the prosecutor, received the packet, he looked for the memo Curnin had cited. He read just a few paragraphs of Bacon's angry prose when he let out a whoop, forgetting for the moment his suspicions that Hutton had been suppressing documents all along.

"This isn't a smoking gun," Murray shouted to a colleague. "This is a nuke. Ha-ha!"

As part of Aubin's laterals between his accounts, he wrote nine checks totaling $9.15 million on February 28, 1985.

The checks seemed ordinary enough. Aubin's neat, wide signature with the confident curlicue at the end of the "G" appeared on the lower right hand corner. All seemed well until they came back to Hutton stamped "Returned Not Paid Because." Below that, the "NSF" box was checked, for "Not Sufficient Funds."

In the next week Aubin bounced nineteen other checks. The total came to $46,430,686.28—a year's worth of profits for E. F. Hutton.

At the same time, Hutton dispatched a midlevel investment banker to devise an exit strategy from Famco and Hutton Mortgage in Little Rock. That sorry disaster had only gotten worse as

Hutton discovered tens of millions of dollars of worthless mortgages in its portfolio. More had been on-sold to its customers. The firm could easily lose $50 million and be sued for much more—another year's worth of earnings down the drain.

A policy was adopted of trying to extricate the firm from the mess by selling off the remaining mortgages and severing its links to the obviously fraudulent Famco. In other words, Hutton would let Famco collapse slowly—hoping that by the time it had gone under, Hutton would be long gone. More important, it would not inform the government of the fraud. It would not alert its hapless customers. It would just try to get itself out of harm's way.

Fomon insisted on one thing: keep it quiet.


On March 8, 1985, George Aubin showed up in New York with J. B. Haralson and his lawyer, Richard Fuqua, to discuss the bounced checks. They met in Bob Fomon's office. Tom Lynch, Scott Pierce, Tom Rae, and another senior retail official, Bob Witt, listened as Aubin issued a sincere-sounding mea culpa and said he wanted to find a way of fixing the problem. He declared that he did not have the capital to cover the $46 million in bounced checks. Fuqua declared that Aubin had a gambling disease and was determined to make good on his debt.

The Hutton executives, managers of one of the nation's largest corporations, did not call Don Sanders to check on the assertions. They did not initiate a credit check. They did not twist arms or demand a personal guarantee. They had so many problems they needed to keep out of the public eye that they agreed to negotiate a deal with Aubin that would maintain the secrecy surrounding his colossal losses.

"Mr. Aubin made a statement to us, and we took him at his word," Rae said.

At about ten-thirty that morning the basic terms had been decided. Lynch went to the offices of Cahill Gordon with Aubin's lawyer to hammer out a final agreement, taking time out only for lunch at the nearby Fulton Fish Market. A few hours later they had an eight-page facility agreement and a two-page promissary note, documents that were bizarre—but signed. It was probably one of the fastest $48 million loans in history.

Hutton agreed to loan Aubin the money through a dummy corporation Aubin had created. Haralson would put up his stock in Mercury Savings as collateral. Hutton would be repaid from the proceeds of the sale, which was said to be imminent.

No matter that the thrifts were known to have financial problems. No matter that Haralson and Aubin were being thrown out of the thrift business by the government. No matter that Aubin had committed what might have been construed as a felony by passing the hot checks. The point for Fomon and his executives was to keep the whole thing quiet.

First Hutton had to move the problem out of the view of regulators. Aubin's securities and commodities dealings had been with E. F. Hutton & Company, the brokerage unit. But the agreements with Aubin cleverly shifted the debt out of the brokerage unit and into the holding company, E. F. Hutton Group, which did not need to make any disclosures to regulators.

Hutton also agreed that the loan would be effectively interest free. Any interest would be charged against commissions Aubin had already paid, a ruse that guaranteed Aubin free use of Hutton's money. (This also appeared to be an indirect admission that the level of commissions produced by Aubin's accounts had been much too high. But Hutton's shareholders would pay for the problem.)

There was another incredible twist. As Lady Luck would have it, Aubin's fortunes rebounded even as the lawyers hashed out the final terms: the market turned. A total of $2 million was knocked off his debt on March 8 because of an improvement in his positions. He now owed Hutton $44 million.

That was good news, because Hutton had agreed to give Aubin enough to cover the debt, plus another $4 million in *cash*. The additional sum was seed money, to finance *more trading*.

In other words, a man who had lost $46 million through one of the most frenzied bouts of trading in the history of the financial markets, and who had then written $46 million in hot checks, was allowed to keep rolling the dice—with Hutton's money. (Not least, Hutton was committing another serious breach of the margin rules.)

According to the terms of the deal, Aubin was only permitted to liquidate his accounts, not trade further. But that was ignored. Tom Lynch personally approved continued heavy trading.

The terms were so wildly favorable to Aubin that everyone who examined the deal afterward believed there had to be something forcing the hand of Lynch and Hutton's executives. A top-secret document prepared as part of an internal investigation provided at least a partial answer—and a remarkable insight into how major decisions were being made at Hutton.

"It would appear that Hutton may have an internal problem of some magnitude which would have far-reaching ramifications," Robert B. Denson, president of Southwest Security & Investigation, a Dallas-based private investigation agency, wrote to Hutton's top outside lawyer. "In reflecting upon the interviews Abbot [another investigator] and I conducted with top Hutton executives, it became a source of wonderment that a group of intelligent, highly educated and experienced men could have accepted a proposition and subsequent agreement as porous (bordering on the absurd) as the 'Facilities [sic] Agreement' engineered and dictated by George Aubin.

"If the allegations made in the attached reports have any substance whatsoever, there appears to be a distinct possibility that George Aubin is also aware of the 'skeletons' and has profited thereby. George Aubin may very well have come to the meeting of March 8, 1985, 'with hat in hand,' unfurled the 'Jolly Roger' and displayed the 'key to the closet.' The rest was easy. I hasten to add that the enclosed allegations represent raw information which has not yet been corroborated."

The letter made clear that the investigator believed Aubin knew of wrongdoing by Hutton's senior executives and blackmailed the firm. Transcripts of the highly confidential interviews Denson conducted provide shocking evidence of what he had uncovered.

Stuart W. Johnson, head of the margin department in Houston, told the investigators of two major problems in accounts controlled by Don Sanders. First, there was the blatant kiting scheme involving Aubin's accounts, which Johnson said he had reported. "However, no one he complained to seemed to want to listen or to do anything about it," the report said.

Second, there were highly suspicious and possibly illegal trades. This was how Johnson described them. Hutton's stock trading desk in New York had what was known as an error account.

Frequently, after large block trades were transacted, there would be a residue of stock odds and ends. These holdings would be placed into the error account. What Johnson noticed was that, often, when these holdings rose in value, they would be transferred to a Sanders account, along with the profit. It would be made to appear that Sanders had purchased the stock in the first place and that it had been placed in the error account only by accident. (That, of course, can happen legitimately. When stocks are later put in the correct account, the transfer is known on Wall Street as an "as of" trade.) According to Johnson, as quoted by the investigator, Sanders and his clients enjoyed riskless profits at Hutton's expense.

That these strange transactions were no accident was backed up by two facts Johnson cited. "These trades normally will have a backdated purchase date of one or two days," the time it usually takes to spot an error, Johnson told the investigators. "However, he noticed that Sanders' accounts would have backdated purchase dates of 5 to 7 days. Furthermore, his investigation revealed that Sanders' accounts always made money on these trades.

"Johnson thinks Sanders, with the cooperation of Bob Brown in New York [head of what was known as the miniblock trading desk], is illegally using Hutton's Trading Account."

Adding credibility to the assertions was a similar interview with Jack Johnstone, the margin clerk in Sanders' office. Johnstone, according to secret notes submitted to Hutton's lawyers, described precisely the same practices. "He believes Sanders is making fraudulent trades using the Hutton Trading Account," the report said. "If Sanders and Brown are working together in a scheme of this type, it would be easy for them to do, especially since no one in Hutton will do anything about it for fear of Sanders." He added in the interview that it was rumored Sanders gave Brown a car and a yacht in return.

When asked about the trades, Sanders at first denied them, then said, "Everything that happened with Bob Brown was above board. Trades that occurred were in the normal course of business." Brown said he never heard of the report. However, three senior Hutton executives confirmed that the suspicions had come to their attention and that actions were taken to halt the practices.

The gifts were another matter. It is highly unorthodox, if not overtly improper, for a broker to pay such a bonus to another official who stands in a position to provide him with unfair advantages. At first Sanders denied the gifts, then he insisted anything Brown got was "normal compensation for doing an exceptional job. If he got paid extra it was because he did a hell of a good job for me. It's just like my secretary, I give her a little something extra when she does a good job."

Brown admitted he received bonuses from Sanders. He said Sanders' payments were in cash, but that, as claimed by Johnstone, he used them to buy a luxury car and a yacht, among other things.

What Hutton's lawyers also knew was that an internal audit of Sanders' special subbranch in August 1984 turned up the same problems. It cited one instance where Sanders earned $65,000 in a span of a few days for one of his accounts by having a block of ten thousand shares of IBM flipped to him from Hutton's error account.

Left unstated in these highly confidential documents was whose accounts had benefited from Sanders' dealings. It was such a sensitive issue that no one was willing to name names in writing. But there is a hint in Denson's letter.

"Interestingly, though, a review of our notes taken during the series of interviews at New York noted a pattern of very close ties, both personal and financial, which allegedly exist between Sanders and Messrs. Fomon, Lynch, Pierce, Rae and Witt, the latter four being present at the meeting of March 8, 1985. A comment by one interviewee—Rae—was, 'Probably 80% of E. F. Hutton's board have bought investments with Don Sanders.'"

The letter raised concerns that Hutton's top executives may have been permitting Sanders to trade illegally because they were profiting from the transactions—or at the least that they were protecting Sanders and those who profited.


By mid-April Hutton's lawyers had concluded their negotiations over Hutton's plea agreement for the overdrafting scheme. Bacon's "smoking gun" memo had blown their defenses out of the water. On April 30 Hutton's directors met to vote formally on accepting the embarrassing guilty plea. (The only outside board member not present was, as usual, Peter Ueberroth.) The board—

which included several of those who knew they would have been indicted had the company not agreed to take the fall for them— listened as a few modest objections were voiced.

Tom Curnin swept them aside with hair-raising stories of the negative publicity Hutton would suffer in the event of a trial. Curnin also emphasized the one thing he had gotten from the prosecutors in return for Hutton's agreement to plead guilty: no individuals at Hutton would be indicted. As it was, the prosecutors had granted immunity to nearly three dozen brokers and executives in an effort to nail senior Hutton executives, such as Tom Morley, Norm Epstein, Mike Castellano, and Tom Lynch. The government had finally agreed to let off all the individuals responsible for the crimes in return for the firm's guilty plea. Once again the shareholders would take the hit for the individuals who worked at Hutton.

Curnin's responses were hardly necessary. Just about everyone in the room knew what other disasters were brewing at the firm. The government's plea deal was like manna from heaven: it did more to protect than hurt them. The agreement, with all its immensely disturbing implications for Hutton's future and reputation, was accepted after less than an hour of discussion. The plea would be made public within a week.

The plea, the deal with Aubin, and the Famco disaster made a shambles of Fomon's rehabilitation campaign. But Fomon still regarded himself as the buccaneer the magazine had depicted on its cover a decade earlier. He believed the mythology, so he leapt at his latest opportunity to act tough.

In the spring of 1985 Hutton won the job of representing Ted Turner, founder of the cable television empire, in an attempted raid on CBS. When Tom Wyman, the CBS chief executive, first got wind of Hutton's role, he called Fomon, hoping to head off an attack.

"Bob, I've just read in the paper that you might be representing Ted Turner in this offer he's trying to put together," Wyman began. "Given our relationship in this building project—and we're looking forward to having you as our neighbor—I was sure it wasn't true. But I wanted to ask if you would confirm that. That's what this is about."

Fomon said that he would have to get back.

"Tom, we talked about this here, and we are going to represent Ted Turner in his offer," Fomon told Wyman a few hours later. "We're going to do everything we can to make it work."

"Why would you do this?" Wyman implored.

"This is a fee-oriented business we're in," said Fomon. "What we have is not the usual fee arrangement. We have an opportunity to make much more." In fact, Hutton stood to earn well over $25 million in the unlikely event the bid succeeded.

"Well, Bob, this'll really take some of the fun out of planning for the party when you move in next door."

"Oh, I wouldn't worry about that," Fomon shot back. "If this works out, I don't think you'll have to worry about opening parties."

# CHAPTER 10

# GREAT NEWS
# FOR THE MAFIA

Morning broke bitter and rain-swept in Bonn on Thursday, May 2, 1985. The weather was appropriate accompaniment to the harsh news out that day. President Reagan's visit to the West German capital for an economic summit had been completely overshadowed by the controversy surrounding his planned visit to a German war cemetery at Bitburg—a cemetery that contained the graves of several dozen members of Hitler's Waffen SS.

The president faced ceaseless criticism because of his insistence on going through with what had been intended as a gesture of conciliation. The economic summit was declared a failure even before it began. The White House was battling to regain the public relations high ground.

On May 1 White House officials had announced, quite unexpectedly, economic sanctions against Nicaragua after Congress rejected military funding for the contras. The press cast a decidedly skeptical eye on the timing of the maneuver, regarding it as a transparent attempt to deflect attention from Bitburg.

"Privately, some American officials acknowledged today that

the action toward Nicaragua may prompt debate of the Administration's policies in Central America," wrote Hedrick Smith, *The New York Times*'s chief political correspondent, in the May 2 edition. "The French and Italians have been critical of President Reagan on this score in the past. But these American officials also concede that the White House hopes that one effect of the President's stern action on Nicaragua will be to drive the furor over his plans to visit Bitburg on Sunday out of the headlines and divert attention from what has been the President's major political embarrassment this spring."

*The Washington Post* quoted a reporter asking whether it was "too cynical to suggest you timed this move in the middle of Europe to take the heat off the President's trip to Bitburg."

"Yes," said Larry Speakes, the presidential spokesman, "it would." The fact that the question was asked seemed more important than the answer, though.

Against this background, Ed Meese made an unusual, last-minute decision. The attorney general and the president's closest adviser chose to lead a press conference, scheduled for May 2, on E. F. Hutton's guilty plea to fraud charges for the bank overdrafting scheme.

Attorneys general rarely put their personal stamps on individual prosecutions, unless they represent broader initiatives or cases of national importance. This was certainly not true with Hutton. Its guilty plea was the result of one dogged prosecutor laboring anonymously, and with a fair amount of luck, in Scranton, Pennsylvania. There was no reason to suspect that other brokerage houses were doing the same thing to their banks. There was, however, the splashiness of a big case against a firm with the upscale image of E. F. Hutton.

For once, Hutton's well-burnished image had turned into a huge liability. A big case against such a well-known financial institution was bound to make headlines.

(Terry Eastland, Meese's chief spokesman, said the Bitburg controversy had not been mentioned openly by Meese in deciding to lead the press conference. Speakes said he could not recall any overt discussion of the matter. Meese denied that he had been influenced to lead the press conference by the Bitburg flap. And Stephen Trott, now a federal district judge who had headed the

Justice Department's criminal division, called assertions that Bitburg influenced the decision "bullshit." One White House insider said, though, that Bitburg could have motivated the move.)

Hutton's executives and lawyers were flabbergasted when they heard that Meese himself would be announcing the plea. The firm had taken more than a month to plan every detail of the plea announcement and had hired two politically well connected PR firms to try to soften the blow. Any last-minute hitches were discouraging. Fomon in particular hated the sense that things were spinning out of control. He had worked hard to anticipate any problems or slips.

Just after 11 A.M., before the plea was finalized, the first calls came in. Some wire service reporters had been tipped off in Washington about the deal. There was a tense moment as Hutton's public relations team tried to decide if they would confirm the plea. Fomon decided to move.

Hutton quickly mobilized a small battalion of messengers, each armed with thick packets of documents. There was a seven-page press release, a six-page question-and-answer-format explanatory document, and a forty-one-page tome describing everything from what money management was to how the check clearing system worked and Hutton's abuses of it. Of course, the releases all put a Hutton spin on the story, downplaying how systematic and abusive the practices had been. But more important to most reporters was the weight of the plea—two thousand felony counts.

Hutton would pay a $2 million fine, reimburse the government $750,000 in costs for the investigation, and set aside $8 million to repay the banks it had defrauded.

The next step in this well-orchestrated campaign was to deliver batteries of letters from Fomon to key business leaders, including the heads of such concerns as Morgan Stanley, Goldman, Sachs, Metropolitan Life, and the Morgan Guaranty Trust Company, reassuring them that Hutton was sound.

Fomon worked the phones, too. He contacted Representatives Ferdinand St Germain, John D. Dingell, Timothy Wirth, and Jack Brooks, and Senators Alphonse D'Amato, William Roth, Jake Garn, and William Proxmire, key members of committees that had some oversight for the brokerage industry. The calls were perfunctory but courteous. Dan Murphy, the head of Hutton's Capitol Hill operations, worked with Tommy Boggs, a prominent lobbyist, calling other members of Congress.

Fomon then faced a press conference for the first time in his career. It had been a controversial decision within Hutton, since everyone feared his penchant for outrageousness. But the PR experts insisted it was essential for the chairman to speak for the company on this grave occasion. Fomon was given weeks of coaching, all of which culminated in his thirty minutes in front of a gang of reporters. Hot television lights glared in his eyes, and dozens of photographers snapped away as Fomon read a statement.

"This is a sad and difficult day for E. F. Hutton and for me personally," Fomon said. "The practices to which the company has pleaded guilty represented violations of our policy and procedures. Nonetheless, the company and its top management assume full responsibility."

Now that the criminal investigation was completed, he added, Hutton would take "appropriate" action against individual employees.

He then stood at the podium, peering above a spiky bouquet of microphones, answering questions. He exhibited a level of patience that none of those present recognized; all the training had clearly worked.

Then came Meese. Because of delays at the courthouse in Scranton, Al Murray and the other Justice Department prosecutors arrived later than scheduled in Washington for a press conference. Once they arrived, they bolted straight to the conference room where the press briefing was supposed to be held. The room was empty.

Murray soon discovered, to his extreme disappointment, that Meese had run the press conference without him. It was over. A few reporters were rounded up later to speak to Murray. But by that time most newspaper stories were written or nearly completed. Meese had been the government's chief interpreter of the plea.

"This action is part of the Justice Department's ongoing effort against economic crime and makes it clear to the business world that so-called white-collar crime will not be tolerated," Meese had said, turning on his trademark scowl for the cameras.

Trott disclosed that several dozen Hutton employees were involved in the illegal practices. The Justice Department had given most of them immunity, however, in its efforts to win their cooperation and pin the blame on senior Hutton executives. However, he said, the evidence had not been strong enough to do that. The result: the perpetrators had gotten away scot-free.

This was "a corporate scheme," Meese said in a completely contradictory statement. "No one personally benefited" from defrauding the banks. The statement was a clear sign that Meese did not understand the matter and was trying to cover up the department's failure to nail the Hutton officials who actually did benefit from the scheme.

Al Murray managed to squeeze a couple of remarks into some of the articles being written.

"It was sort of like, 'When E. F. Hutton talks, the banks listen,'" Murray told reporters, finally enjoying a few moments in the spotlight.

The SEC, meanwhile, granted Hutton a 180-day temporary exemption from the law banning felons from acting as investment advisers. But the SEC said it would be conducting its own investigation of the matter. Soon every state in which Hutton operated would undertake its own investigation.

Back in New York Fomon had not faced very tough questioning, in large part because reporters had been given very little time to digest the enormously complex particulars of the case.

Leaving the Hutton press conference, Fomon was ebullient. He had stood before a hostile crowd and handled himself with aplomb, resisting the impulse to snap at the idiot reporters. He became highly emotional.

"You really beat me up before," Fomon told Orin Kramer, his media consultant, "but I was ready for them."

"You did a terrific job, Bob, really good," Kramer replied.

"No, I have you to thank. Being tough with me was the right thing."

Kramer wrote a memo to Fomon later that day, saying, "Everyone I spoke to following the press conference, including some press, shared the view that you did a really superb job. You have obviously developed a special facility for responding to stupid, antagonistic questions."

Hutton's stock was opened for trading after the announcement, and it promptly tumbled $3.50 a share to $29. However, the next day it rebounded $2.50 to $31.50. That seemed an accurate reflection of how quickly the storm was passing. Dan Murphy in Washington spoke to about one hundred members of Congress and staffers on Friday, May 3. "The reaction is absolutely bland," he told executives in New York.

Monday morning brought a mild surprise. A Justice Department official was quoted as saying that Hutton's scheme involved overdrawn checks totaling about $10 billion, not the $4 billion mentioned in the press conference or the $1 billion mentioned in the plea agreement. Hutton, he added, might be required to repay "between $40 million and $50 million" to the banks it defrauded.

Tom Lynch denied the assertions. That seemed to be the end of that.

But on Tuesday the controversy began to boil up again. A group of Senate Democrats, most of whom had fought against Meese's appointment to the attorney general's post, wrote a sharp letter expressing incredulity over the Justice Department's decision not to prosecute individuals at Hutton—particularly in light of Meese's crowing over the plea.

Ironically, the authors wrote, just a week earlier a woman named Dakota Plumber had received a thirty-day sentence in Washington for stealing four sweaters worth less than $200. "We would appreciate an explanation as to how it would "send a clear signal" that the Justice Department is serious about white-collar crime when it lets E. F. Hutton & Company off the hook while it sends Dakota Plumber (a.k.a. Karen E. Hill) to the slammer."

On May 9 William Safire, *The New York Times*'s conservative columnist, complained that the $2 million fine was "like putting a parking ticket on the Brink's getaway car. . . . No personal disgrace for the perpetrators; no jail terms; not a slap on one individual wrist. Putting on his most severe look, Attorney General Edwin Meese had the chutzpah to announce: 'This makes it clear to the business world that white-collar crime will not be tolerated.' On the contrary, the pretense that no human beings operate E. F. Hutton makes it clear to the business world that if your company is shot through with managers involved in a huge swindle, not to worry—the Meese Justice Department will limit the liability to the corporation."

Safire grew sarcastic. "Says Mr. Meese: 'We are as aggressive in the investigation and prosecution of so-called white-collar crime as narcotics and organized crime.' Based on the immunity white-wash and cozy plea bargain in this case, that's great news for the Mafia."

That was all it took to give the scandal new momentum.

On Monday morning, May 13, the *Times* carried another Safire column that shattered any lingering hopes Hutton executives might have had for a respite: Safire revealed Fomon's Washington lunch with William French Smith.

Safire posed the question of whether Hutton improperly influenced the outcome of its case through the lunch or other channels. Safire mentioned that Scott Pierce's sister was married to Vice President George Bush and that the chairman of the SEC was a former Hutton vice-chairman.

The torrent of bad news had one positive result. It helped Hutton's lawyers and PR experts persuade Fomon that there was only one way for him to regain control—he had to find and penalize the brokers who actually committed the crimes. Fomon had doggedly resisted doing so. Some lawyers felt it was out of fear that, to save their own skins, all those involved would begin to reveal the other problems secretly plaguing Hutton. He could not afford a widespread rebellion. Pressed to come up with a plan to show the public that Hutton would really purge its ranks of wrongdoers, Fomon proposed that he and Scott Pierce conduct their own inquiry.

With some difficulty, Fomon's transparent attempt to fix the "investigation" was brushed aside. Fomon's advisers took a piece-meal approach. First, they suggested, fire the person most obviously involved—Tom Morley, who ran the money management system. If Morley had not noticed the abuses, at the least he had been grossly negligent, and that deserved a dismissal. After much arguing, Fomon gave in. He called Morley into his office, but Morley insisted that the chairman listen to his side of things. He had a two-pronged defense. First, Morley denied responsibility for the activities. He insisted he was in charge of the way the system worked, not the actual running of it. It was a fine semantic distinction that only a firm as Byzantine as Hutton could produce, or believe.

Morley also presented memos from 1980 showing that he tried to set up a computer system to run the money management function. He said he had been turned down for budgetary reasons. The computers would have halted any abusive overdrafting immediately, he argued.

Fomon walked to Scott Pierce's office and interrupted a meeting. "Scott, come into my office. I need to see you," he said.

"Look at these memos," he told Pierce. "We should be giving Morley a promotion, not firing him." Pierce could not believe what he was hearing. Fomon then went into a conference room where a PR consultant was working on a press release.

"Cancel that," Fomon told him. "He stays."

Pierce sputtered an ineffective plea that Fomon bow to reason. But Fomon left the office before Pierce could finish.

The lawyers persisted, arguing that Hutton would suffer until it cleaned house. Fomon finally agreed to take a new approach. An outsider had to be brought in to swing the axe. Hutton needed somebody with impeccable credentials, stature, independence, and—not least—the respect of the Democrats in Congress who were hounding the firm.

Only a few names were tossed around, including Cyrus Vance, the former secretary of state, and Stuart Eizenstat, a former aide to President Carter. Griffin Bell, now a senior partner at the prominent Atlanta law firm King & Spalding, was proposed, too.

Bell, a former federal judge and attorney general with a spotless record, seemed to meet the requirements. He had also just completed an internal investigation for an insurance company, so the job was familiar to him. As usual, Fomon made the arrangements without even telling his board, in whose name Bell was retained.

It was a key moment in Hutton's history. There had been plenty of consultants snooping around before, making recommendations. But this would be the first time an outsider would be granted something of the run of the place with a mandate for rooting out corruption.

• • •

By late May a new problem was cropping up. All the negative publicity was starting to have a direct impact on Hutton's bottom line.

The first public indication of this came on May 20. That morning a large "tombstone" appeared—an ad publicizing a securities offering—for a $591.7 million bond issue by the city of New York. It was the city's largest financing ever and thus a particularly prestigious deal.

The lead managers were Merrill Lynch and Goldman, Sachs. Absent from the bracket of major firms underwriting the bonds—a fact conspicuous to the Wall Street cognoscenti—was a longtime New York City adviser, E. F. Hutton. Because of the growing scandal, the city had dropped Hutton from the syndicate. It was a huge embarrassment.

A month later the Metropolitan Transit Authority, a New York State agency, also decided to drop Hutton as one of its bond underwriters. It was followed by the Massachusetts State Housing Agency and a host of other state and local governments leery of being connected with a tainted brokerage firm. In May and June Hutton fell to eleventh place among underwriters of municipal securities—down from second the year earlier.

Hutton's retail brokers were hit with angry questions from customers and a decline in business. They were furious. Most had been given no warning of the coming plea and felt blindsided.

In fact, just days before the plea was announced Fomon met with a group of Hutton's top brokers—members of the elite Directors Advisory Council, or DAC—in Chicago. During the weekend of fine food and parties, Fomon told the brokers that the toughest problem Hutton faced was sex discrimination in its branch offices. The number of lawsuits against the firm for alleged sexual harassment, he said, had been rising sharply. He asked their help in stamping out the problem.

Brokers who were surprised to hear Bob Fomon, of all people, complain about officers sleeping with secretaries were bitter to learn what he had not told them.

The next bombshell came without warning. Hutton was in the process of selling one of its largest tax shelter deals ever, Silver

Screen II. A total of $200 million was being raised to finance feature films produced by Walt Disney Productions. Adding to the deal's luster was the fact that George W. Bush, Jr., son of the vice-president, sat on Silver Screen's board.

But in late May word started to come back from several states that Hutton had failed to properly register the deal. The matter had been left to Cahill Gordon. Although Hutton had been told that all relevant filings had been made, inexplicably the law firm had not done so.

North Carolina issued an embarrassing cease and desist order. Then Pennsylvania said it was investigating. On May 29 Massachusetts issued a cease and desist order. Cahill Gordon admitted its error, covered all of Hutton's expenses on the matter, and paid a penalty of millions of dollars. But the money hardly mattered. The bad publicity only added to the stain on Hutton's reputation.

What was happening in secret by this time was far more frightening.

Banks collapse from a run by depositors. Securities firms collapse from a run by their creditors, usually banks and large financial institutions. This is one of the least understood, but most critical, aspects of the way Wall Street operates. It is rare, but runs can happen.

Securities firms have relatively little capital compared with the amount of assets they control. They are, in short, highly leveraged. The firms must borrow billions of dollars a day to support that financial edifice.

Imagine that a firm's capital base is the skin of a balloon and the air pressure inside is the firm's assets. The more assets relative to equity capital, the tighter the skin gets stretched. If some of a firm's capital is tied up in investments, that makes it difficult to move around quickly—called being illiquid. The skin cannot stretch and bear the pressure. The optimum condition for earning big profits is to keep the balloon taut but not strained.

The basic point is that if, for any reason, a firm's equity capital base starts to shrink, it must let some air out of the balloon—sell assets quickly—or risk becoming overstretched. Such is the precariousness of this situation that creditors who are happy one day to loan money to a brokerage house can flee the next if they suspect the capital base has been impaired somehow.

Hutton had raised $200 million in 1984 through the sale of

floating rate notes, an ordinary enough transaction. But, in an act of hubris, Hutton chose to distribute the securities itself, becoming the sole market maker for the notes. Most Wall Street firms used other securities houses for such deals. But Hutton wanted to earn all the commissions on trading in its own securities and deny its competitors those profits. That meant the only broker a buyer or seller of the notes could call was Hutton—leaving Hutton as the buyer of last resort if selling of the notes mounted.

Almost immediately after the plea, noteholders got cold feet and decided to sell. As a felon, Hutton's future suddenly looked uncertain.

Hutton was forced to repurchase about $70 million of the notes, which took a direct bite out of its capital and drained off most of its cash supply. It was a dramatic, terrifying, and totally secret development.

If news of the sales leaked to the market, the other noteholders would surely rush to unload their securities in a panic. Undoubtedly that would also cause a stampede by many other Hutton creditors, including Hutton's retail customers. The threat was not hypothetical.

The firm turned to its banks for loans to cover the repurchases and bolster its shaky capital base. That's when Hutton got a worse fright: Tom Lynch had failed to arrange any formal lines of credit. Major companies maintain committed lines of credit for precisely these occasions. They arrange the standby loans when times are good, when they have some negotiating leverage. But the incompetence sanctioned by Fomon and Hutton's fragmented financial apparatus had left the firm unprepared.

The crisis was resolved with enormous difficulty and at great expense. Hutton managed to negotiate a $200 million line of credit from Bankers Trust. But the expense was huge: a $400,000 fee—at the last minute it was lowered from $500,000—on top of the interest payments, which were higher than usual.

The most degrading blow came in the form of Project Drum. It was somehow fitting that the man who, a few months earlier, had been gloating over the disgrace of the chairman of CBS was now the quarry—the ultimate insult on Wall Street.

George Von der Linden, the chief executive of Smith Barney,

Harris Upham, another large brokerage house, decided to try to sell Hutton from under Fomon and win a big fee.

Chrysler was approached and expressed some interest, although it never made a commitment. Smith Barney officials met with executives from Metropolitan Life, U.S. Life, and Transamerica. There was some interest, but no one knew how deep Hutton's problems were. Until that became clearer, potential acquirers kept their distance.

"You don't understand," Von der Linden told the wary companies. "You don't want to buy it cheaper. You want it now— before it gets worse."

# THE CLEANEST FIRM
# ON THE STREET

Fomon's first call went to Donald E. Nickelson. Nick, as he was known, was president of Paine Webber, a key Hutton competitor. He was a polished, gray-haired, cigar-smoking executive who had made his career in the retail side of the brokerage business. What particularly interested Fomon was that he was known for being interested purely in the retail trade, which seemed to make him less threatening—precisely what Fomon was looking for in his new president.

It was incredible to some of Fomon's friends at Hutton, but after years of prodding he was finally going to replace Ball. The plea and the shock of the subsequent controversy had moved him into action—once again, because his own position seemed at risk. He followed no formal process, hired no headhunters to handle the effort in a professional way. He randomly consulted with a few of his cronies and called Nickelson. But somehow the Fomon magic did not work. Nick rebuffed him.

Dick Jones then began to press Fomon on Bob Rittereiser of Merrill Lynch again. Now the timing, from Ritt's perspective, was perfect. He had come close to leaving Merrill a few months earlier to become chief executive at another firm. He had already thrashed out all the personal issues during that process, including the sense of failure he carried from Merrill. It was clear that he was just not taken seriously as a potential head of the huge brokerage house, and he refused to imagine himself as a perpetual also-ran.

Ritt was in something of a hurry, too. Bill Schreyer, Merrill's CEO, was about to name Dan Tully his president, not Ritt. His humiliation would be public. He had to make his move before that announcement.

Fomon contacted Ritt in mid-May. They had drinks at Fomon's antique-filled Fifth Avenue apartment and agreed each had enough interest to move forward. Within days Ritt accepted Fomon's offer that he become president of the E. F. Hutton Group, the holding company. Tom Lynch would give up that post and be named vice-chairman. It was all handled informally. Other than Fomon's assurances that he would be "taken care of" at Hutton, Ritt made the move without a signed agreement.

Hutton made the announcement on June 3, and it was received almost joyously by the market. Hutton's stock jumped $1.50 to $33.25. It was the first sign in a month that Fomon was really ready to tackle the firm's problems. Fomon could not resist, though, showing his mischievous side in announcing Ritt's new job, by poking fun at Ritt's penchant for turning life into a baseball metaphor.

"He plays four positions, he has speed, and he hits with power," Fomon told the press in completely uncharacteristic language that had his cronies laughing quietly in the background.

Ritt did not notice. His lifetime dream had come true. The patrician E. F. Hutton had pursued him and made him its president.

Initially Fomon had told Ritt to take time to get acquainted with the firm and to leave the plea agreement problems alone. Hutton was different from Merrill Lynch, which was known as a regimented sales machine. Hutton prided itself on being more entrepreneurial, less structured, and more focused on the job of serving well-to-do retail clients. Ritt had to make it clear to the troops that he did not intend to Merrill Lynch-ize Hutton.

Fomon knew that Ritt was no George Ball when it came to

company cheerleading. George Ball, however, had never been the manager that Ritt was reputed to be. But the biggest difference between the two was that Ball had extricated himself from a mire he'd helped create; Ritt was stepping right into it, as he would soon learn.

On July 1, Ritt's first official day in the office, there was an ominous article in *The Wall Street Journal*. It reported on newly uncovered Hutton memos that seemed to implicate senior executives in the illegal overdrafting. It directly contradicted the assertions by Meese and Fomon that no one at the top levels of Hutton had known about the crimes. Similar articles followed. The controversy that Ritt had been told was under control was still working its way into the headlines. With each revelation Fomon's credibility sank further.

On July 10 came the even more stunning disclosure from Hutton that it had discovered a cache of important and incriminating documents on the firm's banking practices that had never been shown to the prosecutors. Hutton did not say publicly how they had been found because it was too embarrassing.

Pam O'Neill, Scott Pierce's secretary and Fomon's former mistress, took note of the growing controversy over the overdrafting and remembered something. She had been one of Ball's secretaries before he left Hutton and recalled that when he moved to Prudential-Bache he had left behind two file drawers full of papers.

During three years of governmental investigation, with dozens of lawyers swarming over Hutton's headquarters, the files had never been examined, according to this story.

O'Neill went to Fomon and revealed the trove. Fomon told her to show the files to Pierce. Pierce flipped through the files for five minutes, then stopped, shut the drawer, paused to catch his breath, and called for the attorneys. The grimmer message was that Hutton now faced the prospect of new felony charges for obstruction of justice. There would be months of public questioning over whether it had lied to the government.

The real story of what happened to those documents may never be known outside a tiny handful of people. A school of thought within Hutton held that the memos had been known about much earlier and had been deliberately concealed from the prosecutors. They were brought out, in this view, because Fomon had decided to implicate George Ball, the principal author of the papers in the cache. Fomon and others denied this. What is unquestionably true is that Fomon was irked from the start at how little critical attention was being focused on Ball for the overdrafting. The notion that two file drawers of documents kept twenty feet from the chairman's office would not have been examined in the course of a three-year investigation struck many at Hutton as questionable and another sign of the eagerness to evade responsibility. Hutton would not be charged with obstruction of justice, but only because its lawyers pleaded incompetence instead. Both prospects left Bob Rittereiser shaken.

Fighting to put his spin on the developments, Fomon invited a reporter into his office that day for a long one-on-one interview, a rare event for the press-shy chief executive. He looked defeated. He paced, as usual, drawing deeply on one of his ever-present Winston cigarettes. He self-consciously projected the image of a man lost in thought, preparing to say something difficult.

The plea, Fomon said, had been a colossal error. He was unflinching in his apparent openness.

"If I had to do it over again," he said, his head down, enveloped by curls of blue smoke, his executive assistant eyeing the performance from the side, "I would have pleaded guilty on behalf of the company. The individuals involved would have stood by themselves."

It was "incredible" to him, Fomon said, that no high-level Hutton executives were at least aware of the illegal practices. "I don't believe that those two midlevel executives came up with the entire scheme," Fomon added, responding to a dubious Justice Department assertion that the scheme had been hatched by the two unnamed officials.

Fomon explained that he felt like a victim in the unfolding drama.

"Look, we were guilty," he snapped. "When you look back, this has been incredible. I didn't know what a cash concentration system was until a few months ago. We're going to be the cleanest firm on the street now."

The next day Representative William J. Hughes, chairman of

a congressional subcommittee investigating Hutton, was outraged that Fomon was now admitting that senior Hutton officials were guilty. Hughes charged that Hutton was stonewalling Congress while trying to appear cooperative in public. As a result, an even more aggressive tone would be adopted in the hearings Hughes had lined up.

Rittereiser was increasingly uncomfortable watching the spectacle from the sidelines—in part because he had begun to discover Hutton's long list of ills.

He had learned about Hutton's difficulties in obtaining bank loans to stay afloat. He had discovered the $48 million loan to George Aubin. He'd stumbled on the size of the Famco problems and had started to hear almost macabre tales of the massive tax shelter problems. Hutton's difficulties began long before May 2, and they appeared chronic. Hutton was like a runaway train picking up speed. It began to dawn on Ritt that he might have been overly hasty in grabbing the firm's presidency.

Nonetheless Ritt decided to stick with his schedule. On Friday morning, July 12, he planned to head to Washington, where he would attend a board meeting of the National Association of Securities Dealers, which ran the over-the-counter stock market. It was his first trip as Hutton's president, and he was ready to enjoy a round or two of congratulations from his friends on the board for his high-profile new job.

Ritt had not let the depressing first two weeks at Hutton get him down. He was still enjoying his new status and all the perks that went with it. And whatever criticism he had heard was directed at Hutton, not at the sharp new president. Ritt was the guy who would straighten things out.

Then that changed, too.

On his way to the airport, Ritt was deeply shaken by a front-page *Wall Street Journal* article indicating Hutton was in for a long siege. It also questioned Fomon's—and Ritt's—ability to right the ailing firm. Stunned by the personal attack, the first he had ever experienced in public, he aborted his trip and returned to Hutton's headquarters, only to have an even more dispiriting encounter, this one with Fomon.

It was as though Ritt were meeting his CEO for the first time. Ritt laid out his concerns and insisted on the obvious: that Hutton think more seriously about reformulating its plans for managing the scandal and that it consider a major management realignment. When Fomon simply walked out on him, Ritt's confidence was undermined.

Still, he was not ready to give up. He took his first step into the overdrafting scandal that day and put his weight behind a proposal by some of Hutton's lawyers to retain one powerful attorney to coordinate the mushrooming investigations by Congress, the states, and federal regulators.

Terry Adamson, one of Hutton's outside lawyers, had been a personal lawyer for President Carter, and he recalled how highly Carter had praised Warren Christopher, who had served as assistant secretary of state in his administration.

That Friday afternoon Adamson called Christopher on the West Coast from Fomon's office. Adamson explained the job briefly, and Christopher expressed interest. He called back to say he would fly to New York on Monday with two of his partners to meet with Fomon. An appointment was set for 5:30 P.M., July 15, in Fomon's Fifth Avenue apartment.

Ritt spent the weekend contemplating further bad news. *Business Week* magazine carried an article bluntly headlined, HUTTON MAY GET EVICTED FROM CONNECTICUT.

In fact, Hutton's license to operate in several states was being held hostage by state officials seeking suspensions and fines. The notoriously lax state securities officials were being pressed to demonstrate that, even if they woke up years late, they could be tough.

Monday morning brought more bad news. The anger among Hutton's retail troops had reached the boiling point. They were outraged not only by the plea—which they generally saw as caused by the idiots in New York, not the field—but by the continual pounding Hutton was taking. In their communities, the brokers *were* E. F. Hutton. They were starting to lose business and see their personal reputations questioned. Even the Bell investigation bothered many retail brokers, who saw it as an abdication of responsibility by Hutton's top executives. It was up to Fomon, not some outside lawyer, to ferret out and fire the wrongdoers.

That Monday it was time for action. The top brokers, dubbed the Directors Advisory Council, or DAC, had demanded a meeting in New York to air their views. The meeting was later expanded to include all the regional vice-presidents and a group of top branch managers. They were all livid about the negative publicity.

Monday began with a secret DAC caucus in a suite at the Parker Meridien Hotel. The group reached a consensus after less than an hour of debate: Fomon had to resign. He had lost all credibility in their eyes. They were much less clear on who would spearhead the attack on the old king and who would replace him, but they were convinced the time had come.

Unbeknownst to the brokers, Hutton's top executives were also planning their strategy for the encounter. Fomon was asked at the planning session what he perceived to be the worst-case scenario for the firm. Fomon said that heavy defections of account executives, or AEs, was a real possibility—ignoring what he knew to be the truth, that his own job was at stake.

"We've told people we'll break their legs if they try to leave my departments," Dick Locke said angrily, insisting that, for the time being, threats had to be used to keep people in line. He went on to propose a vigorous communications campaign later to rebuild morale.

"There's no question, it's in an AE's best interests to ride this thing out, to sit it out, not to leave at the bottom," Ritt offered, trying to take the rational approach. "They should make their decision wisely, not in an atmosphere of hot heads."

Fomon was asked about contingency plans after someone suggested that maybe the firm should be sold, or it should do a leveraged buyout.

"Those are not contingency plans," Fomon snarled. "At present, there are no suitors." He went on to explain that a leveraged buyout—an acquisition in which a company buys out its public shareholders using mostly borrowed money—would force Hutton to take on an enormous debt burden that posed untenable risks.

The tough but obvious question was finally asked. Was there a cover-up? Fomon answered that that was one of the questions Griffin Bell was investigating, as though he had no idea himself.

An hour later Bruce Tuthill, a Boston-based broker and leader of the DAC, began the real session in a Parker Meridien conference room. He explained that the anger in the field had reached a critical level. "The firm is out of time, key brokers are preparing to leave, and entire offices are ready to defect," Tuthill began.

A wave of departures in Chicago was imminent, he said. He also told the story of a Hutton broker who went to Shearson for an interview and had to hide in a room for several minutes to avoid running into one of his colleagues, also interviewing there.

Another AE then piped up with a suggestion that was vintage Hutton. The firm, he said, should increase the payout to brokers by 5 percent to win back their respect. Two other brokers quickly cut off that angle.

"Brokers in the field have lost confidence in management," one broker said bluntly. "Five percent won't help that."

"We have to let someone go at this point," said another broker as the group grew bolder in pushing toward its real goal.

Fomon responded that a trickle of firings would create another string of negative articles, which was just what the wolves in the press and Congress wanted. He counseled the rebels to wait for Bell's report. "There is no possible chance of a cover-up here," he insisted.

"I know this is repetitive," said Jerry Rosenstein, a branch manager. "But what we have to do is get someplace where we can stop the publicity. Now."

Fomon snapped, "You have to understand, to the congressmen this is show business, a road to stardom. I don't know what you do about stopping it."

That did not mollify the brokers. "Every person at the meeting today feels we have no time," said Harold Rubin, a DAC member. "We have to figure out a way today." He added that neither Fomon nor Pierce nor Rittereiser could handle the retail side of the firm properly.

Fomon sought to give assurances that Hutton would not be put out of business, although he admitted that Connecticut was a particular problem. He added, in a classic Fomon maneuver, that he would personally give everyone in the room $1,000 if Hutton was barred from the state. Besides, he said, if the state attempted a ban, Hutton could obtain a court injunction blocking the move "within an hour."

"Injunctive relief is a hand job," countered Tuthill. "You don't seem to understand. Our brokers are ready to bolt, and our customers are concerned. The field has lost its pride. We need something."

Someone asked if there was anyone in the room who could

take over the retail side of the firm right away. Clarence Catallo, the regional vice-president in Detroit, was mentioned as a candidate.

"The bottom line," said Bud Jordan, a DAC member particularly disgruntled about the tax shelter disasters, "is that at a meeting we had prior to this meeting, the DAC felt Bob Witt was not in the right job."

Dick Locke leaned over to Fomon and said in an aside, "Do you know whose blood they're calling for?"

"Yeah," Fomon whispered. "Witt's and Pierce's."

"And yours, Bob. They're calling for your head, too," Locke told him. Fomon was suddenly on his feet, pacing.

Bud Jordan found himself standing and speaking at the decisive moment. He was working up to the call for both Fomon and Witt to resign. Suddenly Fomon interrupted him.

"Hold it. I know what you're going to say," Fomon said. "I should fire Bob Witt." His crackly voice was almost drowned out by the din as he argued that that would be too easy. It would not solve anything but would create uncertainty at a time when the firm needed to ply a steady course.

The raucous chorus continued. Rittereiser began an impromptu speech to deflect the criticism from the chairman.

"I believe this company has the best chance to be the champion in the investment services business," he began, sounding as though he were trying to recruit brokers at a Rotary Club meeting. "I believe that relative to Shearson/American Express, Merrill Lynch, Prudential-Bache, this is the place to be."

Ritt tried to leaven the atmosphere by recalling a line from one of his favorite movies, *Cool Hand Luke:* "What we have here is a failure to communicate." Nobody laughed.

With that, the pacing Bob Fomon bent over to whisper something to Dick Locke. "I'm going to go to my apartment to meet with Warren Christopher, I'll be back later."

"Bob, I don't think you should do that," said Locke. "He can wait. That's what you have a butler for. You need to be here."

But Fomon insisted. With that, he paced back and forth a few more times, then limped right out of the room. Few noticed, since the discussion was still focusing on Bob Witt. Some thought Fomon was heading to the men's room. It took several minutes for the brokers to realize that he had escaped. Several whispered among themselves angrily.

John Latshaw, head of the central region and a director, made a last effort anyway. "I told Bob Fomon that we want someone else to be chairman of the board of the securities company, whether it's Clarence Catallo or someone else." Still, nothing happened. They did not have the power to force Fomon out. Fomon had shown he could simply ignore them. The great rebellion had fizzled.

Rittereiser concluded the meeting by proposing that a new communications task force be formed to give the field direct access to Hutton's senior executives, as though that had been the point of the rebellion. He also proposed giving more board positions to top brokers.

"If you send this group home today with the message that you are going to form a committee, you may as well board up the doors," said an obviously disappointed broker.

"Where would we be if we did put some person in a job that's not thought out?" Rittereiser countered. "What happens in two or three months if it doesn't work out?" Nobody had an answer. Anyway, the game was already over. The meeting adjourned for drinks and dinner. It was a dismal anticlimax. Things just sputtered out.

Ritt lingered only briefly. He had promised his family that he would join them for dinner to celebrate his birthday—his forty-seventh. He decided he had to stay for cocktails. Bob Fomon returned later, and aside from a few glum faces, spirits appeared to have picked up a bit. Ritt finally departed to a chorus of empty Happy Birthdays. Meanwhile, Fomon was informed of Ritt's promise that more brokers would be placed on the E. F. Hutton & Company board of directors.

The next morning Fomon was determined to set Ritt straight.

"I want to know what's going on," Fomon snapped after putting away the last triangle of toast on his tray and pouring another cup of black coffee. "I heard reports that you agreed to put people on the Inc. board. What authority do you have to make those kinds of decisions? That's not your fucking board to give away."

"Bob, let me tell you something," Ritt responded. "Yes, I did say that we would put some of those people on the Inc. board. First of all, you have no choice. You heard those guys. They are demanding that they be heard. Second, it's the right thing to do. But last, we have a lot to do around here with this management. This is just a start. A lot of decisions are going to have to be made. We have work to do defining our markets, coming up with our game plans, and executing in an organized fashion. I want you to understand the kind of game I want us to play and that we do not have much time. It's late in the fourth quarter."

Ritt felt he was in a position of strength. Fomon might bristle, but surely he had to recognize the threat that those angry brokers presented. If Fomon had any interest in restoring the brokerage house, he had to listen to his president.

Fomon thought otherwise. This "game plan" stuff meant nothing to him. All he knew was that Ritt was pretending to make decisions that were the CEO's. The issue for him was not Hutton's future, but the perks of power. Hutton was collapsing. There was no doubt of that. It could make cosmetic changes or real changes. It was a question of who had the nerve—and the self-confidence—to fight openly.

That moment was the pivot around which Hutton's future turned, as Ritt found himself staring at a trail of cigarette smoke in Fomon's otherwise empty office.

A few days later Hutton launched a communications offensive, approved by Fomon and guided by his PR consultants. The firm took out a full-page ad in *The New York Times* headed, E. F. HUTTON TALKS . . .

" 'Thank You.' That's the most important thing we can say to our 17,500 employees and our thousands of customers and clients," the ad read.

Fomon also delivered a rare speech to his troops over Hutton's internal communications system, the Profit Line, normally used to tout stocks. Written by the PR staff, it was a candid appraisal of what had gone wrong and how he was handling the problems.

The subject of naming names, he admitted, was central. Fomon insisted that the matter rested in Griffin Bell's hands. "If Judge Bell points the finger at me, I'm gone," Fomon vowed. "If he points it at others, they're gone."

Fomon assured Hutton's employees that none of the outside forces buffeting the firm could destroy it. "The only thing," he said, "that can destroy this firm could come from the *inside*."

Then came the clincher. "Common sense says that when questionable practices involve billions of dollars and dozens of a firm's offices, top management knows about it."

Yet, Fomon added, "there are times—they don't happen often, but there are times—when the reality of a situation defies what our common sense tells us. This is one of those times."

The only question was whether Griffin Bell would buy that line.

# THE HUTTON SALUTE

August 1985 was like the playing out of a piece of surrealistic theater at Hutton. Griffin Bell's investigation was in full swing, with one aim—to make heads roll. When you met someone in the hall, even the imperious Bob Fomon, you might have been talking to a wraith who would disappear at the report's delivery in early September.

This owlish former judge—a tall, slender, slightly stooped man with thinning dark hair and round, tortoiseshell-rimmed glasses, an unfailingly courteous southern manner and a heavy deep South accent—controlled their fates, and they hated him for that.

Hutton's executives feared Bell more, in fact, than the government prosecutors. The government could have sent them to prison, but at least in the courts there were rules their lawyers could manipulate. There were limits. Bell had to answer, effectively, to no one. He had a mandate to turn any stone at the firm and come up with broad judgments about the performance of Hutton's executives.

Fomon had never made such judgments, had never held his

team to any standards. True, every consultant he'd ever called in had been appalled by the way Hutton was run, but Fomon could ignore them and rely on advertising and the Hutton myth to bamboozle the public. Accountability was a completely alien concept in his regime; none of those responsible for fiascos like the loan to George Aubin, the tax shelters, the upper floaters, or Famco were fired or penalized. Even after Arnie Phelan's embarrassing involvement with the Pizza Connection became public, his status at the firm went unchanged.

In order to hold his unquestioned grip on power, Fomon had tacitly agreed not to insist on performance; that was the compact between him and his ruling barons that kept him on the throne. Now Fomon had allowed this outsider to come in and shed some light on his shadowy world.

The investigation began as a laborious, mechanical exercise. Every branch's bank accounts were checked for signs of overdrafting and pinwheeling. Branch managers were then questioned as the investigators worked their way up the Hutton hierarchy. The principal question was how independent Bell would be in drawing conclusions.

The early signs were not good. For starters, Bell asked the Justice Department for help. Al Murray in Scranton and the top Justice Department lawyers in Washington provided what Bell called "tips," encouraging him down certain paths and discouraging him from others.

The investigation was also a trial for the Justice Department, given the intense criticism of its failure to prosecute individuals at Hutton and the remaining question of whether Fomon had improperly influenced the Justice Department through back channels. The government had a clear interest in having Bell agree with its own findings. But Bell was providing them with an early opportunity to sway the course of his inquiry, even though Bell insisted that his judgments were unaffected by the government.

By mid-August Bell was circling the key suspects, setting off a vicious fight for survival. Paul Hines, the head of accounting, planning, and financial control, had coveted Tom Lynch's chief financial officer title, and the two barely spoke, giving each the incentive to finger the other. Many also regarded Lynch as Fomon's lackey and struck at the CEO by pinning the blame on Lynch.

Others pointed to Ball, who had been so enthusiastic in encouraging the overdrafting. Several Hutton officials blamed Norm Epstein, the head of operations and Tom Morley's boss.

"The big fight was over whether Epstein was going to take the fall or if Lynch was going to take the fall," Bell said. "Epstein was not a beloved figure. There's no question that that's the one people wanted us to get. There was no one there to protect Epstein, I can tell you that."

The trickiest call was Fomon. No evidence connected him directly with the illegal overdrafting. But what broader responsibility did he have as CEO? If this was a "corporate scheme," as Meese had claimed, should the head of the corporation be penalized?

On this issue, too, Bell sent out odd signals. He and his staff carried on friendly meetings with their prime suspect, sometimes over lunch—an unorthodox tactic for a prosecutor.

In a June 27 letter to Fomon, for instance, Bell wrote in a markedly unprosecutorial tone, "My lawyers report that in all of their contacts with Hutton people, they are finding a spirit which looks to putting the Hutton cash management chapter behind them.

"This spirit," he added, rendering a judgment before he'd even completed his investigation, "will help us complete our investigation on schedule but, in the interest of Hutton, it bespeaks a viable organization made up of loyal people, looking to the future rather than the cash management problems of 1981–1982."

Adding to the increasingly bizarre atmosphere was the role that Cahill Gordon, Hutton's outside law firm, was playing. Cahill's lawyers insisted on representing Hutton officials before the Bell inquiry. However, Cahill also represented the board. It was a classic conflict of interest; if the company was going to end up firing some of these people, how could Cahill be on both sides of a dispute?

Warren Christopher, fed up with the problem, threatened to resign if the situation was not corrected and had to be persuaded to stay. Cahill was unwilling to give up the power, or the fees, it would get. Fomon, willing to grab at anything that might provide a bit more control, acquiesced.

Despite the care exercised by Bell and his team, they were in a quandary that only deepened as the steamy summer days dragged on. Lines of responsibility at Hutton seemed to lead into a fog. It was almost impossible to determine who worked for whom in Hutton's money management area, the heart of the crime, because everyone told a different story or simply denied stories related by others.

It was an appalling situation: here was the system through which more than three-quarters of all of Hutton's revenues flowed, yet it appeared that no one was in charge. At least no one admitted to being in charge.

Griffin Bell came up with his "Hutton salute" to describe what he encountered: he would wind each arm across his chest and point in opposite directions, like the scarecrow in the *Wizard of Oz* giving directions to Dorothy. In the context of E. F. Hutton, the gesture meant, "Him, not me."

Bell wrestled with what seemed an incoherent corporate structure. For Fomon, refreshingly direct as usual, it was a far simpler matter.

"Of course they lied," Fomon said. "Nobody is going to stand up and say, *'Moi.'*"

Hutton's executives were not under oath, and Fomon had made clear that the whole point was to fire people. There was, to put it mildly, not a lot of incentive to be frank or courageous. As a result, Tom Morley, head of the cash management system at blame, had become like Harvey, the invisible six-foot rabbit in the Jimmy Stewart movie; Griffin Bell was the only person who seemed to be able to see him.

But Bell was not being paid $2.5 million to conclude that an invisible rabbit was responsible for two thousand felonies and a crippling scandal. A decision had to be made, and that decision came down to one interview, one exchange, one moment.

In mid-August Bell's lawyers met with Loren Schechter, Hutton's former deputy general counsel and the attorney who performed the initial investigation in 1982 when the government had first confronted Hutton with evidence of its crime. (He had then gone on to work for George Ball as general counsel at Pru-Bache.)

Schechter was being questioned by Perry Pearce, a young lawyer in Bell's office.

"Whom did Morley report to?"

"He seemed to report to different people for different things. It wasn't always clear from what people told me."

"But when you investigated after the meeting [on February 10, 1982] with the banking regulators, whom did Morley deal with?"

"When we spoke to Morley on the Saturday afterward, he said, 'On things like this, I report to Lynch.'"

By late August Bell's staff ran a series of what they called "due process" interviews with their targets, even though they had reached their basic conclusion. The interviews took place in what was known as "the wallpaper room," the conference room across from Bob Fomon's office that had held wallpaper samples in those glorious days when a Hutton executive's toughest assignment was figuring out how to redecorate his office. The comings and goings from that conference room were being scrutinized anxiously now.

Tom Lynch knew there was some heat on him as overseer of Hutton's financial apparatus, but he felt he'd persuaded Bell that he had no direct supervisory responsibility for Morley. He had three interviews, believing each time that he had made his case— only to discover later that he had not. Eventually he bargained with Bell to settle the matter once and for all.

Lynch agreed to give up his role as de facto chief financial officer, while retaining the title of vice-chairman and his seat on the board. It would give Bell an opening to mandate a reorganization of Hutton's financial operations, a sensible thing, Lynch thought. But things had not gone quite as he expected.

"If I were Tom Lynch," Bell told Scott Pierce a few days later, dropping a bombshell, "I'd resign now, before the report is completed."

Pierce called his friend immediately.

"We can't control him," Pierce said. "I thought I ought to tell you as a friend that he's after you."

"No way," snapped the usually calm Lynch. "That's unacceptable."

Lynch went to Fomon, long the protector of the status quo. Fomon, with his growing list of infirmities, relied so heavily on Lynch that, Lynch hoped, the CEO would shield him.

"What are you going to do about this?" Lynch demanded. His old friend gave him assurances that, as he always had, he would take care of the problem.

Shortly before midnight on Wednesday, September 4, Lynch received a call from Tom Curnin of Cahill Gordon, the senior partner on the case and the lawyer who had been representing Lynch throughout the proceedings. Curnin had just gotten word on Bell's recommendations—due out the next day—and said it claimed Lynch had agreed to give up all of his titles and would be leaving Hutton.

"This is crazy," Lynch said, flustered and growing agitated. "This isn't what we agreed to."

"That's basically what he's going to say in the report," Curnin replied. "We just found out."

"You know that's not the deal. He can't do that. We'll take it to the board. You can make the arguments better than I," said Lynch.

Then Lynch received another shock.

"I'm sorry, Tom, I can't represent you if you do that," Curnin said, ending the long-standing charade. "I represent the board. I would have a conflict representing both of you."

Lynch was out there alone. Fomon had his scapegoat.

At close to noon the next day, the directors of both E. F. Hutton Group and E. F. Hutton & Company assembled. They were handed copies of Bell's report, whose conclusions were then outlined and explained by the lawyers. The atmosphere was funereal. Word had spread that Lynch was going to take the fall. Everyone felt it was a little unfair. However, the dominant feeling was, "Better him than me."

The report selected six branch managers (including Perry Bacon, author of the "smoking gun" memo) and four regional executives as the principal perpetrators of the scheme. The choices seemed almost random. Bell stated that twenty branches had been involved in the abusive overdrafting. Only six had been "egregious" and "excessive," he said, without providing criteria for the selections. In the case of the Louisville branch manager, for instance, Bell agreed to let him off the hook if his bank provided a letter stating that it knew of the overdrafting and approved it. The bank wrote, saying that it was aware of the overdrafting without saying it had approved the abuses. But Bell accepted the letter anyway and did not cite the manager, a friend of Scott Pierce's.

The reaction of many board members was ambivalent. On the one hand, the 183-page report and its 300-page appendix neatly laid out a series of conclusions that, if accepted, just might end this nightmare once and for all.

However, the report raised more questions than it answered. It was little more than a number of bread crumb trails. The trails bifurcated at times, led into the dark at other times, but never reached a satisfying destination because of the contradictory information Bell was provided by the executives supposedly cooperating with the inquiry. Bell's report was filled with implausible explanations.

In one respect it was strong. Bell described a chaotic organization—a frightening thought considering that this was one of America's largest and best-known corporations, handling billions of dollars' worth of securities transactions every day. The report also described the medieval structure in which Fomon arranged his barons so that he would maintain control.

But the emphasis on organizational shortcomings had a strange side effect: it became a dodge. The system was the culprit, in Bell's view, not the individuals who constructed and ran it.

Bell recommended, for instance, that Morley be reassigned, but not fired, "because his defalcations was [sic] more than just *his* defalcations; they were part of a failing in a management system." Bell ignored the possibility that the organization had been described to him chaotically for a purpose.

Bell pointed out that Hutton's accounting department kept elaborate records by branch of the firm's financial performance, including its interest earnings. He then made this curious observation: "While nearly all of the senior people at Hutton were focusing on the idea of increasing interest earnings, no one was taking note of any unusual interest earnings, other than to urge those with low interest earnings to follow the examples of those who had high earnings."

In other words, Bell argued, there was a firmwide drive to squeeze as much interest profit out of the banks as possible. Branches that earned the most were identified, as were the branches that underperformed. The methods of those that excelled were explored and disseminated in the hopes that others would emulate them. And yet "no one was taking note of any unusual interest earnings."

In another instance Bell discussed the May 1981 memo in which the assistant controller praised a good cashier as a better source of profits than a broker because of the interest the cashier could earn from overdrafting.

The accountant wrote that memo, he told Bell, in response to an inquiry from the branch manager in Hartford, Connecticut. The branch manager, who denied any memory of making such a request, was identified as a key culprit in the overdrafting.

"This is almost a classic example," Bell wrote, "of the accounting department's dwelling on interest earnings rather than interest problems, although, in fairness, unlike today, interest problems control had not been assigned."

Inexplicably Bell did not find it a classic example of how Hutton officials did, in fact, spot the aggressive overdrafting. He applied blame to an abstract accounting shortcoming rather than to the individuals involved.

But the best example of his failure was the brick wall he ran into with Harvey the rabbit. "Morley is now an orphan, seemingly lost or at least in limbo along with his corporate function somewhere in the Hutton corporate structure," Bell wrote. "An old saying may be applicable: Victory has a hundred feathers and defeat is an orphan."

Bell's colorful description elicited some chuckles, but it evaded the darker truth. Hutton's executives were lying to him, and he was unable to cut through the dissembling. Calling Morley an orphan was not describing a system; it was an admission that Bell had failed to find the system. The lying, in other words, succeeded.

George Ball received remarkable treatment. Ball was the prototype of a Hutton manager; he had a say in everything that happened, but clear responsibility for almost nothing. For several years he built impressive increases in revenues, for which he claimed credit. He was not held responsible, however, for Hutton's mounting cost problems.

That left Ball free to exhort his branches to earn interest prof- its, to specifically encourage "overdrafting" of bank accounts, to choose as models branches that were breaking the law—and then to claim, as he told Bell, that "he was in effect an executive sales manager." Ball had always claimed that "overdrafting" itself was not illegal, only systematic and abusive overdrafting, which he knew nothing about.

"The overdraft interest data showing aberrations," which Ball often cited, "did not constitute sufficient notice of overdrafting problems," Judge Bell concluded.

The final conclusions were thus fairly predictable. Bell ex- onerated Fomon cleanly. Lynch would have to go, but only be- cause of supervisory lapses. Tom Rae, the general counsel, would have to go because of his incompetence in not replying fully to the government subpoenas. Tom Morley was out. A few branch man- agers and regional operations officials would receive modest fines and something most board members had never heard of before—a "letter of reprimand" to be kept in their "permanent records," whatever that was.

Secretly a number of board members were disappointed most by the treatment of Fomon, particularly the anguished Scott Pierce. There was no way they could kill the king themselves. They wanted Bell to do the job for them. It was an opportunity missed. Some came to the board meeting prepared to hear their names put in nomination for Fomon's job—Bob Rittereiser among them. Ritt had been jolted by Fomon's power politics a couple of months earlier.

At noon the directors assembled around the imposingly large, wheellike board table. Fomon, who would normally lurk around the periphery of the table, smoking heavily, practically stumbled into his seat. In a tense chat that morning with Tom Lynch, Fomon had looked awful, his complexion gray, his movements slower than usual, his voice pinched up. He looked even worse now. He managed to call the meeting to order, and the debate over the Bell report began.

Tom Lynch, his usually ruddy face infused a deeper red, his gray hair pushed straight back, wearing one of his standard dark, pin-striped suits, stood up to defend himself.

"I have to disagree with what this report says about my responsibility for this matter," he began, his confident, mellow voice dry and cracked. "Look, the cash management department did not report to me. I had no responsibility for the control functions. Those reported to other people here, and all of you know that. I am being unfairly singled out. This is just unfair.

"I cannot understand why Bell decided that the vice-chairman was responsible if those other people were not. It doesn't make sense.

"And his saying that I agreed to give up all my titles is just wrong. That is not acceptable. When it was made clear to me earlier by the lawyers that something would have to happen with the chief financial officer's job, I agreed to give that up. I never really was chief financial officer. Paul Hines acted as CFO, and you know that. I agreed to give up that title so that Bell would be able to call for the hiring of a new CFO and a reorganization of the department. We had a deal, and Bell changed it at the last minute. We have to reject the recommendations."

Silence followed. It was embarrassing and awkward. Most of the directors stared at their hands, folded in front of them. Tom Lynch was begging for his professional life, and they were not going to grant it to him because, for many of those present, that would mean taking some responsibility themselves.

"The fix was in," said one board member. "The feeling of everyone was, 'There but for the grace of God go I.'"

Seeing that he was not moving the directors—especially with no lawyer to speak up for him—Lynch's appeal grew more pathetic. He reached into a stack of papers and fished out an E. F. Hutton & Company telephone book. He opened it up and waved it in front of the directors.

"We put our organizational structure in this book. You just have to know how to read it. Look, my name appears here. But look where Morley's is, it's in operations, not under my name. You see, if you know how to read the telephone book, it's obvious that I did not have any authority for cash management, that I had nothing to do with it."

(Three years later, when asked to explain his organizational responsibilities, Lynch interrupted an interview in his living room to rummage through a closet and pull out the E. F. Hutton phone book to prove his point.)

Hutton had secretly begun to run out of control and it was at the height of its illegal bank overdrafting, but chairman Bob Fomon (left) and president George Ball cut impressive, patrician figures for the cover of the firm's 1980 annual report. *(Cheryl Rossum)*

In better days, Bob Fomon, at the peak of his powers, and his father-figure, Al Jack, admire an award Hutton bestowed on the old chairman in the mid-1970s. *(Wagner International Photos)*

Jim Lopp's aggressive business style, success in public finance and shared interests made him a favorite of Bob Fomon. Lopp oversaw the slow crumbling of Hutton's corporate finance department, but remained close to Fomon and eventually became one of his key allies on the board. *(Cheryl Rossum)*

George Aubin was a Texas rancher and deal maker with a gambler's temperament and a checkered business history, but through his relationship to superbroker Don Sanders he became E. F. Hutton's single largest customer in 1984. Aubin's orgy of trading and Hutton's efforts to bend the rules to allow him to stay in business cost the firm more than $50 million, and nearly exposed some of Hutton's most tightly held secrets.

A stolid Tom Lynch, the ultimate scapegoat for the overdrafting, looks on as Bob Fomon attempts to persuade congressmen at a hearing in 1985 that no senior executives were involved in the illegal banking activities. *(Bettmann Archive)*

Former Hutton president George Ball, whose memos linked him to the push to overdraft, explained at a congressional hearing that he was just a sales manager and had no responsibility for the illegal activities. *(Bettmann Archive)*

Bob Rittereiser could rarely resist hamming it up for cameras. Shortly after joining Hutton, he put on a relaxed, presidential air in the firm's boardroom. *(Joyce Ravid)*

Shearson chairman Peter Cohen, in a festive mood after concluding the Hutton acquisition in 1987, clowns with a grim but smiling Bob Rittereiser. Cohen mocks the old "When E. F. Hutton talks, people listen" ad, unaware of the career-shattering mistake he has made. *(Bettman Archive)*

Tom Rae, Hutton's general counsel (right) shares a thought with Scott Pierce, Hutton's president and George Bush's brother-in-law, testifying at a congressional hearing in 1985. Pierce was one of the Hutton executives who could credibly claim to have no involvement in the overdrafting. *(Bettmann Archive)*

Dina Merrill, famed movie actress, daughter of company founder Edward F. Hutton, and one of the least informed members of Hutton's board, became a tool helping Bob Fomon gain revenge against Bob Rittereiser. *(Bettmann Archive)*

Poker-faced Peter Ueberroth deftly controlled Bob Fomon and the E. F. Hutton board. He led Hutton's sale to Shearson and personally earned $1 million from it, while avoiding any visible role in the firm's collapse. *(Bettmann Archive)*

One-time Hutton vice-chairman John Shad was out-maneuvered and then humiliated by Bob Fomon, but finally escaped to become chairman of the Securities and Exchange Commission. A secret tip from his old tormentor helped launch one of the commission's largest insider-trading cases against a Fomon enemy, Giuseppe Tome. *(Bettmann Archive)*

Griffin Bell was a Southern gentleman, respected former judge and attorney general whose credibility was expected to halt congressional attacks on Hutton for the overdrafting scheme. He failed to find those responsible, but his investigation produced one lasting product: his aptly named "Hutton salute," a metaphor for evasion of responsibility. *(Bettmann Archive)*

American Express chairman James D. Robinson III (right), known for his warm and confident manner, was never personally close to Peter Cohen, Shearson's sharp, sometimes brusque chief executive, but they developed a solid partnership based on what Robinson called Cohen's "terrific money-making ability." Robinson fully supported Cohen in the dash to acquire E. F. Hutton, which nearly destroyed Shearson and left the two executives bitterly divided. *(John S. Abbott)*

It was a pitiful finale. All he had to defend himself was a dog-eared copy of the company phone book. Lynch finally sat, the strain showing in his clenched jaw.

Fomon, although sickly, spoke up. "Griffin Bell says certain things that I think we should debate because I disagree with them," he began.

John Latshaw, the head of the central region, which had been one of the more egregious offenders in the overdrafting—Perry Bacon came under its authority—added his voice for rejection of Bell's conclusions.

"We do not have to accept this report," he began. "We run this company, not Griffin Bell. Tom is right. He had no authority for the problems. Bell is making him the scapegoat."

Jim Lopp delivered an impassioned speech on behalf of Lynch. It was time to close ranks, he said, not do something unfair for expediency.

Dina Merrill, held in high regard as the founder's daughter, spoke briefly on behalf of Tom Lynch's loyalty.

Bob Rittereiser then cut in.

"I frankly don't think we have any choice," he said. "You cannot come this far and then say we think the report is wrong. We have no basis for rejecting it. The public just will not accept that. There's no question that Tom may have had no clear responsibility for Tom Morley or any of this. I've known Tom for twenty years, and I have the highest regard for him. I am not about to sit in judgment on anybody. But from the standpoint of looking at this as an ongoing business that shows some corporate responsibility, we have to implement these recommendations."

Dick Locke followed. "We have next to no credibility to the public already," he said. "I can tell you, we might as well close the doors on the public finance department if we reject this report. We'll be out of business."

Ed Cazier, Bob Fomon's law school classmate and his staunchest ally on the board, added his view that it would be awkward to reject Bell's report.

(Some claimed that Cazier threatened to have all the outside board members resign if the report were rejected, but Fomon flatly denied that. "Cazier is a wimp," he said. "He would never have the balls to do that." Cazier refused to be interviewed.)

It was painfully clear what had to be done. Warren Law, the

Harvard Business School professor and the longest-serving outside board member, recommended on behalf of the audit committee that the board accept all the report's conclusions. Law's motion was passed.

"If that's the board's view, then I will accept it," replied Lynch, who had just been forced out of E. F. Hutton after twenty-three years.

Latshaw offered a meager consolation prize. What the board was doing was wrong, he said, but at the least the company had to show its appreciation for Tom's contributions. It was an ambiguous suggestion at best, offering solemn praise for a man whom the board was also blaming for the worst problem in the firm's eighty-one-year history.

Nonetheless, the resolution was passed. A committee of directors later drew up a four-paragraph testimonial to Lynch, who was taking the rap for the firm.

"For those who benefitted from his counsel, warmth and genuine concern," the plaque said of Lynch, "he has come to embody the very spirit of E. F. Hutton."

The blow was also softened by the multimillion-dollar severance package worked out. Lynch would receive more than $600,-000 a year for life, medical insurance, reimbursement of legal costs, and two club memberships.

The deal was done. Hutton had "purged" itself, and Fomon had been defeated. All the board members stood to leave—save one. Bob Fomon was already gone.

Late in the meeting he had grown paler and more visibly ill as his political potency was sapped. Jay Moorhead, his assistant, watched with growing dismay. Moorhead's father had suffered a stroke earlier, and he knew the frightening symptoms. He feared that the weary, beaten Fomon was slipping into a similar attack.

At one point during the afternoon, Fomon had taken Ritt aside and, surprising his president, said, "Rittereiser, if I should die and you're named chairman to replace me, dammit, I don't want you to make Scott Pierce president of the holding company." Somewhat taken aback, Ritt just told Fomon not to worry about such things. But he too grew worried as Fomon sank onto his chair. Fomon's speech was becoming slurred. His face was red, and one side was sagging. His mouth was getting contorted.

The vote was taken and before anyone noticed, Fomon was quietly escorted out of the room. The chairman was spirited out the back of the building, put in a waiting limousine, and rushed to his doctor's office, where he was given medication and told to get some rest. Neither Hutton's employees nor the public was told of the attack.

When everyone had cleared out, Ritt took a few minutes in his office to consider the ironic closing words Griffin Bell had gratuitously added to the report.

"A new Hutton," he'd written, "with a majority of outside Directors, a reorganized management, with tight internal controls and a renewed commitment to its shareholders, customers and employees should give it a fresh start." It was a conclusion Ritt struggled to accept.

# 13

# BEHIND THE CURTAIN

"The image of a securities firm is very much like the Wizard of Oz—it's bigger than life with lots of smoke," Samuel L. Hayes III, a Harvard Business School professor and expert on the securities industry, was quoted as saying in *The New York Times* the day after Bell's report was released. "But that image can collapse, deflate when you see the little man behind the curtain. If that happens, you have to figure out how to pump it up again."

Bell had been discreet—after all, it was Fomon who brought him in and was paying his bill—but even Fomon could not miss the obvious signal: he had been exonerated only to make clear that his rule was over. It was, everyone believed, and certainly Ritt hoped, no longer necessary to do violence to unseat Fomon. The weight of opinion would do the job for them. The Fomon myth had atrophied, and now the Hutton myth would, too, if it did not get "pumped up" again.

A hundred flowers bloomed as the sweetness of spring filled the nostrils of all at Hutton. It was suddenly all right, even fashionable, to criticize the old CEO—as though he were already gone.

Words that would have been treasonous weeks earlier now seemed as sensible as galoshes on a rainy day.

"What Bob has always needed is someone to tell him when he's wrong," said Jim Lopp, one of Fomon's most intimate friends, in an interview shortly after the Bell report. "He didn't have enough of those people."

Lopp—who had left Hutton to form a corporate bond insurance firm but remained on Hutton's board—openly described Fomon as an often grumpy meddler who monopolized power and encouraged people to go around their bosses' backs. He even told the story of a young analyst who had done that to him.

The firm had not just slipped, Lopp added, it had suffered a "breakdown," heavy language for someone who was still a director of Hutton. "You've got to run like hell just to stay even in this business today. It was too much for him."

"He's not broken," Lopp added in the interview, "but he's weary."

"The kind of philosophy we had with so many people reporting to Bob and such a loose organization was probably okay until the late seventies or early eighties, but our business has gotten much too complex to be run by one person now," said Scott Pierce in another interview. "Go easy on him."

Even George Ball broke a long public silence to comment on his former mentor. "He gave a lot of thought to getting the right people and to dealing with them. But he gave little detailed thought to structures or processes. That's how he really controlled the company—through individuals, not the systems they worked in," he told an interviewer.

But most striking were the remarks made by an emboldened Bob Rittereiser. The loyal staff officer was suddenly demonstrating a powerfully independent streak as he candidly discussed a brokerage house in disarray. For over an hour, twenty feet from the king's throne room, Rittereiser opined during an interview on what had gone wrong and how he would fix it.

"Strong leadership and good ideas could push this business extremely well for a long time. And Hutton really benefited from that. But clearly there is a change now toward more teamwork. Your strategy has to be toward a whole business system, how the parts relate. At this place people are good at their functions, but there is no interrelation among them. That's why this has happened," explained Hutton's new president, a cheerful man in a dark, pin-striped suit, its lapels covered with a light dusting of dandruff.

"We have some accidental synergy in a few instances. But that's it. Strangely enough, this company has a tradition of teamwork. But with the departure of Ball some of the natural linkages disappeared, and people admit to that. I also sense that everyone here wants out of this era and wants to go back to the teamwork era."

Ritt summed things up in his inimitable style: "If you just stand in center, you can't say you're doing okay if there are problems elsewhere. There was an atmosphere where the ball could roll through the third baseman's legs, and then through the left fielder's legs, and the center fielder could say, 'It's not my problem.' That's not the way winners play."

In case the point had been missed, Ritt spelled it out. "Bob's vision was that he wanted to work until he was sixty-five. But in many ways personally this has been a real blow."

Fomon missed several weeks as he recuperated from his collapse at the board meeting. When he wandered back into the office shortly afterward, he continued a series of interviews that had begun before Bell's report had been released. He was tired-looking and old for his sixty-one years. The subject of Hutton and how it was managed bored him visibly. He relished talking about himself instead. He puffed constantly on his Winston cigarettes, never unbuttoned or removed his double-breasted suit coats, and paced slowly around his leafy corner office, weighing his comments with care. He encouraged talk on racier, personal subjects.

"I don't like women who've been around the block," he snapped when asked why he only dated young models in their late teens or twenties. "All an older women has is problems."

Asked what he could possibly talk about with what he described as often less than brilliant companions, Fomon looked at his interviewer as though he had just dropped from the moon. "What do you think?" he replied in his nasal, scratchy voice.

When the subject did drift back to Hutton, Fomon was relentless in refusing blame for the problems. Nor would he admit in the slightest that his rule might be in trouble.

It was odd. Fomon refused to deliver the valedictory that everyone expected of him.

"I've thought about whether we made a mistake here," he said. "The problem was that I was not aware really of the hatred of the Democrats for Republicans. We're a victim of that hatred."

Was his management of Hutton at fault? "Nobody has convinced me of that."

Told of the hints by other Hutton executives that his days were numbered, he replied, "I'll leave February 1990, when I'm sixty-five. The Bell report made me firm in my resolve. I would never leave Hutton in the present condition it's in.

"I'm going to stay here until this is cleared up," he insisted, pulling on a cigarette as he stood by the telescope at the floor-to-ceiling windows of his office, "and then some."


As things began to quiet in the fall of 1985, Fomon got back to his most important project, the new headquarters. Ritt observed with concern but kept his distance. At one planning meeting, Bill Clayton, in charge of portions of the project, explained that he intended to leave six of the hugely expensive floors vacant temporarily so that Hutton could grow into them over time.

"This is a fucking joke," howled Rich Carbone, the deputy controller. "This is crazy. What makes you think we're going to grow like that, and what makes you think we can afford that space? I want fifteen floors of that building sublet. You cannot produce the goddamn revenues you need to cover the expenses. We need fifteen fucking floors to cover our asses on this thing."

After a few minutes of arguing, Fomon, who had been silent up to that moment, arbitrarily told Clayton, "Sublet eight floors."

Carbone was not satisfied. "I want twelve floors. We don't need and cannot afford all this goddamn space at these prices."

Within a few weeks it was clear that none of the floors would be sublet. But Ritt let well enough alone. He was trying to work out the least confrontational relationship with the old chairman so that he could focus on what he considered more substantive matters. Ritt was trying to recruit a new chief financial officer to replace Tom Lynch and a new general counsel to take Tom Rae's job. He was eager to bring in executives who would be beholden to him, not Fomon. And Fomon appeared to stand back.

Then, to his surprise, Ed Cazier called to say that he had been rounding up candidates for the general counsel's job and wanted to discuss them with Ritt. Ritt was angry at this infringement of his prerogatives, but he listened to the suggestions and even spoke with some of the candidates. Cazier then flew to New York from his home in Los Angeles to press Rittereiser on hiring his man.

"Ed, I do appreciate your help in this in any way you can," he said. "But I want you to know that I am going to have the final say on whom we hire."

"Well, if that's the way you feel and you have no use for the board, then you just have to say so," a peevish Cazier replied. He added that Fomon, the chief executive, had asked him personally to screen potential recruits. Now Ritt understood.

"Ed, I didn't say I didn't want you to help. I don't want you to run it. The people who are going to be taking this company forward have to be in a position to select the people who are going to work closely with them. Nobody's going to come in here who can't work with me. And I'll make the final decision."

Such behind-the-scenes maneuvering was a distraction, in Ritt's view, peripheral to his main concern of building the great firm's future. But increasingly he found himself putting out fires and tackling an endless list of daily problems. For instance, there were the arbs now.

"Arb" is Wall Street argot for arbitrageur, a high-risk trader who speculates in takeover stocks or stocks rumored to be takeover targets. Like wolf packs, the arbs pursue the weakened. And when they circle, even the strong can become vulnerable. The arbs are essential components of takeover attacks.

By mid-September 1985 rumors streamed through the market about the beleaguered Hutton. On September 19 Hutton's stock jumped $2.375 to $36.25 a share in anticipation that a bid might be launched. Shortly afterward financial columnist Dan Dorfman reported that Smith Barney was shopping Hutton to potential buyers, under the code name "Project Drum." That just brought out more arbs.

There was, in fact, a solid logic to the rumors. Hutton was one of the last independent large retail brokerage firms on Wall Street. It was also regarded as among the choicest picks left, with its extensive sales system. If a major corporation wanted to buy a foothold on Wall Street, perceived to be a hot area, Hutton was sure to get a good looking over.

To Dan Good, the head of Hutton's small mergers department and adviser to Ted Turner in his unsuccessful run at CBS, it was coming down to a simple choice: Hutton could make something happen by arranging a marriage, or it could wait to get hunted down.

The matter was of more than academic importance to Good. The plea agreement and resulting controversy had devastated his business and his ability to recruit talented investment bankers. The firm had to be strengthened so that Good could get back into action, or he would have to quit.

Good had his staff pull together extensive studies of three likely merger candidates: Kidder, Peabody & Company, Paine Webber, and Smith Barney. Like Hutton, all three firms were perceived as strong in some areas, but too small to go it alone in the new global era.

Kidder was Good's first choice because it had a well-regarded corporate finance department and strong trading operations, two of Hutton's greatest weaknesses. He brought his ideas to Ritt and waited for a decision to move ahead. And then he waited some more.

Ritt accepted Good's analyses, but he seemed unable to act. Fomon was clearly interested in the idea, although he chose to appear uninvolved. It was all up to Ritt. The curious thing was that Ritt would neither shut things down nor push them ahead decisively. He just let them drift. Was Hutton for sale or not? The answer was, sort of.

The first real opportunity to force Ritt into action arrived at the end of 1985 with U.S. West, the Denver-based Baby Bell. After the earlier introduction, the conversations between Fomon and U.S. West had continued. Ritt had seemed to climb on board, too. Finally even a price was floated: $1.8 billion. U.S. West was prepared to move, and a date was set for the first serious negotiation. Then everything collapsed, after one real session, led by Dan Good. U.S. West's negotiators were put off by Good's gruff manner and insistence on forcing his terms on U.S. West. They packed up and went home.

But not long afterward Good pushed his Kidder, Peabody idea.

Rittereiser met with Ralph DeNunzio and Jack Roche, the chief executive and president of Kidder, Peabody. DeNunzio later called back to ask what kind of a price Ritt had in mind. Ritt's reply: $400 million. This was a major development; Ritt had put an offer on the table.

But to Ritt's great surprise, Kidder announced shortly afterward that it was selling an 80 percent stake to General Electric for $600 million. Ritt had not realized that he was being used by Kidder as a stalking horse to try and drive GE's offer higher. It was a tellingly naïve stumble.

That was illustrative of how Ritt spent his days. It seemed that the more he wanted to devise long-term strategies and realize his dream of creating a Wall Street powerhouse, the more he was consumed by day-to-day operating disasters and Fomon's maneuverings.

For instance, in October 1985 Hutton suffered its second liquidity crisis of the year. What triggered the latest capital problem was a junk bond issue Hutton had arranged. Hutton underwrote $200 million in these low-grade, high-yielding bonds for the Dart Group, a company run by the Haft family, well-known corporate raiders.

The source of the problem was that Dan Good was trying to break the near monopoly that Drexel Burnham Lambert had on the junk bond market. So Hutton managed Dart's $200 million issue alone, even though it was inexperienced in this realm. When Hutton tried to market the securities, Drexel discouraged its regular customers from buying Hutton's junk. Not surprisingly, the merchandise sat on Hutton's shelves. Hutton had to buy nearly the entire issue itself.

For a healthy brokerage house, tying up $200 million of capital would not be easy, but it could be done without disrupting business. But this was E. F. Hutton. The firm was in a terrible bind.

Throughout the fall Hutton engaged in tense negotiations with the New York Stock Exchange, which was pressing Hutton to unload the bonds. Hutton was unwilling to sell because the bonds were "under water"—they were worth less than what Hutton had paid for them, and it was reluctant to show that loss. But to hold them Hutton would have to take a "haircut," a mandatory reduction in their value of about 25 percent, as represented on Hutton's books. That would wipe nearly $50 million from the company's already strained balance sheet.

As year end approached, Hutton's accountants undertook some urgent financial legerdemain to remove the crucial problem. The trick was—as in the case with the loan to George Aubin—to move the problem to the holding company and out of the brokerage unit.

At year end, when Hutton's accountants calculated how much capital the brokerage unit had in excess of the regulatory minimum, they found just $20 million. In other words, had the brokerage unit not cleared up that $50 million problem from its balance sheet, it would have faced severe action by the stock exchange—or it might have been forced to find a buyer. Ritt escaped by a hairbreadth.

While that was occupying Ritt in secret, some older brushfires were starting to become public. The Aubin tale had taken such a macabre turn that the plot sounded as though it had been woven by a financially inclined Edgar Allan Poe.

Because of a tremendous rally in the bond markets, Aubin's $4 million stake, given him by Hutton in March, had blossomed into tens of millions of dollars in profits. It was an astonishing streak of luck and a direct result of Aubin's high-rolling methods. By summer the winnings totaled a whopping $49 million.

The good news seemed to be that now Aubin had the capital to repay Hutton its $48 million—and not a moment too soon. By summer the attempts to sell Mercury Savings and Ben Milam Savings—whose proceeds had been promised to Hutton—had gone nowhere. All the potential buyers had taken a brief look at the mess and then fled. It was finally starting to dawn on many senior officials at Hutton, including Ritt, that the firm might have fallen prey to a massive scam. The brokerage house had handed over $48 million for what now seemed worthless paper.

To get a better fix on the situation, Ritt had Rich Carbone, the deputy controller, examine the two thrifts. Carbone took just a few days to draw his conclusions.

"Those things are bankrupt," he told Ritt in his nasal Brooklyn accent.

"No, there is some ongoing business value. They are worth something to a buyer. Just the business itself is worth something," Ritt insisted.

"Bob, you don't understand," Carbone continued, a bit perplexed that Ritt would not face up to reality. "They are worth nothing. They have no net worth. They are bankrupt. We lost our money. Don't you understand?"

At one point Ritt gave serious thought to acquiring the thrifts for Hutton and then trying to locate a buyer after straightening out the management. That eventually fell through, too.

Hutton's last hope seemed to be in grabbing the pot of cash Aubin had built up in his accounts through his trading. Aubin, however, seemed to have anticipated that possibility.

In fact, with the cooperation of Hutton's eagle-eyed lawyers and executives, Aubin had crafted the terms of the promissory note so that it forbade Hutton from any other recourse than the proceeds from the sale of the thrifts. Not only did Hutton have no right to touch the cash in Aubin's accounts, but if it went for the cash, Aubin threatened to sue—for triple damages, or three years' worth of profits for Hutton. Hutton's lawyers insisted that the firm had no right to the cash.

Then came the final Poe-like twist. Aubin withdrew all the money and took his business to another brokerage house. That was it; the money was lost.

The next blow came on November 15. The First American Mortgage Company, Famco, the fraudulent operation from which Hutton had bought more than $50 million in high-risk second mortgages, locked its doors at midday. The company's two hundred employees were sent home and told they no longer had jobs.

Now that it was too late, Hutton filed a suit to reclaim its losses. The matter received heavy press coverage. A year later Famco's chairman was convicted of fraud. He had lent money at rates of more than 100 percent and then resold many of the mortgages three and four times. Hutton had been duped by a flimflam man.

For years Hutton had managed to conceal such disasters from the public, but that was no longer possible. The press knew about Famco, and they got just a peek at the Aubin mess when Hutton made some regulatory filings.

To shore up its battered financial foundation, Hutton raised

$125 million in December 1985 by selling 3.8 million new shares at $33.50 each. Because of SEC disclosure laws, Hutton had to reveal the write-offs for Famco and Aubin. It said it would set aside $15 million to cover the Famco situation and $11 million for a "note receivable" from a customer. Aubin's name and the terms of the loan were not disclosed.

In reality, the losses were total. The write-off would grow to $41 million for the two events just a month later, and then more.

As if that were not bad enough, Hutton got creamed in the bond market at the end of the year—in the midst of a powerful bond market rally. The firm lost $30 million from the debacle, while the rest of Wall Street was raking in money that seemed to be falling from the sky.

There was a fitting closing chapter to the Job-like year. Just getting from December 31, 1985, to January 1, 1986, proved an exceptional exercise.

Over the previous several years, Hutton's public finance department had sold hundreds of millions of dollars of tax-exempt bonds to its customers with an implicit guarantee that Hutton would buy them back at a preset price if the investor chose to sell. They were called "lower floaters," to distinguish them from the failed "upper floaters" sold previously.

Many of the investors in the lower floaters discovered a handy tax dodge that included selling the bonds at year end and then repurchasing them in the new year.

The only flaw was that Hutton then had to produce several hundred million dollars of cash temporarily to acquire the bonds for that short period of time. That was no problem for a sound company that had strong relations with its banks. For Hutton it produced yet another secret crisis that forced Ritt and several accountants to spend the New Year's holiday pleading with the banks for the cash to stay alive.

Hutton had sold a product to earn fees and commissions for its coddled brokers, but it had not planned for the future. Peeking behind the curtain for himself, Ritt was discovering just what kind of E. F. Hutton Fomon had designed.

# 14

---

# BUILDING
# THE PARTNERSHIP

On January 14, 1986, Ritt announced "the broadest reorganization in E. F. Hutton's modern history." Despite the constant distractions and the firm's dire needs, Ritt would not permit his moment in the sun to be put off. The organization was his, and this was the day he finally got to boast of it.

Hutton was split into two divisions: retail, called Individual Investment Services, and investment banking, called Institutional and Capital Markets.

Jerry Miller, who had been exiled to the equity division by George Ball and then Fomon, was put on top of the retail machine. On the ailing capital markets side, an unhappy compromise was struck. Dick Locke, who had succeeded Jim Lopp as the head of a broken and diminished investment banking department, was put in charge of the wholesale operations. He was regarded as a stand-in until Ritt recruited his own man.

For all Ritt's talk of introducing a new kind of "teamwork" to the ailing firm, and mending its many rifts, it seemed odd that he would engineer such a sharp split between the areas that had always found it most difficult to work together. Ritt's new organization institutionalized a problem that he claimed he was fighting to overcome.

But that was not the point. From the time he had first realized what a swamp his ambition had drawn him into, Ritt had been trying to assert himself, to conquer his inner doubts and prove himself the helmsman. On this day Ritt was in charge. Six words in the announcement demonstrated his triumph.

"Both men report to Mr. Rittereiser," it said of Miller and Locke.

This was Bob Rittereiser's finest moment at E. F. Hutton. He made a decision and implemented it. He commanded, even if briefly, peoples' respect. At the same time he began to articulate his conception of the reborn Hutton. It was an interesting intellectual construct that was oddly detached from the everyday reality he was battling. But it sounded impressive.

Hutton, Ritt insisted, would narrow its mission. "We are not and do not seek to become a financial services supermarket. We are an investment services company," he blared from the cover of Hutton's 1985 annual report.

The future would reward firms that specialized in a few things and did them well, he said. Ritt made it clear in interviews that he was out to recapture Hutton's core constituency, wealthy individuals. Confidential surveys had increasingly shown how disaffected and untrusting those customers had become.

The flip side to the new strategy was that high-stakes investment banking and securities trading would take a backseat. It was another slap at Fomon, who for so long had tried to model Hutton as an investment bank.

Riding the high of his announcement, Ritt proceeded to the next step in his campaign: concluding the recruitment of his new team. Ed Lill, a big, conservative, sad-eyed man who headed the financial services division of accounting firm Deloitte Haskins & Sells, was named chief financial officer. Lill's credentials were impeccable. He had helped salvage Goodbody & Company with Ritt in 1970, then had helped Hutton acquire more than a dozen branches from du Pont Walston in 1974.

Some worried about his inexperience inside a securities firm. Lill was a planner and adviser, not a man of action. But Ritt was satisfied with Lill's résumé and their long-standing relationship.

Shortly afterward Ritt announced that Stephen Friedman, a

partner at Debevoise & Plimpton and a former SEC commissioner, would become general counsel. Again, his credentials were impressive—on paper. But he had little experience in the minutiae of managing a securities firm's legal operations. In his first interview after being hired, Friedman also made it clear that his ambition was to run the firm, or a substantial part of it, not just operate the legal department. To Ritt that was secondary. He was Ritt's man.

To all appearances Fomon seemed satisfied with the developments and worked at what Ritt liked to call their new partnership. He appeared content working on his beloved new headquarters. Ritt knew better than to meddle. If it kept Fomon happy and out of the way, Ritt decided to let it slide. In fact, Ritt acquiesced on a long list of issues as he sought to keep clear of the cranky chairman. He was trying to buy peace.

On top of the list was the task of rebuilding Hutton's board. The board is, in theory, the real source of power at a publicly held corporation. But Ritt took it as a given that any rational person would accept his blueprints for the future and not take the discredited old CEO seriously. Just as he failed to take charge at the moment when he first found himself squared off against Fomon, Ritt failed to grasp the board's potential.

As Bell had recommended, Hutton restructured its board so that a majority of directors were outsiders. All of the insiders except for Ritt, Fomon, and Scott Pierce were thrown off. Fomon appointed Peter Ueberroth head of a so-called nominating committee to find new outsiders.

Predictably, Ueberroth took little interest and deferred to Fomon in what could well prove to be the most important measures in Hutton's future. Fomon wrote a memo to Ueberroth on January 6 making it clear who was calling the shots. Fomon said that he had approved Ed Cazier's speaking with former Michigan governor William G. Milliken about joining Hutton's board. Milliken would join the board in February.

One interesting candidate Fomon discussed was William P. Clark, the former Reagan administration cabinet member. Clark had agreed in early 1985 to become a director, Fomon said. But when the plea agreement hit the headlines, Fomon added, he had told Clark to wait. Fomon was confident that if he asked now, Clark would accept. He said the time was not right, however. The nomination never took place.

Ueberroth himself made by far the most interesting nomination—Bruce Springsteen, the rock balladeer and blue jeans–clad poet of the working guy. Fomon was polite in handling the zany suggestion.

"I personally think that the name Bruce Springsteen represents a person who is more than a teenage idol," Fomon wrote. "I can see more logic to a Bruce Springsteen than to Shearson's putting Jerry Ford on their Board."

That nomination also died a quiet death, but not before eliciting a few chuckles around the executive suite.

(Ueberroth denied having suggested Springsteen and said he could not remember the Fomon memo. But several others confirmed that they heard Ueberroth propose the rock star for a board seat.)

A pattern was emerging. Fomon was frustrating efforts to develop a tough, smart board of directors who could make informed judgments and think independently. Ueberroth was a happy accomplice.

Ritt was not even in the picture. As an afterthought, Fomon's memo mentioned several nominations put forward by Ritt, including a senior officer at Bell Atlantic, a Baby Bell. Each was noted, without comment, and forgotten.

Ritt acquiesced in another major move initiated by Fomon—the dumping of the old Hutton advertising strategy and the hiring of a new company spokesman—Bill Cosby, the popular comedian and television personality.

The aim was not just to bolster the firm's public image; Fomon agreed with some of his marketing staff that a new campaign might raise the spirits of Hutton's battered and angry brokers. After the rebellion the previous July, an entire branch office in Connecticut had defected. Numerous top producers had jumped to other firms for the first time in Hutton's history. Cosby, Fomon thought, might be able to help revive the troops. His television show was an enormous success, giving him great name recognition. And Cosby's ads for Jell-O appeared to be effective.

The negotiations were, in Fomon's style, swift and incredibly lucrative. Cosby negotiated a four-year contract that would pay him about $12 million. In addition, the contract granted him control over the content of his messages.

It was a gutsy choice. Cosby was extremely wealthy, articulate, funny, and black. The selection of a black man to represent an overwhelmingly white business—the first time that had happened—was bound to fuel some debate at Hutton. (The firm had never brought a black into any position of prominence.) But, Fomon thought, times had changed.

Major corporations often initiate extensive surveys and studies before radically altering their public message to gain some advance feeling for the reaction. Not Fomon. He worked from the seat of his pants. On that basis the firm dropped its famous "When E. F. Hutton talks, people listen" line for Bill Cosby's "Because it's *my* money."

Ritt was not about to stand in Fomon's way for something he considered peripheral to his design for the future. Anyway, he believed the two were enjoying a peaceful coexistence. A trip the executives took to Houston in mid-April seemed to capture the growing amity. The occasion was a four-day bash Hutton threw for its top brokers and their wives, the so-called Directors Advisory Council.

The big theme event in Houston was a rodeo. Fomon relaxed, even if it was the kind of hokey evening he usually detested. Feeling mischievous, he ordered one of his executives, "Go and find Rittereiser."

Fomon then had himself hoisted atop a huge—quieted—bull, with Ritt standing alongside. The amicable scene was preserved in a photo—the chairman, his president, and a mound of explosive force between them.

Weeks later Fomon and Ritt prepared for yet another congressional hearing into the plea agreement, this one before the Senate Judiciary Committee. Fomon chafed at the necessity of politely accepting another public drubbing. He accepted his penance irritably. The fallen but well-trained Catholic had confessed to his abstract sin. That was enough. Ritt had to beg Fomon to hold his tongue and let the scandal blow itself out.

Ritt and Fomon flew to Washington on a New York Air commercial flight at an hour that usually found Bob Fomon barely awake, adding to his foul temper. As they made themselves comfortable in the first-class section, a stewardess passed out a soggy, prepackaged breakfast, consisting of a bagel and some condiments. The famous Fomon tongue was suddenly loosened.

"Don't you have anything other than this Jew food?" a grouchy Fomon barked.

Ritt's face dropped, taking on a deeply pained, sad, puppy-dog look. Ritt's impotant rage drained him of color and seemed to sap his ability to speak. Nearly everyone in the cabin turned to stare at the boor who delivered the incredible line and saw the defiant, gray-haired man in the double-breasted suit scowling back at them.

"Bob, don't you ever again pull that sort of stunt in public," Ritt whined when they landed and could talk privately. "You have got to recognize that you are chairman of a major public company and people could recognize you. It's not you this reflects on, but E. F. Hutton. Christ, you're going down to sit in front of a bunch of senators after our hides, and you pull that kind of shit? What is wrong with you?"

"Don't get so excited," Fomon replied, not displeased at the reaction his remark elicited.


Throughout the first half of 1986 it was increasingly obvious that the unspoken compromise Ritt thought he had struck with Fomon was not holding. But Ritt was not about to say no or challenge Fomon directly. Nor was anyone else.

Ritt was, in fact, becoming an accomplice in Hutton's conspiracy of silence. He hoped. He planned. He cut wider detours around Fomon to avoid problems. And he watched with dismay as Fomon did as he pleased. Fomon had always treated Hutton as a personal domain, whether it was in paying for his shooting trips in Europe, taking the company plane for long weekends, or using the company apartments in Europe for himself and his family. Ritt now watched idly as the practice reached new peaks.

When Fomon's daughter, Anne Q. Fomon, a Hutton broker, married a Shearson stockbroker on May 8, 1986, Fomon threw a lavish wedding and reception. The white-tie ceremony was held at St. Thomas Episcopal Church in Manhattan, and the reception was at the posh Metropolitan Club. Visitors, many of them Hutton officials who flew in for the occasion, were put up at some of New

York's best hotels, including the Carlyle and the Pierre—at company expense.

At the Pierre alone, where only a dozen or so guests stayed, the bill came to $10,861.08. The total bill at the various hotels came to three times that, nearly all of which was footed by Hutton, according to Hutton accountants. Ed Lill decided later that the firm would not pay for guests who were not Hutton officials. But meetings were concocted for the officers so that they could claim their visit was a matter of company business—and expense. Lill did not object.

Ever the opportunist, Fomon also met his newest girlfriend at the celebration. He became acquainted with a young-events coordinator at the Metropolitan Club who soon became his next escort. Not long after the wedding, she was hired by Hutton to book dinners for the firm's corporate finance department. Ritt interviewed her and approved the $50,000-a-year job.

Fomon's son, Robert Q., also enjoyed the largess of Hutton's shareholders, with no resistance from Ritt. He had worked for the firm for several years after receiving an MBA from Harvard. Young Bobby was known as a jet-setting playboy who was bright and very reckless. His aim at Hutton was to move into international money management, an area that would allow him to travel abroad extensively, mix with the wealthy of Europe, and lead the sort of lifestyle his father aspired to.

In 1986 he began a mission to study the possibility of Hutton's forming its own international mutual fund. Hutton's executives were decidedly skeptical and resisted; despite years of wasteful spending, the firm had completely failed to establish any international expertise and so was unfamiliar with the markets in which Bobby Fomon hoped to operate. But no one, especially Ritt, was going to say no to the chairman's son.

It was to be a most interesting year for the young man. According to a summary of his expense account prepared by Lill's staff, Bobby Fomon spent $102,400 of Hutton's money during 1986 in his quixotic adventure. That was, of course, over and above his six-figure salary.

Airfare, $24,100; hotels, $20,500; meals, $24,800; entertainment, $7,400; local transportation, $12,900; other, $12,700.

The year included fifty-five days in Europe and twenty-four days in Hong Kong and Tokyo.

At the end, Bobby presented to Hutton's equity department officials his proposal for running a fund. It was politely rejected. The spending had been for nothing.

Loud, anti-Semitic remarks and nepotism were the least of Ritt's problems, however. In May came the next disaster: the bond department lost $55 million from trading in a turbulent market.

In the preceding months Ritt had delayed Standard & Poor's, the credit rating agency, from downgrading Hutton by promising that the firm had put in place systematic controls. Even the usually sympathetic rating experts could not ignore the bond trading losses, though. In late July Standard & Poor's reduced Hutton's rating for the second time in a year. It was a signal to the financial community that Hutton was deteriorating.

The huge bond trading losses had brought Ritt back to the here and now. The head of the department was dismissed, and Ritt began to search for a replacement. His eventual choice bore an unsettling resemblance to his other recruits—a man at the top of his field, but with experience that was largely irrelevant to Hutton's specific needs.

The newcomer was Mark F. Kessenich, Jr. Kessenich, a hard-nosed bond trader, had been head of Citibank's North American investment banking operations. One of its principal businesses was dealing in bonds, handling billions of dollars of transactions a day.

Kessenich, known for his brusque manner, was of the old school. He was used to making snap judgments and committing huge sums when he had a hunch on which way the markets were heading. He rode herd over a group of highly trained, risk-taking professionals.

His prickly personality had turned into a problem at Citibank. Thomas Theobald had been put in charge of all Citibank's investment banking activities. The personal chemistry between the two executives was poor. Kessenich chafed under Theobald, thinking he should have been considered for the job. The conflicts worsened when Kessenich's department took on large trading losses in the spring of 1986.

Ritt heard that Kessenich might be available. He consulted no one at Hutton before making an offer. Kessenich was given an extraordinarily rich, multiyear contract, and he brought with him a small group of senior traders dealing in the most complex areas of the bond business. Hutton had a ready-made bond department.

There was only one problem: Hutton did not have, nor did it intend to build, the kind of bond trading capability the high-powered group was used to. Ritt had said earlier that the firm would focus on the individual investor. Now he was placing Formula One race car drivers into the retail business Chevy of E. F. Hutton.

By chance, a reporter was scheduled to have lunch with Ritt and a small group of his senior executives on July 17, 1986, the day news of Kessenich's hiring began to circulate on Wall Street.

The purpose was to discuss an article the reporter had proposed on Ritt's efforts to rebuild Hutton from the ashes of the plea. He wanted to sit in on some of Ritt's management committee meetings to see firsthand how the new partnership Ritt spoke of was working. Ritt had agreed initially. A few weeks later, however, he reversed himself. Ritt had brought up the subject at a management committee meeting and had been voted down.

"Are you kidding?" Ed Lill had said when Ritt described the proposed article. "This will look like *Ted Mack's Amateur Hour.* There's no way we can let an outsider sit in on this."

That Thursday the reporter had been invited to lunch to make one last pitch for his idea. Lill, Steve Friedman, and Jay Moorhead joined Ritt in the private dining room, which commanded a sweeping view of New York harbor. It was pro forma. They listened politely and spoke about how Hutton was developing, but they did not budge on the article.

As the meal ended Ritt walked the reporter down the long hall, lined with antiques and equestrian prints, toward the elevator. That was the moment the reporter had waited for.

"I didn't want to mention this before, but I just happened to hear this morning that you guys are going to hire Mark Kessenich and some of his people from Citibank," the reporter said. "It didn't sound right, given his reputation, but I wanted to ask you what the story was."

"No," Ritt said. "That's pretty much what's going on. But look, this thing isn't all completed. It's more complicated than it looks, and you shouldn't jump off too fast here."

"I can't ignore it," the reporter said.

"Well, the truth of the matter is that it is not certain yet," Ritt replied. "We may make an announcement later today. We heard the rumors, too."

"The rumors are that this is a pretty unusual choice," the reporter added. "I'm not sure I completely understand. By reputation, this guy has never had any involvement with a retail brokerage. How's he going to fit in with what you're trying to do? You've said repeatedly that you want your capital markets businesses to serve the retail side of the firm."

"Don't jump to conclusions," Ritt commented. "This is already a different firm than it used to be. I've talked to you a lot about this. We have put in place a whole range of controls that never existed. There is no such thing as someone who can go and take big risks in the market without my knowing about it, I can tell you that. It does not affect the retail focus to have a strong institutional group. You can't not be in that business."

By this time the two were near the lobby and had stopped at the end of the long hall. Suddenly they were interrupted by a rustling noise. Fomon, who had not been invited to the lunch, was limping toward them.

Fomon knew the reporter well after a long series of interviews just before and after the Bell report. He had fumed over the resulting article in *The New York Times*, THE UNDOING OF ROBERT FOMON, and had not spoken to the reporter since. He did not speak to him that July afternoon, either. Fomon spun Rittereiser around by his arm.

"Rittereiser, don't you have better things to do than stand around the hall talking to fucking reporters?" he growled. "Let's get to it. Get back to your office."

The smile the reporter had put on to greet the approaching chairman dropped. At first he thought the remark was certainly a sort of gag. But he waited in vain for Fomon to crack a smile. This was no joke.

Rittereiser's face turned ashen and sank as impotent rage filled his moistening eyes. He looked at the reporter with a pathetic expression that was difficult to witness. It was an expression of helplessness.

Fomon turned and limped away. Rittereiser let go in silence what he could not say and, utterly humiliated, dragged himself back to his office.

# OPERATION
# FRUITBASKET

September 7, 1986, a sunny, mild Sunday, was a big day for Bob Rittereiser. He was thrilled to be heading to the finals of the United States Open. Ritt is a good athlete who moves well on a tennis court, particularly for a person with his beefy physique. He attempts to master his opponents through consistency rather than power or stealth. Methodically, with long-winded analyses of strategies and talent—that was how he approached both tennis and the brokerage industry.

That Sunday afternoon Ivan Lendl blew away another Czech contender, Miloslav Mecir, in three straight sets. It was a bracing display of competence, strength, and consistency—a reassuring demonstration for the Hutton president.

Just hours later Ritt found himself a participant rather than a spectator. This time he was on the briskly competitive, unforgiving playing field of the corporate elite—an elegantly appointed Manhattan dining room lorded over by an influential Wall Street deal maker. It was the night that yet another part of Hutton slipped away from him.

Ritt had agreed with Bob Fomon to have dinner in a private room at the posh Carlyle Hotel with Fred Whittemore, an old friend of Fomon's and a senior investment banker at Morgan Stanley & Company. A top executive of the Transamerica Corporation would be joining them. Ritt had not figured it out, but this was a setup.

Increasingly distrustful of Rittereiser and anxious about his legacy, Bob Fomon was determined that he would be the last on the throne of an independent E. F. Hutton. It was more a compulsion than a strategy, but then Fomon was an executive who had always trusted his impulses.

The underlying truth was that the king would become exceedingly rich from a sale. Not least, he would not suffer the ignominy of being tossed from his own firm; he had learned that lesson from Sylvan Coleman. It was the most graceful exit he could make. It would also help conceal all the skeletons hidden in Hutton's closets.

Fomon did nothing to squelch the periodic rumors that Hutton was for sale. Fred Whittemore was trained at picking up the kinds of signals Fomon was sending out. Whittemore, in fact, had already had lunch with Fomon to discuss the idea of a sale. Hutton's chairman had been tactful. He'd said Whittemore could continue the overtures and could tell his client, Transamerica, a big insurance and financial concern based in a pyramid-shaped tower in San Francisco, that Fomon was aware of them. He'd insisted that Whittemore not say the contacts had been approved. But Bob Fomon did not wear coyness well; a big For Sale sign had been hoisted.

The only potential hurdle was Hutton's president. If a friendly deal was to be arranged, Ritt had to be on board. In Wall Street's Darwinistic order, that was the meaning of the dinner at the Carlyle. Anything but a sharp "no" meant "yes."

Adding to the momentum for a deal was the fact that this would be the second flirtation between Hutton and a suitor in two months. The Chrysler Corporation had wooed Hutton over the summer, with Ritt's approval. Chrysler had decided to diversify into financial services and had already acquired Hutton's commercial finance operation. In the summer of 1986 Chrysler's investment bank, Shearson, tried to encourage the automaker to buy all of Hutton.

In early summer Fomon and Ritt met with Lee Iacocca,

Chrysler's high-profile chairman; Steve Miller, the CFO; and the advisers from Shearson. Not aware of the impetus the process would develop, Ritt permitted the talks with Chrysler to start in the naïve hope that he could switch them off at will. Both Shearson and Chrysler signed confidentiality statements in return for Hutton's inside financial statements and projections.

The climactic moment came in late July at a suburban Detroit country club, at a meeting of the finance committee of Chrysler's board. Miller, prodded on by Shearson, was ready to consider a bid and had Peter Cohen, Shearson's chairman, make a presentation.

Felix Rohatyn, the influential senior partner at Lazard Frères & Company, was asked by Lee Iacocca to speak at the meeting, too. Investment bankers have, if nothing else, an uncanny ability to say what their clients want to hear. In this case, Iacocca was not thrilled about the prospect of a Hutton purchase. Rohatyn would play his part.

Cohen began by arguing that the financial services industry was booming and that, with Chrysler's capital and reputation, Hutton could be stabilized and would prosper. Rohatyn, on the other hand, emphasized that Chrysler would be paying a turnaround price, when Hutton still had a long way to go before regaining its health. He asked whether Chrysler's management really knew how to rebuild a business as different from auto manufacturing as securities. In addition, he pointed out how risky the business was. You could get a call from a trading desk one day and be told that the firm had just lost $50 million—something Hutton's executives knew all too well.

"You have to think carefully about that sort of earnings volatility," Rohatyn said. "And you have to think about your management resources, and if that's what you want them focused on."

Without a formal vote the finance committee members quickly came to a consensus. With Iacocca lukewarm on the idea, the deal was dead.

Before he left the meeting, Cohen spoke up again. He told the committee that, if Chrysler passed up Hutton, he just might buy it for Shearson.


It was not long before the gossip network crackled with news of Hutton's failed talks with Chrysler. The stock was starting to jump again, like a barometer reacting to the influence of an approaching storm.

Fred Whittemore picked up the signals and sought a way to get in on the action. He had quickly settled on Transamerica as a good candidate to buy Hutton and win a multimillion-dollar fee. Transamerica, Whittemore knew, had long been close to Hutton, buying and selling large blocks of its stock for a decade.

This time Fomon faced a tougher job in getting Ritt interested. For starters Ritt had grown uncomfortable during Chrysler's perusal of the brokerage house's books, knowing how shabby the figures were. Among other things Hutton had reported a miserable $5 million loss for the second quarter of 1986 because of the bond losses.

"Maybe this is time that should be spent doing our homework here," Ritt told Fomon, trying to get the chairman to stop shopping Hutton. "Maybe we should not be spending any more time entertaining these kinds of things because they really take us away from what we need to be doing."

Ritt was also concerned about the increasing number of Fomon's public outrages. Ritt and the other senior executives even began to wrestle with such mundane matters as whether or not to invite Fomon to dinners because of his drunken scenes. It was not, Ritt felt, the way to impress a potential buyer.

One evening in particular fed these worries. Around this time Rittereiser hired a British securities executive, Perry Moncrief, to head up Hutton's dwarflike European operations. He threw a dinner in New York to introduce Moncrief to the rest of the management team. Ritt had sought a private room so that the executives could speak openly. But they ended up in a screened-off area at Le Perigord, a midtown Manhattan corporate haunt. Fomon, as usual, grew louder and more abusive as he polished off drink after drink, then capped the performance by exchanging several anti-Semitic gibes, loud enough that others in the restaurant could hear, embarrassing everyone.

Around the same time Fomon gave an interview to *M*, a fashion magazine, in which he spoke with his trademark tartness, taking shots at the congressman who had been questioning Hutton and candidly offering his unflattering views of women.

"Most women of any maturity have been married, and most have emotional problems," he said.

He confessed to preferring the company of younger, more attractive women who were "decorative, nice to look at." To make the point, the article included a photo of Fomon at a party in black tie, being hugged and kissed by two fetchingly clad, vixenish young women. Hutton's executives, long used to Fomon's antics, were shocked. Fomon shrugged off the criticisms as prudish.

Weeks later, after Ritt thought he had put the merger genie back in the bottle, Fred Whittemore called with an invitation to dinner at the Carlyle Hotel. Not quite knowing what was coming, Ritt accepted. Ritt had insisted that he not miss the tennis finals and that he be able to bring his wife along; he did not want to pack her up in a limousine after the match and then ship her back along to their home in New Jersey. Obligingly, Lendl made short work of Mecir, so Ritt and his wife, Pat, arrived shortly after seven P.M. at the hotel on Madison Avenue, the neutral site chosen with great care by Whittemore.

It was an evening that Whittemore had choreographed with enormous precision. He had reserved a private room, ordered a dinner of veal that he thought all would find agreeable, and prepped his client on what to say and what to avoid.

Ritt's misapprehension of what this was all about did not last long. As the group settled at the elegant dining table, Whittemore said in his bass voice, "We aren't here just to socialize. The question is, Does this discussion have some validity? I'll be very open. We're trying to see if a deal can be forged. These are two great companies, and it might make a lot of sense to get them together."

Whittemore asked the Transamerica official to explain why he thought a merger made sense. He spoke of Transamerica's desire to diversify and of ventures the two could pursue together.

Whittemore then turned to the Hutton executives, asking them to talk about their future needs and hopes. Ritt, barely over his surprise at what was happening, made clear that he believed Hutton needed time to be turned around.

On these sorts of blind dates, Whittemore knew, the participants had to have reasonable expectations. Here the aim was simply to get to the next step.

The two sides agreed to schedule a second meeting—more confirmation that the firm was on the block. By the end of September Transamerica and Morgan Stanley had sent several teams to meet with Hutton's top executives and review the firm's internal financial records. If Ritt thought he was saying no, he was doing it with imperceptible subtlety.

True to his word, Peter Cohen went on the prowl for a major acquisition shortly after the Chrysler-Hutton talks fizzled. Shearson had grown explosively in the late 1970s by gobbling up competitors and laying off hundreds of employees to reduce expenses. Then, in 1981, Shearson's executives sold the firm to American Express, a savvy move that gave it the financial heft to pull out of the pack—leaving competitors like Hutton far behind.

In 1984 Shearson acquired Lehman Brothers Kuhn Loeb, the venerable, once prestigious investment banking firm. Although many of Lehman's disaffected deal makers left, Shearson kept enough of them to do what Hutton had failed to achieve over the past decade—develop a powerful investment banking operation.

Now it was time to make another quantum leap. Shearson began Operation Fruitbasket in the summer of 1986 to achieve Peter Cohen's goal. A small group of investment bankers secretly compiled data on the remaining independent retail brokerage firms. Two leading candidates emerged: Paine Webber and Hutton. Paine Webber was Peach. But Hutton was the Plum.

Ritt was stumbling along naïvely. Belatedly he telephoned Hutton's financial advisers at Salomon Brothers to tell them about the overture from Transamerica. Ritt spoke with John Gutfreund, Salomon's chairman, and Gutfreund called in Ken Wilson, a senior official in the firm's financial institutions group. Wilson was already deeply involved in helping the Bank of America out of a financial crisis. Now he took a leading role in trying to help Hutton choose from its array of options.

Wilson was stunned to learn that Ritt had permitted the talks to get so far without having come to the basic decision of whether he wanted to sell and without having sought expert advice on how to proceed.

"Bob," Wilson told him, using a standard Wall Street metaphor, "you rolled over and spread your legs for these guys. It's a little late to be saying you're not sure you want to do it, for chris-sakes."

Wilson called Transamerica and said that they had to move soon if they were serious. People at Hutton were seeing teams of Morgan Stanley and Transamerica officials troop around Hutton's headquarters. The chances for a leak were growing, and that could kill a deal. To advance the process, Wilson and a team of Salomon professionals met with Whittemore and Transamerica officials at Morgan Stanley's offices.

They wasted little time. In the verbal tango that deal makers have to dance to get around requirements that serious takeover discussions between publicly owned companies be disclosed, explicit discussions of prices are generally avoided. The investment bankers provide, instead, what are euphemistically known as "indications."

In other words, they make offers that, for the purposes of a legal fiction, are not offers. It is not unlike the way a young man asks a girl for a date when he is afraid of an outright rejection; he frames the question in such a way that, if the answer is no, he can pretend it was never posed.

Within the rules of this game, Whittemore set out Transamerica's terms. It would offer both cash and Transamerica stock. Whittemore said the offer was worth nearly $50 a share to Hutton. Salomon's investment bankers, looking more critically at Transamerica's stock, determined that the offer was worth in the low forties.

Wilson promised that Hutton would get back to him but told his colleagues that Transamerica was trying to steal the company.

Wilson thought that was the end of that, but he soon learned otherwise. Ritt had not even told him of yet another overture. By this time Peter Cohen had begun his courtship of the Plum.

"Bob, I think it would make a lot of sense to put our two organizations together," Cohen explained in his no-nonsense fashion. "We could produce a powerful distribution system that neither of us could build by ourselves. This would give you a chance to be with a real winner here." Ritt was not enthusiastic, but, once again, he did not dissuade Cohen from proceeding.

"That's a big idea," Ritt replied. "A very big idea." He added that he would think about it and that they would talk again soon.

Cohen, a short, tightly wound Napoleon of a man, quickly consulted his second-in-command, Jeff Lane, Shearson's president, and they plotted their next steps. Unbeknown to Ritt, this marked just another stage in Shearson's attack, which was already well advanced. Under Cohen's direction, his firm had acquired 1.5 million Hutton shares in secret, starting in mid-August. To further conceal the purchases, Shearson's traders had not denoted that some of the trades were for the firm, as regulations required, leaving the impression that they were for customers. By the time Cohen spoke with Ritt, Shearson held just under the 5 percent level that would require a public filing of the holding. It was an aggressive move that helped boost Hutton's stock and encouraged rumors that the sharks were circling. It would also win big profits for Shearson if, for some reason, another bidder stepped in and outbid it, or if the talks fell apart.

In late September Cohen called Ritt to set up a meeting. That proved difficult. The first week of October Ritt would be on vacation. Every year he took two vacations, one with his kids and one just with his wife. The first week in October was generally reserved for him and his wife to go to Bermuda.

Cohen, meanwhile, had plans to be away the following week on business. He did not want the subject to slide, so he offered to fly to Bermuda. He took Shearson's corporate jet, departing in the morning and returning that afternoon. The rendezvous was held in strict secrecy.

Cohen set the agenda. He indicated that several top executives—in particular Tom Stiles, head of stock trading and research; Jerry Miller, head of Hutton's retail division; and Norm Epstein, head of operations—would have jobs in a combined firm. On Ritt Cohen was vaguer. He indicated that Ritt would become a vice-chairman, part of a triumvirate running the combined firm with himself and Jeff Lane. But he left unclear just how much responsibility Ritt would have.

In truth Cohen did not plan much of a role for Rittereiser. He formed opinions quickly, and his opinion of Ritt was less than flattering. Ritt did nothing to improve the perception in Bermuda. Ritt liked to ramble, while Cohen was spare with words. And in Bermuda Ritt did ramble.

Nonetheless Cohen gave Ritt an "indication" of what Shearson and American Express would pay, about $50 a share, or slightly more than $1.5 billion in total. However, he insisted, the price would only stand a short while. For tax reasons the deal would have to be consummated by year end.

The conversation ended with Ritt telling Cohen he ought to speak with Bob Fomon. Cohen flew back the same day, still slightly confused by Ritt's meandering comments.

"What did he say?" Lane implored.

"I'm not sure," Cohen said.

He then telephoned Jim Robinson, American Express's chairman, who was in Japan at the time. Cohen said he was almost embarrassed at having to explain the brokerage business to Ritt, but that that should not stand in the way of a takeover.

Rumors swirled through the stock market the next day that some buyer—and the list included Shearson—was stalking Hutton. Hutton's stock jumped $1.75 to $47. As usual the grapevine was on the mark, clearly a sign that it was being fed by someone with knowledge of the Bermuda tryst.

Ritt returned from Bermuda on Monday, October 13, with the discussions gaining momentum. He spoke to a few of his executives and found them just as unenthusiastic about being swallowed by Cohen's crew. On Wednesday, he told Fomon to end the talks, and Fomon relayed the message to Cohen. It proved a useful piece of information, even if temporarily disappointing. The market had been fed stories of Shearson's interest, but not of its being spurned. As Hutton's stock shot up nearly $2 to $48.75 Shearson unloaded about 800,000 shares for a multimillion-dollar profit—taking unfair advantage of its undisclosed information.

The next day *The New York Times* reported Shearson had offered at least $50 a share for Hutton, but had been turned down. Hutton's stock plummeted. Hutton lied by simply denying it had received or rejected any offers. Cohen was still determined to push ahead, but the rumors gave him pause.

The market's reaction made Shearson nervous enough that Cohen decided to approach his second choice, Paine Webber, the Peach. He contacted Donald Marron, the chairman of Paine Webber, to feel him out. The door was closed almost as soon as it was opened. It was Plum or nothing.

On Thursday, October 16, 1986, the executive committee of

American Express's board held a conference by telephone. Cohen had been in constant contact with Jim Robinson, American Express's chairman, about the progress of Operation Fruitbasket, and Robinson felt it was time to inform the board.

Once the electronic hook-up was completed, Cohen explained that he had held preliminary discussions with both Peach and Plum. He briefly discussed his strategy, which was to strip out the best branch offices and brokers and combine them with Shearson's, while laying off much of the remaining staff.

Cohen and Robinson added that, although it would take a big investment, the combination could help elevate Shearson into the number-one or number-two firm on Wall Street. Robinson raised the issue of earnings volatility but said that he believed the risk was worth taking.

The executive committee authorized Cohen to explore an acquisition. On October 17 Cohen spoke with Fomon. Fomon needed no convincing. He passed the ball back to his president, telling Cohen that it would be Ritt's call. The chairman was on board. It was up to Ritt and the rest of Hutton's senior management.

"What the fuck is going on?" Fomon asked of no one in particular as he entered the apartment, his voice hard with the edge it took on when he had been drinking.

Not waiting for an answer, Fomon walked into the kitchen. Around the long oval conference table, Hutton's management committee tensed instinctively as it heard the bell-like ring of ice cubes bouncing off the bottom of a crystal tumbler, followed by a lively liquid tinkle.

Two investment bankers from Salomon Brothers, seated on a couch, saw what Hutton's top executives already knew from experience to be the case—Fomon was pouring himself a nice tall Scotch.

"The issue here, Bob, is Transamerica and whether it makes sense to do anything with them," Rittereiser said.

It was October 23, a Thursday. Hutton's management committee, which comprised the heads of each of its operating divisions, had been summoned to meet at 4:30 P.M. in one of the apartments

Hutton leased at 800 Fifth Avenue, the "bordello." The company apartment had been chosen because, in addition to being a good place to carry on affairs, it was also a place where sensitive meetings could be held. At times it made sense to get people together away from prying eyes.

Ritt felt obliged to let his executive team know more about the merger discussions. He had invited Ken Wilson and two of Wilson's colleagues to advise the group. They were in a difficult position, since Ritt had only mentioned Shearson's approach to Wilson the day before. Ritt had let things get terribly far, with not one, but two suitors, to be having second thoughts.

"It's a pretty good bid," Fomon said of the Transamerica offer as he pulled on his drink, lit a Winston, and paced around the table. "We ought to go ahead and sell the company. It's goddamn good money."

The other executives made it clear that they felt the Transamerica bid was much too low. They also felt that Transamerica was simply not strong enough to take Hutton on.

"That's not even the real issue here anymore," Wilson pointed out. "You have to decide what your future is. It's a basic decision."

After another thirty minutes of discussion, with Fomon making repeated sallies to the kitchen for refills, Ritt turned to Wilson and asked, "What are the firm's chances of Hutton's staying independent?"

"Bob, I have to tell you that there's about a 20 percent chance you'll remain independent at this point," Wilson replied. "There are just too many things that you have to do, and you can't do them alone. This place is a mess."

The room became silent as the executives absorbed that sobering thought. Fomon paced and jiggled the ice cubes in his glass.

Norm Epstein, the hulking head of operations, repeated what he'd said from the start, that he did not think Hutton should be sold. Epstein had a strong emotional bond to the firm and had a powerful grip over his fiefdom. He resisted letting that go.

Fomon, who had consumed nearly half the bottle of Scotch by this time, fumed at the effort to block the sale he wanted so badly. He blurted out, "You asshole, you're only interested in your job. That's good money. The firm ought to be sold. What you're doing is just greenmail. You're just trying to hold out for more money."

"You've always waited for a chance to sell the firm," Epstein retorted defiantly. "What do you have at stake? Nothing."

"I wouldn't be the chief honcho anymore."

"You're gutless," Epstein replied.

"You bastard," Fomon snapped, and then did something that nobody in the room could believe. He lunged forward at the seated Epstein, grabbing at a brass floor lamp next to the table. Everyone expected Fomon to swing the fixture at the heavily built, six-foot-tall executive.

Fomon stumbled just short of his target and glowered at Epstein, who looked up at Fomon with an expression that said, "Go ahead and try something."

Ken Wilson may have saved Fomon's life at that instant, or at least spared him yet another long stay in the hospital. He restrained Fomon, who was swaying from the effects of the tumblers of alcohol he'd been quaffing.

"You're gutless," Epstein repeated.

Though no violence had been done, Fomon's startling action seemed to break the dam. The discussion grew more agitated. Shouting broke out.

Wilson decided to go to an adjoining room, the bedroom, and make some telephone calls just to get away. His two colleagues from Salomon Brothers, flushed with embarrassment, slipped out of the apartment altogether and milled in the hall. Even from that distance the verbal fisticuffs ricocheted through the building. The Salomon officials paced awkwardly, feeling humiliated.

Ritt took on that same hurt puppy-dog look as his broad black eyebrows bent under the weight of his own humiliation. He tried several times to restore his dignity. But it was too late. The Hutton tragedy was turning into a farce.

"Let's calm down here," he implored. "Let's not get too excited and just discuss this.

"Please, guys," he repeated. "Let's discuss this."

# WHAT'S AN ARB?

$W$hile E. F. Hutton's managers jockeyed for position and debated whether the firm was worth $45 or $50 or $55 a share, the brokerage house was balanced on a financial knife's edge. Hutton's business was declining further. The board, in theory all that stood between Hutton's shareholders and a financial abyss, drifted through the crisis without doing a thing. After all, that was how Bob Fomon had designed it.

Just a couple of dismal facts were controlling Hutton's destiny.

First, Hutton had become a break-even company. It was saddled with the additional $50 million a year in costs for the new building, tens of millions of dollars more for a fancy new computer system that Fomon had approved, and scores of millions of dollars of reserves to cover the management fiascoes. In addition, it was top-heavy with layers of superfluous staff and paid its brokers about the highest commissions on Wall Street.

The expenses had become so overwhelming that, in good times, Hutton's basic businesses simply broke even. If anything went wrong, the firm's already depleted capital would be reduced even further. Ritt organized and reorganized Hutton, but he refused to make any serious efforts to reduce the firm's expense burden. He did not have the stomach for challenging the ruling barons.

Second, there was by now a matter that could sink Hutton far more swiftly—the deferred compensation time bomb. For several years Hutton had offered its better-paid brokers and executives an opportunity to reduce their tax bills by deferring some of their annual pay. The deferred funds, which added up to tens of millions of dollars a year, were lent back to Hutton as what is called a subordinated loan and were counted as part of the firm's capital.

The Hutton officials did not have to book the money as income until tax rates declined and they withdrew it. Hutton, meanwhile, had use of the capital, which was growing sharply. From $129 million at the end of 1985, the total exploded to $200 million at the end of 1986 and to $280 million a year later—roughly a fourth of Hutton's total capital base.

The money, however, was a short-term loan. It would have to be repaid soon. When it was, Hutton would have to replace it or shrink. But what outsider would put up several hundred million dollars as a subordinated loan to a break-even company? Hutton's executives were lending the firm capital when few if any others would have.

The firm was also about to report a huge write-off to cover the long hidden upper floater and tax shelter losses, as Lill had told Hutton's management committee and board. The brokerage house was like a spiffy race car, all chrome and polish on the outside, but running on just four of six cylinders and facing the prospect of having to return a borrowed wheel midrace. Meanwhile its drivers were arguing about which direction to head.

As if that were not enough, by late 1986 the New York Stock Exchange had started warning Hutton's executives quietly that it would not permit the firm to pay out the deferred compensation if doing so would cause financial stress. But telling Hutton's employees they could not have access to their accumulated wealth would have been like the Chase Manhattan Bank suddenly telling its depositors they could not withdraw their money. Whatever confidence remained in Hutton would have evaporated.

In the second half of 1986 Hutton worked out two five-year

loans from municipalities, in the form of what were known as guaranteed investment contracts, of GICs, to try to plug the deferred compensation hole. But those were also temporary Band-Aids.

The next step was asset sales to raise cash. Hutton had sold its commercial credit company the year before. By late 1986 it was planning to sell its life insurance operation, a business that had shown promise of becoming more profitable than Hutton's brokerage subsidiary. Hutton was selling off the profitable pieces of its business to support the dead weight of its retail system.

Still, takeover maneuverings occupied Hutton's senior executives. On October 29, 1986, Hutton's stock price soared by nearly $5 a share as the whispers about a pending merger spread. Hutton's stock hit a record high of $54.50.

Behind the scenes, Peter Cohen waited in vain for someone to take charge and conclude the deal. Ritt equivocated. Fomon withdrew slightly, to avoid appearing too eager.

Jim Robinson, Cohen's boss, thus went to a backdoor source to add some impetus to the discussions. He called Peter Ueberroth, a good friend. The two served together on the board of Coca-Cola and so spoke regularly. Robinson used him to convey the seriousness of American Express's approach and to elicit some information. Robinson's message was of critical importance, because it insured that the proposal would be high on the board's agenda, that Ritt would not be able to sweep it aside.

Robinson then telephoned Ritt himself to discuss the merger. He came away disappointed, as Cohen had been, with how long-winded and vague Ritt could be when discussing the brokerage business. But there was no intention of leaving Ritt in charge of the firm. The aim was to get the deal done.

The suitors persuaded Fomon and Ritt to meet with them again. On Sunday afternoon, November 2, Robinson and Cohen showed up at Fomon's Fifth Avenue apartment and settled onto the rosy, chintz-covered couch and burnished antique chairs in the living room, with its cozy view of Central Park. Cohen had drawn up a series of papers to show how Hutton and a handful of its senior executives would fit into the combined organization. He wanted to scream at Ritt to get his act together and make up his mind.

The documents brought a revelation to Ritt—he would not be

an equal member of a management triumvirate after all, but one of many divisional heads. Despite the high-sounding title promised him, vice-chairman, he would be an overseer of parts of the retail business alone. He was stunned.

Fomon was not surprised to learn that there was no specific role for himself. But that did not bother him. He would be getting rid of Ritt, earning a fortune, and removing the Hutton throne for good.

Next, Cohen and Robinson again tossed out the $50 a share offer, a total of $1.6 billion. Cohen knew that once his sharp financial team scoured Hutton's records, it would find ample reason for lowering the bid. But the point was to get Fomon and Ritt to take the bait. That suited Fomon. He tried to accentuate the positive to influence his wavering president. The discussions even covered what the new firm would be called. Cohen mentioned the idea of just calling it Lehman Brothers, a name that still carried cachet from its former days of glory.

"That's probably the one name that would really scare the rest of the street," Fomon said approvingly.

After nearly two hours Robinson and Cohen tried to corner Ritt, suggesting that the two sides retain lawyers to hammer out a contract. To their dismay Ritt said that, before he went any farther, he wanted to consult with Hutton's board. A meeting was already scheduled for Friday, November 7.

"If you really have an interest in doing something, you should come to some terms before going to the board so you have something real to present them with; right now you're operating in a vacuum," Cohen countered. But Ritt held firm.

Cohen and Robinson left in the separate chauffeur-driven cars in which they had arrived. "Talking to these guys is like putting your hands in a bucket of eels," Robinson complained to Cohen. "I cannot understand how they run that place."

This was where Robinson's secret contacts with Peter Ueberroth began to pay off. The back door insured that Ritt would not control the agenda.

Hutton's management committee met on Monday, far less tempestuously this time because Fomon was absent. Assurances aside, the Hutton executives knew they would take on secondary jobs, or lose their jobs entirely, if Shearson absorbed Hutton. The discussion no longer focused on whether a sale was desirable. The subject was how to derail it. The answer: promises. Hastily the executives prepared profit projections for 1987. The aim was to convince the board that they would be selling too cheaply at $50 a share.

After a frantic week of back-of-the-envelope estimating, the management team decided to tell the board that the firm could earn more than $120 million. (That did not include an additional $50–$60 million after-tax profit from the expected sale of Hutton's insurance company or an $80 million tax benefit the firm planned to book in 1987.)

It was a ridiculous number. Were 1987 to prove the best year in Wall Street history, the goals were barely within reach. Absolutely everything would have to go just right. If it were merely a good year, Hutton would come up short by more than half. If conditions were mediocre or difficult, Hutton would be teetering.

Hutton's confidential records for 1986 made clear how fanciful the new projections were. After being hit with the huge trading losses in May, the brokerage unit had posted operating losses, before taxes, of $7 million in June, $581,000 in July, $8 million in August, and $2.5 million in September. After eking out a $2.6 million operating profit in October, Hutton would lose $4 million in November and $34 million in December.

Such inconvenient facts were peripheral to the main issue, which was to put the firm in the best-possible light. That was the fiction with which Ritt and his team hoped to save their hides at the Friday board meeting.


Ritt convened the board at 10:00 A.M. by handing out his proposed agenda. At the top was a discussion of the sale of the insurance company and then a discussion of Hutton's 1987 prospects, division by division. He barely got out a few sentences when he was interrupted by Peter Ueberroth.

"Bob, there's only one subject on the agenda today, which is how we're going to respond to the American Express proposal," he said, showing no emotion, as usual, behind his well-tanned poker face. "I think we need to hear more about what has happened and where things stand."

"There's no question that if you begin with the insurance company, you get to a broader discussion of where this firm is going," Ritt began. "We think that you should understand the process here before we take the next step.

"The management has really decided that we are not in a good position to negotiate a merger. We are still trying to understand the financial underpinnings of this firm. I think there's a risk here that we start something and then Shearson comes in and says we've found some things and we're going to have to adjust our price. If that gets out, you could have real problems, and then you have nothing left to sell. We believe there is potential for Hutton to perform much better than it has."

"We'll listen to your views, but I want to make clear that you brought this process a long way, and you've forced us to come to some kind of decision," Ueberroth said.

The members of the management committee had spent the morning waiting nervously for a sign of how the deliberations were progressing. The board now called them in, one by one, to discuss the profit projections and to hear their views on a sale.

Jerry Miller, rarely neutral on any issue, spoke out strongly against a deal. As was often the case, he backed his argument with dire warnings about mayhem in the ranks of brokers if the status quo were altered. Scores of Hutton brokers would simply leave, he predicted.

Scott Pierce also opposed the deal, but in large part out of anger at the way Shearson was handling the matter. He described the leaks to the market and the run-up in Hutton's share price as a deliberate form of "bear hug" by Shearson and American Express, a takeover tactic designed to force a company into agreeing to a sale.

Nonetheless Pierce said that the profit projections were, as he put it, "aggressive."

Ueberroth argued that the directors still had to try to get the best price for shareholders.

"Look, if you're worried about the shareholders, consider who they are," Dick Locke said. "With all the rumors in the past few weeks, all the shareholders are arbs by now."

Suddenly a female voice chirped up. "What's an arb?" Dina Merrill asked.

There was a long pause. Several board members exchanged embarrassed glances.

Locke, suppressing a chuckle, explained what an arbitrageur was. He thought with some concern that E. F. Hutton's future rested partly in the hands of someone with so little basic knowledge of Wall Street. (Merrill did not answer several interview requests.)

Ken Wilson of Salomon Brothers arrived at Hutton's lower Manhattan headquarters at about 1:30 P.M. He had spoken to Ritt that morning and found him anxious.

The prospect of the sale of a major corporation is, even for seasoned professionals, an unnerving experience. Thousands of jobs, and huge sums, are usually at stake. The market, the press, and the courts stand by to render judgment. Wilson was told that the board wanted to talk with John Gutfreund, Salomon's chairman. Wilson called his boss and asked that he come over right away.

Gutfreund was delighted by the summons. As luck would have it, he was in the middle of a lengthy interview with a *New York Times* reporter. An article was being prepared on Salomon Brothers' internally divisive attempts to enter the riskiest and most lucrative new realm on Wall Street, merchant banking, where securities firms both arrange and help finance takeovers. Gutfreund was not thrilled to be discussing the matter. When a secretary told him of Ken Wilson's call, he snapped up the opportunity to excuse himself. The silver-haired, imperturbable Salomon chairman got up from a stylish leather Donghia chair, strolled over to a bulbous antique chest, fished out a fistful of the thick cigars he puffed on constantly, and slid them into the breast pocket of his reassuringly conservative, dark gray suit coat. He told the reporter he had urgent business and sauntered confidently out of the building.

By the time Gutfreund had walked the two blocks to Hutton's headquarters, the outside directors had given Ritt and Fomon a good going over. Lopp in particular was relentless in questioning the basis of Ritt's ambitious projections. If the projections fell, so would opposition to the sale.

"We've never done this well in the past," Lopp said to Rittereiser. "What makes you think you can do this well now? I just can't see us earning this much without spectacular markets."

Dina Merrill opposed a sale. She thought $50 a share was a steal, adding that the new management had been approved by the board and deserved a chance before the company was sold from under them.

These discussions took place largely behind closed doors. Hutton's executives were asked to file in and answer questions, then were asked to leave. Even Ritt and Fomon, though directors themselves, had to step out. For Ritt it was a painful experience. He was not just being questioned—grave doubts over his abilities were being expressed. Those shafts wounded him deeply. Lopp had been the bluntest. He'd suggested, none too subtly, that Ritt was not up to the job.

Fomon also grew angrier as the afternoon progressed. Although pleased that the directors were giving Ritt such a going-over, he was stunned that he had been shut out. Ueberroth had, in fact, wrested the chairman's role and was exercising it fully. At one point the board called Fomon in to solicit his comments on the best course. "You talked about it without me, so make your decision without me," he snarled. "I'm not going to answer that question."

The directors were particularly eager to hear Gutfreund's opinion of Rittereiser's profit projections. Gutfreund was reluctant to state flatly that he believed them ridiculous, so he couched his view in diplomatic circumlocutions.

"This environment has some uncertainties," he said in his trademark low-key, gravelly voice. "These projections are very aggressive."

Gutfreund also offered advice to the board on various strategies for responding to American Express. He and Wilson told the directors that they could not negotiate a deal over an extended period of time. The uncertainty at the firm, if prolonged, could trigger a serious deterioration of its finances and a crippling loss of brokers.

Gutfreund also explained that, once the board made a commitment, it would have no more bargaining leverage. If it wanted concessions, such as guarantees on jobs for Hutton's senior executives, it would have to obtain them before the two sides shook hands. He indicated that Shearson wanted Hutton so badly, it would pay a rich price. The two investment bankers were then asked to leave.

When they returned a little before 8:00 P.M. the word came.

Peter Ueberroth ordered in the Salomon officials and proceeded to give them the terms he wanted conveyed to Robinson and Cohen. Hutton was to be sold.

"The minimum price has to be fifty-five," Ueberroth told his investment bankers. "There has to be a bulletproof contract by Monday morning if they want a deal. And the management has to be taken care of."

For $1.6 billion, eighty-three years of independence were about to end. The rest of the directors listened in silence.

"We'll call," Gutfreund said, concealing behind his cool demeanor and a puff of thick white smoke his surprise that a board that had vacillated so much during the day had suddenly become so decisive.

The members of the management committee, milling about in Ritt's office, were stunned. Scott Pierce went home, thinking about life after Hutton. Ritt was taken aback. He refused to blame his own lack of action on reducing Hutton's costs for his situation. The company had just been yanked out from under him.

"The truth of the matter is that these guys just cooked their own deal. Period. Over and fucking out," he said to a colleague in one of his rare moments of white-hot anger.

Robinson and Cohen had grown weary of waiting for an answer, so each had gone home, Robinson to his horse farm in Connecticut and Cohen to his Manhattan apartment, where he prepared his family for their usual weekend jaunt to the Hamptons.

Gutfreund and Wilson walked into Scott Pierce's empty office and reached Robinson at his home at 8:30 P.M. In sparse language Gutfreund laid out Ueberroth's terms. He indicated that this was a take-it-or-leave-it proposition, confident that American Express would take it.

"I'll talk to Peter about this, but I don't think that's doable," Robinson replied.

"No way," Cohen responded when Robinson told him the terms. "They think we want it so bad that they're trying to force this through. We can wait."

Cohen phoned Gutfreund. The Salomon chairman ran through the terms again briefly.

"What do you want to do?" Gutfreund asked.

"I'm going to the beach," Cohen replied tartly. "Have a nice weekend."

Minutes later he and his family were on their way to Long Island. The firm that was sold twenty minutes earlier was suddenly unsold. The board's strategy had backfired.

"Robinson's out," Gutfreund told Hutton's executives after giving the board the dismaying news.

Jerry Miller, already agitated, could not contain his irritation. "I don't understand," he said. "This is the most important call in our lives and he's not there to take it? What the hell is going on?"

"You misunderstood," Gutfreund said. "He's out of the deal."

A strange mix of emotions flooded through the weary executives, of relief and apprehension. "I guess we owe you one," said Dick Locke.

"We'll see," Gutfreund replied.

Fomon, plastered by this time, interrupted. "Let's go back to them at fifty," he suggested. Gutfreund did not respond.

The board, rudderless in the best of times, was totally at sea now. Ueberroth and the other directors had committed a blunder of oceanic proportions. By far the worst situation for a company to be in is to agree to be sold and then have a buyer walk away. From that moment on the company is regarded in the market as damaged merchandise. Hutton was known to be ailing prior to that fateful Friday. But the name still had an attractive aura. The board had just marred that sheen with a display of prodigious ineptitude.

The predicament was almost too awful to contemplate: a board that had demonstrated its complete lack of confidence in Hutton's management now had to figure out how that same management could lead the firm forward. In a fit of desperation they asked whether the talks could be salvaged. Gutfreund assured them that it was over.

As the meeting broke up, Fomon offered Gutfreund a lift home in his waiting limousine. Gutfreund helped the unsteady chairman in the car, and they headed into the darkness, both exhausted, leaving the day's bizarre developments unmentioned.

"Good night," Gutfreund said as he exited the car at East Sixty-fourth Street and Madison Avenue, around the corner from his Fifth Avenue home.

"And good luck."

· · ·

Hutton's executives were still absorbing the remarkable turn of events. They exchanged sometimes angry comments about the board and filed toward the elevator. Rittereiser ran into Jim Lopp in the men's room.

"Jim, I just want you to know what I think of what you did there today; it was just plain sneaky," Ritt said. "What right have you got to talk about management like that after what you left at this firm? You forced us to basically discuss this thing out of context. I just want you to know that as far as I'm concerned our relationship is over."

"Bob, I don't have to listen to this," Lopp replied. "You don't understand a board's obligations."

"I do know that you have an obligation to be up-front and not hide like that," Ritt answered.

Ueberroth then found Ritt and pulled him into an office, dropping the next bombshell of the evening.

"Bob, it's clear that you and Fomon have a different view of where things are going," Ueberroth said. "You have to work this out. We're not going to get into the middle of it. It's up to you to make the changes." Ueberroth then made clear that Fomon was to resign as CEO and that Ritt would succeed him.

Ritt was surprised, not just at what seemed in store for him, but at how this was being presented. The underling was supposed to fire his boss?

"You sure you want me to handle this?" he asked.

"Yes, and it needs to be done by tomorrow's board meeting."


"Rittereiser, this is Bob Fomon. I think we need to get together and work some things out before the board meeting."

"There are some things I'd like to go over, too," Ritt answered.

Fomon invited Ritt to his house for lunch that afternoon, Saturday. Ritt replied quickly that it would be better to meet at a restaurant. He did not want to give Fomon the chance to pull off one of his famous disappearing acts if he heard something he did not like. They agreed to meet just after noon at the elegant Polo Restaurant, at the Westbury Hotel on Madison Avenue.

"Look, Bob, I'm here to tell you that the firm thinks the time has come to make a change in the leadership," Rittereiser said, wasting little time once the two were face to face.

"I don't think things are working the way they are. We have to change it to move ahead. Really, what I'm here to say is that you have become a problem. I've told you many times that you cannot embarrass the firm the way that you do. You have to understand the responsibilities of someone in your position. I've defended you publicly on many occasions, but people are starting to ask why I tolerate this stuff.

"I've been asked to say to you today that at the board meeting you should nominate me as the CEO."

Fomon was not entirely surprised, but actually being told that he had to go was a jolt. "Are you telling me that this is something others on the board accept?" he asked, his scratchy voice pinched.

"Yes," Ritt answered. "They are expecting some action on this today."

The two picked at their food. This should have been the greatest moment in Ritt's odyssey from the rough streets where he grew up—about a mile from where he sat now—to the top of his field. But he did not feel the triumph he had expected. The board's doubts had troubled him deeply. It was an ambiguous victory at best.

Fomon prodded Ritt to get a sense of how much Ritt had pushed for his ouster.

"Bob, I am where I am on this," Ritt said. "I'm here because we have to go on to the next step. It's not what either of us envisioned when I joined Hutton, but it's what we need to do now."

Fomon showed none of the bitterness welling up in him, and he said nothing of the strategies he was mulling. He could not permit this to be as final as Ritt was indicating. They finished their generally polite repast, and then Ritt said he had a car waiting to take them to the board meeting.

"Does the board expect me to give up everything, or do I remain chairman?" Fomon asked anxiously in the car.

"Yes, I do expect you to continue in the role as chairman," Ritt replied, seeking to reassure Fomon and avoid any open battles. "But it has to be clear who is running the firm."

"I'll go along," Fomon said tersely after they had traveled a few blocks. He had found his opening.

The ride was brief. Instead of stepping out onto the familiar harborside scene at the Battery, the chairman and CEO-to-be of E. F. Hutton found themselves standing on Fifty-second Street, in front of the new Hutton World Headquarters, with its brittle skin of pink granite.

The Saturday board meeting would be the first ever held in this monument to Bob Fomon—and his last in the role he had snared sixteen years earlier with a deft political double cross.

Together they strode between the theatrically oversized columns, across a lobby whose soaring, mosaic-tiled ceiling had been freshly buffed, and to the elevator. Ritt would soon hold a job that his rivals at Merrill Lynch had never appreciated he was capable of. With a few minutes before the climactic board meeting, he decided to survey his domain, to savor the moment.

He bypassed the elaborate trading desks and the shiny staff gymnasium and headed up to twenty-eight, the executive floor. It should have been a grand and satisfying moment. But Ritt was not proud as he perused the small but elegant offices, the heavy chairs covered with green leather, the mahogany desks polished to a bright sheen, and the grand stairway with a brass banister leading to the executive dining room.

Standing, alone, with his hands in the pockets of his dark pinstriped suit, scraps of buff-colored carpet stacked along the walls and sunshine streaming through the dusty floor-to-ceiling windows, Ritt felt physically sick. Only now did it dawn on him that he had been so busy devising strategies that he had hardly paid attention to this impossibly burdensome albatross.

There would be hundreds, if not thousands, of layoffs. A huge write-off and losses were imminent. The long pampered retail brokers were going to have their payouts cut. And this would all be decreed from one of the most expensive buildings in New York City.

# THE KING IS DEAD—
# LONG LIVE THE KING

"I understand that this was an emotional experience for all of you," Ueberroth said in opening the Saturday board meeting. The de facto chairman had adopted a schoolmaster's tone as he began to lecture Hutton's senior managers.

"I want you to know that it was emotional for us, too. But you have to understand that we have a fiduciary duty to do what is best for the shareholders. We feel that the reaction from the management committee was inappropriate, and we want you to know that we will not stand for it. Going forward, we are going to work together. The management is going to have to show proper respect for the directors and the position they hold."

Lopp followed. "I am dedicated to making this the great firm it ought to be," he said. "I am going to put any personal remarks aside because we have bigger things to worry about."

Before Lopp finished, Ueberroth cut in, no longer able to contain the real source of his anger—how foolish he and the board looked, offering the company up for sale and being rejected. He fancied himself a master negotiator, but he had blown it this time, and everyone on Wall Street would soon know.

"You guys kept bringing dance partners in here. Then, when the gorilla wanted to dance, you said, 'No thanks,' " Ueberroth said. "You put us in a very difficult position. You brought us this nice package all tied up with a ribbon, and then you tell us we can't open it."

He added that he had spoken that morning with Jim Robinson and could confirm that American Express was not coming back with a counteroffer. Gutfreund and Ken Wilson, sitting in on the meeting, exchanged a knowing look; it occurred to both at that moment that Robinson and Ueberroth had been communicating all along as a secret back channel, exchanging information and pushing the talks forward without telling either Salomon Brothers or the other members of the board.

Once the lecture was over it was Ritt's turn. He said that he had met with Fomon earlier and that it would be best if the chairman spoke.

"I have the impression that some of the directors want me to step down as chief executive of E. F. Hutton," Fomon said. "Is that the view of the board?"

"Bob, I do think we have to clarify the leadership," Ueberroth replied.

Fomon began to defend himself in his scratchy tones but was stopped. With Ueberroth having indicated his desire for change, the other directors, desperate for a lead to follow, snapped into line. Dina Merrill spoke about the embarrassments the firm was suffering because of Fomon's outrageous public behavior. She complained heatedly about the *M* magazine interview. Even Ed Cazier expressed sympathy with the need for a change. There did not seem to be much more to discuss. Fomon nominated Rittereiser as CEO.

Before the board voted, however, it took more than an hour to debate what Fomon's functions would be as chairman. While Ueberroth insisted he should not have any operating authority, Lopp and Cazier said his experience could still prove valuable. They did not wish to completely humiliate their friend. Fomon fought to retain control of the thing that had always obsessed him: image. He simply could not imagine leaving the good name of E.

F. Hutton in any other hands, and he said so. Finally it was agreed. Fomon would continue to run advertising and public relations.

That done, the board voted to make Ritt CEO. Fomon's reign was over. Or so it seemed.

Fomon remained subdued on the surface, but inside he was fuming—and thinking. He mentally reviewed each member of the board and felt little more than condescension and disdain. The bold thing to have done, he thought, would have been to throw out Rittereiser and his crew. But the board had not had the balls to do that. They did not have the balls to do anything tough. They could not even throw out the old chairman properly, he thought. The directors had to be shown what to do. That thought gave him pause, lifting the darkness of his anger for a moment. The board was an empty vessel that someone had to fill, or it had no purpose, no meaning. The failed Shearson talks had proven that. Ueberroth could be decisive, but he had no idea in which direction to head.

Fomon then looked at Ritt, babbling away in what Fomon considered semi-English. That bastard who calls himself CEO, Fomon thought, engineered this chaos and Fomon's disgrace. He could hardly blame the board. He thought about that, too, for a moment. How could this long-winded technocrat run Hutton? What did he know about the psychology of controlling the firm's big egos? What did he really know about money, about how to use it as a tool of control? Forget the firm, Fomon thought. Focus on the board. He had created it. Taking away one of his titles did not erase that fact. He still had the ability to manipulate these directors. That was the key to righting the wrong he had just suffered. Behind his humiliation and his scowl, Fomon suddenly found some comfort.

Ueberroth and the other board members then delivered more speeches on a most uncomfortable subject, the future. The board had displayed its lack of confidence in Rittereiser the previous day in the most severe manner a board could: it had tried to sell the company against the president's wishes. Now it told Ritt that he would be held to the impossible profit projections. If he missed them, he was out.

Ritt leapt at the chance to present his agenda. A buyer had already been found for the insurance company, he said, who would pay $300 million. That would produce a profit of over $50 million after taxes. He also discussed his need to hire several new senior executives.

The board then took up a matter not on Ritt's agenda—the election of a new outside director. Ueberroth had been chairman of the nominating committee for over a year but had produced nobody. Fomon was behind the new arrival.

The candidate was Sadao Yasuda, general manager of the international investment department of the Sumitomo Life Insurance Company, a huge Japanese insurer. Fomon had paid a visit to Hutton's newly opened Tokyo office some months earlier and, as part of a round of introductions, had had dinner with the chairman of Sumitomo Life. The two got along well and quickly decided to take steps toward building business ties. Fomon had offered Sumitomo Life a seat on Hutton's board.

The move fit a pattern on Wall Street. The Sumitomo Bank, a separate institution, had acquired 12.5 percent of Goldman, Sachs & Company months earlier. The Industrial Bank of Japan had acquired a Wall Street bond firm.

Hutton was not aware of it yet, but Jim Robinson was planning to sell a major interest in Shearson to the Nippon Life Insurance Company. Nomura Securities would come within a whisker of acquiring a large minority share in Kidder, Peabody from General Electric. And before long Paine Webber would take on a Japanese insurer as a large minority shareholder. The Japanese were regarded as attractive partners because of their massive capital bases and the access it was believed they would provide to their country's booming financial markets.

Those deals usually involved elaborate planning. But Fomon and Hutton's board gave no thought to precisely what Sumitomo Life would be doing or whether it should make an investment in Hutton. Fomon was improvising.

Yasuda's introduction to the board had been botched badly already. His first board meeting was to have been the tumultuous session on Friday, November 7, when the firm was nearly sold.

Yasuda had not been told of the purpose of the meeting or that it might be better for him to miss it. But the directors had decided that it was not appropriate for him to participate. So Yasuda spent his first Hutton board meeting sitting in Scott Pierce's office, chatting and waiting, in vain, to be called in. Finally, on Saturday Yasuda was formally nominated as a director and elected.

The board then took up the delicate question of what it should say publicly about the near sale. The directors fought for no disclosure, but the lawyers cautioned that the securities laws would force some comment. Of course, they also had to plan for the announcement of Ritt's succession to the CEO's title, Yasuda's election to the board, and the sale of the insurance company.

They asked the public relations department to draft a press release, and Jay Moorhead, Fomon's assistant, was called in to clear it. A moment far tenser than Ritt's election as CEO followed. Fomon bristled as Moorhead read a manufactured declaration of how delighted the chairman was with the developments. Fomon was being asked to approve the announcement of his own defeat.

The directors also chose to issue a brief, misleading release stating that Hutton had had some "preliminary discussions" of an unspecified nature with American Express's Shearson unit. "No formal offers were made in the course of these discussions," the firm insisted, adding nothing on its $55 counteroffer.

After the meeting ended, Cazier joined Fomon. He told Fomon he had been surprised at how quickly he had folded.

"Maybe I was a dumb shit, but I thought that was what you wanted," he snapped. "All you people want to destroy my whole life. Well, I'm not going to stand for that," he added, putting Cazier on notice that this was not the final showdown.

Meanwhile Ritt called his brother, Fred, chief executive of Sherwood Securities, a small, struggling brokerage firm that specialized in obscure over-the-counter stocks.

"Freddy, I think they're going to name me CEO in an announcement at about four this afternoon," he said. "I just wanted you to know before you heard it somewhere else."

"You must have had a hell of a weekend, but congratulations," Fred said.

"Yeah," Ritt replied. "Say a prayer for me."


The flush of success wore off quickly when Ritt actually faced his inheritance. Within days his profit projections, to nobody's surprise, unraveled. Shortly before Christmas, in a series of planning meetings, the sobering truth came out.

- The head of the international division admitted that he had no plan. As for cost cutting, the executives discussed closing down Fomon's Paris apartment.
- The operations division proposed eliminating free lunches for traders, for a savings of about $175,000 a year.
- Jerry Miller conceded that the retail division's revenues would come in from $32 million to $64 million lower than the board had been told. Hutton's mutual fund business would produce $20 million less in fees.
- The administration division said there was no plan for advertising. Neither was there a plan for cutting expenses firmwide. The executives proposed closing down an unusual operation run by Ron Lopp, Jim Lopp's brother. He ran a clothing shop inside the firm that provided business suits to Hutton brokers and executives at cut-rate prices. The outfit cost Hutton $200,000 a year. The division also proposed selling one of the firm's two aircraft. Eliminating the Christmas parties would save $400,000 annually.
- Dick Locke said that the investment banking projections had been overstated by at least $15 million. He also raised serious questions about whether Hutton was making any money from its tax shelter business, given the huge number of lawsuits it was being hit with.

A week later Ritt went before the board again. He said nothing of the expected shortfalls in earnings but focused on the write-offs. He wanted to move ahead without that baggage left over from the Fomon era.

The tally was huge: $70 million for losses on the upper floaters and another type of municipal bond, $40 million to rehabilitate some failed tax shelter deals and to cover litigation costs, $16.5 million in extra costs for moving into the new headquarters, and $5 million for severance payments to executives who would be dismissed.

Hutton would report a $90.3 million loss for 1986, Fomon's last year as CEO, one of the largest losses in Wall Street history. By contrast other firms on Wall Street had enjoyed an almost ridiculously profitable year.

When Hutton announced the write-offs in early January, Standard & Poor's followed with another downgrading of the firm's credit rating. Hutton, the seventh-largest brokerage house on Wall Street, held the lowest rating of any major firm. Another downgrade and it would face the prospect of having its lenders pull out.

From outward appearances Fomon seemed to be taking his demise philosophically. He tried to enjoy himself a bit more. During December he went on a hunting trip to the White Deer Ranch in Nebraska to shoot duck and pheasant with a group that included his son, Jim Lopp, and Tom Rae, the former general counsel.

Initially Fomon was eager to prove his worth around Hutton. He was measured and temperate as he struggled to remain involved in important company matters. As Ritt prepared for the series of planning meetings near Christmas, he warned Fomon he would not tolerate gratuitous attacks.

For the first three days Fomon spoke infrequently, but when he did he was incisive. He still knew the firm better than the new CEO. But he could not sustain the pose for long. Ritt was calling the shots. Fomon could suggest or cajole, but the key decisions were in Ritt's hands. By the end of the week Fomon had grown testy. He sniped at the division heads and made capricious demands. He tried to embarrass people. Ritt asked him to stay away. That was the final break.

The next week Fomon began his campaign in earnest.

Hutton's corporate by-laws did not draw a sharp distinction between the roles of chairman and chief executive, on the assumption that they would be held by the same person. The wording thus granted most powers to the chairman rather than the CEO.

Steve Friedman, Hutton's general counsel, had already suggested to Ritt that the by-laws be rewritten to clarify the roles and avoid arguments with Fomon. The board had clearly intended to vest the CEO with the principal authority over the firm, and that ought to be codified, Friedman told him. Ritt, choosing not to see the potential for trouble, said he had enough to do without worrying about the by-laws.

Then Fomon seized his opportunity. He proposed that Ritt negotiate a new set of by-laws on his terms. It was a clear attempt to win back some of the power he had lost. Ritt was incensed.

"Bob, I have bigger fish to fry," he said. "I'm not going to negotiate with you on an issue that was already decided. I'm just not going to get involved."

Fomon then went to Cazier, who called Ritt, proposing that the three of them sit down to work out the problem.

"I don't think that's necessary," Ritt replied, growing irritated with a man he saw as Fomon's pawn. "Look, you know what the board intended. Wherever it says 'chairman' in the by-laws, you just write 'CEO' and leave it at that. That does not have to be negotiated. We have to get on with more important things, Ed, and you know that."

What Rittereiser did not want to acknowledge was the graveness of his tactical error in not ousting Fomon completely. You had to kill the king in this game or not take the risk of showing defiance. There was no partial victory over Fomon.

For a change, the markets began to cooperate, providing a silver lining to the otherwise black clouds gathering over Hutton. The bull market came back with a vengeance in January 1987. E. F. Hutton & Company, the brokerage unit, took in net earnings of $14.9 million in January. The results were 50 percent above the plan.

Ritt also took a remarkably lucid look at the firm and wrote a landmark memo to his management team. In the pithy six-page document he used a new word, "urgency." He described as "crucial" the need to let Hutton's managers know that the firm's problems required immediate action.

"In short, we are only now, in January 1987, at the starting line," Ritt said, adding, "The Firm is a wonderful organization with a great history, but more change rather than less is required to secure a winning position."

Then the seesaw dipped down again.

Fomon was furious at the weakness of Hutton's investment banking division under Dick Locke and its failure to recuperate from Lopp's tenure. Fomon, whose office was adjacent to Ritt's, wandered in constantly to harangue him about Locke's incompetence. By January the criticism had gone from anger to a demand that Ritt fire Locke.

"Bob, I'll tell you what," Ritt said on one of the rare occasions when he lost his patience. "I have a real good idea. If you're so concerned about the guy, why don't you take some time and do a little exploring and find the son of a bitch who put him in that job? He's the really incompetent one because Locke never belonged in that job. You find him and I'll fire the son of a bitch."

In silence Fomon walked out of Ritt's office.

Ritt had had enough. For two years he had avoided the inevitable break with Fomon. Now, however, he sensed that he had the board's ear. The January performance had strengthened his hand. Everything was in place for Fomon's elimination. The venue would be the February board meeting.

Catching wind of what was in store, Fomon called Scott Pierce beforehand to feel him out. Pierce, pushed almost completely out of the firm by Rittereiser, had decided it was time to leave. The first week of February he announced his resignation, effective March 1. This would be his last board meeting.

"Do you think I should stay on as chairman?" Fomon asked Pierce.

"No, I don't think so," came the reply. "Bob, it just isn't working. You've become obstructive. It's time."

"Well, then I don't want you at that meeting," Fomon said, his runty voice turning into a snarl.

"Bob, you can't ask a director not to go to a meeting because you don't like what he'll say," Pierce replied.

The pièce de résistance of Fomon's headquarters building was the gym-size boardroom. It occupied the whole west end of the twenty-eighth floor, just below the zigguratlike crown of the building. In the center of the room sat a huge table polished to the brilliance of patent leather. Surrounding it were oversize soft leather chairs. That was where the minions sat.

A platform had been built along the room's eastern wall on which a special, elevated chairman's seat had been erected. It was a dramatic aerie from which to look down on the directors below.

But the modest-size Fomon had never ascended his throne's grand heights, and Ritt felt ridiculous even thinking about climbing up on the pompous thing. As the February board meeting began, the board members gathered like mere mortals at the half acre or so of table to decide the fate of Bob Fomon once and for all.

Ueberroth called the meeting to order, and the outside directors asked the insiders to leave so that they could discuss the matter alone. Ritt, Fomon, and Pierce stood to exit. Ueberroth stopped Pierce and asked him to stay.

"You don't need Pierce here," Fomon snapped. "He should leave, too." Ueberroth, firmly in charge, waved Fomon off.

"Scott, what's your view?" Ueberroth asked when the others had left. "Are the employees still loyal to Bob?"

Pierce did not deliver the speech he had prepared. But he was finally ready to speak his mind after two years of failing to ease Fomon out quietly. Pierce's anguish over what he felt was Fomon's destructiveness had reached a climax.

"He's become an enormous embarrassment," Pierce said. "There was the *M* magazine piece. That was just awful to our customers. He's also been interfering with policy decisions. He's doing stupid things, like the new dining room. It's a nuisance. He's made a fool of himself."

(Fomon had engaged in months of bickering over how much Hutton's executives should be charged for eating in the firm's dining room when they were not there on company business. Hours and hours were spent on the delicate matter of whether the executives should pay by the meal or an annual fee.)

Pierce added that even the location of Fomon's office was a problem. It was right next to Ritt's, which meant that he could intercept people heading to meetings and bully them or simply spy on Ritt's doings.

Lopp defended Fomon, asking the directors not to forget how much he had done for Hutton. Cazier, eager to save face for his friend, seized on Pierce's comment about office geography. He proposed a compromise—as though a ghost glared at him from that empty throne behind the board table: let Fomon remain chairman in name, he said, but move his office out of the headquarters building so that he could not interfere.

It was a remarkable suggestion: throw the man out of his office ignominiously but call him chairman, the firm's highest title. The board could not make the break clean.

Ueberroth and Pierce said that it would be better to end the farce and ask Fomon to resign. But Cazier, Lopp, and Dina Merrill were insistent. They were at a stalemate. Finally Cazier's compromise won out. Incredible as it sounded, Fomon was told he could remain chairman only if he left the building.

"This is outrageous, and I don't think you should stand for it," Lopp told Fomon after the board meeting. The two had gone to lunch at Jim McMullen's, a well-known East Side watering hole.

Fomon alternated between fatigue and fury. "I should have said, 'No fucking way,' " he fumed. "Shit, I built the fucking building."

"I suggest that you just resign as chairman and let me work out your severance," Lopp said. "I'm going to go out and get you ten million bucks."

"You won't get that," Fomon replied.

"Hell I won't," said Lopp.

CHAPTER

# 18

ATTACK OF THE
REGISTERED REPTILES

The split on the board was mirrored within the firm. By the beginning of 1987 Hutton's retail system, a simmering caldron of resentments for two years, was at war with Hutton's capital markets division. Jerry Miller railed about the lack of attention his division received, and he even threatened to resign.

The brokers developed a venomous antipathy for "New York"—meaning the managers, particularly Ritt, whom they blamed for their plight. All the while Hutton's retail customers were fleeing, stirring the ire of Hutton's brokers even more.

Yankelovich Clancy Shulman, the market research specialists, were hired to get a precise measure of customer attitudes. The results were frightening. Tellingly, Hutton's best customers, the so-called heavy traders, held the lowest opinion of the firm and expressed a lack of trust in Hutton's brokers. That was significant, since about 10 percent of Hutton's top retail customers produced 90 percent of its business. The survey showed that Hutton's account executives had lost confidence in New York, too.

And then there was Mark Kessenich. One of the first things Kessenich had done when he'd arrived at Hutton was to assess the profitability of all Hutton's bond-related businesses. He was shocked by what he had found.

First, there were the upper floaters. He proposed that Hutton merely stop paying the ridiculously inflated prices for the bonds and buy them from Hutton's customers at an appropriate market price. The brokers went crazy, arguing that even if Hutton had wrongly promised to buy them at par, it had to stand by its word.

If Kessenich's plan went through, their customers would take huge losses, which could hurt the brokers' business. Better, they said, to stick Hutton itself with the bill. In other words, the brokers fought to have Hutton's shareholders pay. Forced to make a decision, Ritt had crumbled. That led to the long delayed write-off.

Kessenich had also stumbled onto one of the secrets to Hutton's chronic weakness—a sales system that permitted brokers to sell nearly anything to anybody. If the brokers could land an institutional account—say, a thrift institution, a bank trust department, or the pension fund of a regional corporation—they could keep it, receiving retail-level payouts. By paying the retail brokers their standard commissions on these institutional accounts, Hutton was earning nothing, or even losing money, on transactions that earned thousands of dollars for the brokers. Hutton's shareholders were being beggared to support the excesses of the system.

Kessenich was not alone in his view of the profligacy of the retail brokers. Tom Stiles, the head of Hutton's equity division, had found that Hutton was losing money on a money management product the brokers were permitted to sell. For every dollar of commission the brokers earned on the product, Hutton's shareholders lost a few cents. On Wall Street brokers are called registered representatives, or registered reps, because they must register with regulatory organizations to do business. Kessenich took to referring to them as "registered reptiles." Hutton had turned into a B-grade science-fiction thriller, with those registered reptiles poised to attack.

Despite his earlier declaration of the need for urgent action, Ritt once again permitted the problem to fester by putting off a decisive solution to Kessenich's war. Fearful of a misstep, Ritt took no steps. Once again, he felt that, if he could just get his plan in place, such problems would be resolved. So he focused on recruiting the last two members of his management all-star team.

First, he hired Ken Wilson, who had been one of Hutton's key advisers at Salomon Brothers. Wilson, bright and plainspoken, was a well-regarded investment banker; also, he was often pessimistic, one reason he was generally viewed as a solid adviser. Early in the year, he agreed to become head of Hutton's investment banking division—with an implicit promise that he would be named president when Ritt rose to chairman, which he expected later in 1987.

For Wilson, the draw was clear. He escaped a growing political tangle at Salomon and received an opportunity to run a major brokerage house. Not least, Ritt gave him an extraordinarily lucrative contract that guaranteed him millions of dollars no matter what happened at Hutton. At worst he would walk away with nearly $10 million.

That left one slot open—marketing. Ritt showed up with Jerry Welsh, by far his most unusual choice.

Jerry Welsh was recruited from American Express, where he had developed a reputation as a sporadically brilliant, volatile, and extraordinarily energetic head of marketing. He spouted ideas from morning to night, which he would describe with the fervor of a revival-show preacher in his self-consciously homey Tennessee accent.

A former professor of Russian, Welsh was credited with inventing "cause-related marketing" when he started a campaign in which American Express contributed a penny toward the restoration of the Statue of Liberty every time a customer used one of the company's charge cards. There is, as Welsh unfailingly reminds interviewers, a Harvard Business School study of some of his marketing innovations.

American Express's top executives had come to regard him as something of a mad scientist, an unpredictable, erratic crackpot whose solid ideas had to be culled carefully from the torrent of loonier suggestions that gushed from him. All the same, American Express's executives were sorry to lose him. If properly controlled, he was an asset. Jim Robinson let him know that Hutton was not long for this world. But Welsh would not be dissuaded. The preacher in Welsh had found a new mission—to bring his ebullient brand of marketing to Wall Street.

"Bob Rittereiser is going to be remembered," Welsh promised his new colleagues soon after joining Hutton with another one of Ritt's whopping guaranteed contracts, "as the executive who introduced real marketing to the brokerage industry."

Internecine warfare aside, the omens seemed good for Ritt's new lineup. The spectacular run in the markets continued through February and March of 1987. The rally was as inexplicable as it was unstoppable. E. F. Hutton earned an astounding $66.1 million in the first quarter—$44 million above Ritt's projections.

That news greeted Ken Wilson on his first day of work, Monday, April 6. At the weekly management committee meeting that day an exuberant Ed Lill provided a sneak preview of the quarterly profit figures.

"What do you think of the numbers, Ken?" Ritt asked proudly.

"I think we have a real problem," came the reply.

Silence.

"What do you mean?"

"Just look at them," Wilson said, speaking in his usual fast-paced, blunt manner. "We don't make any money. This is all non-recurring stuff. If we don't make money in this environment, you're going to have a real problem if the business gets tougher. Your costs are way out of line."

The room went quiet again.

"Ken, no offense, but you've only been here one day, and I don't think you understand the company," said Jerry Miller in a calm, avuncular tone, not wishing to upset the newcomer. "We don't have a cost problem; we have a revenue problem. We just need to generate more revenues by expanding the system."

More frightening than the fact that Wilson was right was Miller's response. For starters $27 million of the first-quarter "profit" was accounted for by a tax gimmick. Another $3 million represented profits from the insurance company, which was being sold.

Of the remainder, $15.4 million simply came from the increase in value of some investments Hutton had made, principally a large stake in the Vista Chemical Company. Those profits had nothing to do with regular operating earnings from Hutton's core business. Vista Chemical's stock price could go down as well as up—as the firm would later discover.

Factoring that out, Hutton earned only about $20 million from operations. But even that was an illusion; it was interest income.

Hutton's commissions soared to $459 million in the quarter, nearly $30 million higher than the plan and $90 million above the previous year. Yet none of that made it to the bottom line. Expenses ate it up. Head count, for instance, had jumped from 17,500 employees in mid-1986 to 18,400.

"You have to understand," explained Wilson, "if you want to get this firm on track, you've got to get your costs under control."

Wilson and Welsh may have been disabused of their grandiose visions as soon as they joined Hutton, but they were still men of action and tore into their assignments. They became Ritt's agents of change, taking the steps that the CEO could only dream about.

Wilson laid off more than a dozen highly paid professionals from the investment banking division, an unthinkable act under Fomon. Hutton's old-timers were angered because Wilson also hired several people close to him, considered cronies, with large guaranteed contracts. But Ritt was glad to see some action for a change.

Wilson also began to say no to some of the deals Hutton's investment bankers brought in. For instance, some of Hutton's deal makers had proposed offering a tax shelter for the new owners of Sardi's, the famous, if down-in-the-mouth, restaurant in the Broadway theater district. A new group of investors had bought it and wanted to franchise the restaurant, but the deal seemed to provide tons of cash to the new owners and few assets to the investors. Wilson put the kibosh on that.

Welsh had a grander shake-up in mind. He, too, wasted little time bowing before Hutton's sacred cows. Within a few months he had authored a series of scathing memos that spelled out the firm's basic problems and proposed radical solutions. He proposed slashing the payout to the retail brokers and cutting back on headquarters staff and overhead. Welsh also abandoned Fomon's advertising strategy, unceremoniously dumping Bill Cosby. Privately he ridiculed the notion of using a black spokesman in a white-dominated business. He called Cosby "a used Jell-O salesman."

In a magazine interview Welsh was cynical in dismissing the old campaign.

"It's *my* money!" he sneered, mocking Cosby's tag line. "Screw you, Bill. Our new message has got to be this: We're hard-nosed businessmen, and we've come to the conclusion that people are our best business."

But Welsh did recognize the difference between image and substance. He had quickly learned the retail industry's dirty little secret—only a fraction of retail clients are profitable for the firms that service them. The more profitable clients subsidize the rest.

That affects the firm, but not the individual broker, since a broker's income is based on the gross revenues he brings in, not the profit after all the firm's expenses are paid. The system allows brokers to hold on to these marginal clients in the hope that someday they might evolve into more active traders. Until then the brokerage house, meaning the shareholders, foots the bill.

Welsh wanted to create what would be, in effect, two separate brokerage houses under the same roof. Under this tiering strategy, only the identifiably profitable clients would get full-service treatment. The rest would receive a low-cost, depersonalized form of brokerage service. It would amount to a practical application of the adage, "You get what you pay for." For Wall Street, it was a radical suggestion.

Welsh next proposed lavishing an array of services on the more active investors. They would become members of a supposedly elite 1904 Society—named for the year E. F. Hutton was founded. It would provide special account statements, club memberships, and access to prestigious events.

Beneath them would reside the hoi polloi. They would receive cut-rate service, largely through direct mail and from dialing toll-free telephone numbers. The customers would no longer have their own broker to call for advice and would be steered principally into packaged products such as mutual funds and unit trusts. As wild as Welsh could be in pitching his ideas, this one was down-to-earth and shrewd.

Such bold strategies appealed to Ritt. But Wilson and Welsh insisted that they would fail unless he got Hutton's mushrooming expenses under control first. Expenses and head count had to be slashed dramatically, or the firm would not survive. It was Ritt's last chance. His solution was NOVA—National Overhead Valuation Analysis.

The project had two purposes: to plan the needed cuts with care so that valuable employees and assets were not lopped off; and, most important to Ritt, to persuade even the most reluctant Hutton manager or broker of the necessity of the cuts. Ritt was terrified of a misstep that could incite the destructive retail riot Jerry Miller constantly warned of. NOVA was, in other words, a massive public relations exercise.

The head of the twenty-three-member NOVA staff was Rich

Carbone, the deputy controller and longtime gadfly. The stated aim: to reduce Hutton's expenses by $100 million a year. It was by far the most important item on Ritt's agenda.

Like clockwork, as soon as Ritt began to implement the strategy, a grimmer reality struck. Hutton's bond department was laying down huge bets. Once again the market turned against the firm, and Kessenich's traders took a shellacking. They lost $65 million in late April, then another $13 million in May.

Kessenich might just as well have enjoyed a $75 million pop in profits had the markets gone the other way. But that was the point—bond trading was a high-risk business. You could lose big just as easily as you could win. What business did Ritt have sanctioning those sorts of risks at a firm as capital weak as Hutton? Where were the controls he kept promising the rating agencies?

The retail executives were both shocked and secretly pleased at the losses. The red ink bolstered their resistance to Kessenich's assault on the registered reptiles.

Publicly the firm would report net earnings of $46 million for the second quarter of 1987. But once again the numbers were illusory. Hutton actually lost $41 million in the period before taxes. The reported profit was accounted for by a one-time gain from the sale of the insurance company and tens of millions of dollars in tax benefits.


As Lopp had promised to his dear friend, Fomon's severance terms were generous. As the package was wrapped up in early May, he could congratulate his friend on the generosity of Hutton's shareholders.

Fomon would be paid $4 million in cash, plus $500,000 a year as a "consultant's fee" for seven years. The consulting entailed overseeing several investments, including the Vista Chemical stake, giving Fomon a window onto Hutton's true financial condition.

On top of that, the board voted to pay Fomon a pension of $612,450 a year for life, about four times what he would have been entitled to under the corporate pension plan. And 76,000 shares of Hutton stock or options for shares that the board had granted him earlier were immediately vested. The shares were worth approximately $3 million.

There was an odd counterpoint to the board's generosity with the discredited old chairman. At the same time that the talks with Fomon's lawyer had been under way, the board had agreed to negotiate a contract with Ritt. He was to be given the same sort of golden parachute as his new recruits. However, while Fomon's contract talks breezed to completion, Ritt's were bogged down. The directors niggled over small details.

Ritt thought he was about to become Hutton's chairman. But the directors were sending him a crisp signal that they had other ideas. For Fomon that was just the first of a two-part humiliation he wished to deliver on the would-be usurper. Fomon had big plans for his final board meeting in May. He wanted Peter Ueberroth to succeed him, not Ritt. None of the directors expressed misgivings about the proposal, especially since Ueberroth was already functioning as the chairman. Fomon lunched with Ueberroth and encouraged the plan. Everything was falling into place. High-level departures were usually an occasion for gold watches and expressions of affection. Not for Fomon. He made sure that he would not go gently into the good night of retirement.

Things began on schedule and hewed to Fomon's script at the May 6 gathering. His contract was accepted quickly. Next the directors began, one by one, to praise Ueberroth's leadership. The climax was approaching.

"Bob, what are your thoughts?" Cazier asked Ritt.

"The time has come to run this like a real company," he began, unable to control his anger as he realized what was happening. "No, I don't think Peter Ueberroth is the answer. That kind of a signal to the firm is not what I need to get things done around here. I'm going to have nothing but bad news for the next six months, and I don't need to be getting undermined."

Fomon made his move.

"The board already looks up to him as the leader here," he said. "I nominate Peter Ueberroth to be chairman of E. F. Hutton."

"Bob, there's no use in making the motion," Ueberroth said quickly. "It just doesn't make sense, and I'm not going to do it. Don't even bother seconding the motion."

Fomon was flabbergasted. He paused as he absorbed what had happened. Everything had been lined up, yet Ueberroth had just said no. Fomon had thrown what he thought would be his trump card, and it had failed. He had created that goddamn board. How dare anyone on it defy him!

Fomon had accurately gauged Ueberroth's interest in the prestige and financial reward of becoming Hutton's chairman, but he'd underestimated how sensitive Ueberroth was about his public image. Should Hutton collapse on Ueberroth's watch, his name could be stained. That was not a risk that he was going to take. Victory, so sweet and near a moment ago, was slipping through Fomon's fingers as Ueberroth's well-tanned face stared at him blankly.

"You wimp," Fomon snapped.

The other directors stared at the table or at their feet, embarrassed by the outburst. Those were Fomon's second-to-last official words to the board he had dominated for seventeen years.

"I can tell you that my first piece of business will be the sale of this firm," Fomon added in his final comment.

"Effective today I am resigning as chairman of E. F. Hutton," Fomon began his address over Profit Line, Hutton's internal communications system. "I have been at Hutton for thirty-six years, having served as a director for twenty years and CEO for seventeen years. I was the fifth CEO in the history of E. F. Hutton, which shows a certain continuity of management, for better or worse. Only five CEOs in eighty-four years.

"Edward F. Hutton, one of the most respected individuals of his time, in addition to founding E. F. Hutton and Company, was the founder of the General Foods Corporation and chairman of the finance committee of the Chrysler Corporation.

"Before I joined the firm in 1951, Hutton used to move its offices around the country as the clients moved, depending on the season, from Pebble Beach to the Plaza Hotel in New York, to Palm Beach, Florida, to the Ambassador Hotel in Los Angeles—wherever the clients were. I never really knew whether the partners moved to Palm Beach because Mr. Hutton was the founder of the Everglades Club or whether they moved to the Ambassador Hotel in Los Angeles because it was the home of the famous nightclub, the Coconut Grove. But they sure had great tans. They tried to move the Bisbee, Arizona, office, but the manager wouldn't let them because he was attached to his wooden sidewalks out front.

"The firm has come a long way since the days we were dependent for business on traders like Joe Kennedy, who later became the first chairman of the SEC, Jesse Livermore, 'Bet a Million' Gates, and J. Paul Getty, all of whom contributed to the extraordinary mystique of the firm.

"There are still men around the country today who remember Mr. Hutton and his considerable contributions to society. For example, during the Depression, the company ran soup kitchens for the poor. One of the most respected individuals of his time, when he became a limited partner, he wrote a syndicated column espousing capitalism. This column appeared in hundreds of newspapers around the country.

"When I joined E. F. Hutton in 1951, I thought it was the closest to knighthood that one could achieve in the securities industry. Nineteen years later, in 1970, two strong contenders for the CEO position knocked each other off, and I was unanimously elected. At that time, *The New York Times* said, OBSCURE VICE-PRESIDENT FROM CALIFORNIA TAKES OVER E. F. HUTTON. [Fomon's supposed quote was incorrect.] I did not know at that time that the firm was on the verge of bankruptcy. Somehow I don't think things worked out too badly.

"For the past seventeen years I have really considered myself the prime keeper of the good name of E. F. Hutton and Company. Over the years many employees have resigned from the firm to join competitors. However, in almost all those cases the resignations were not the result of unhappiness at E. F. Hutton, but the result of their being proselytized by competitors who recognized that E. F. Hutton was a good recruiting ground for highly trained, skilled, and professional employees. Today there are E. F. Hutton alumni associations where men meet not to complain about E. F. Hutton, but rather to praise nostalgically the qualities of the firm.

"On balance I think we all have done a terrific job as we built Hutton from the seventeenth-largest securities firm in 1970 to one of the largest and most successful today. It's been a lot of work and a lot of fun.

"I thank you for the successes we have shared in the past and wish you all success and prosperity in the future. And until we meet again, may God bless you and hold you in the palm of his hand."

CHAPTER

# 19

---

# A SMALL REVOLUTION

The four hundred and fifty stockbrokers sipped cocktails or slid from one cheerful knot to another exchanging broad salesman's smiles. Models dressed as flappers and molls strolled between the gleaming, Roaring Twenties–era automobiles, and filling the air with brass, a big band blared over the din in the hotel ballroom. It was a joyous event—the rebirth of E. F. Hutton & Company, courtesy of Jerry Welsh.

Welsh liked the idea of a born-again brokerage firm, whipped up at a prayer meeting–style bash. It fit his self-image as an inspired leader of the unwashed salesmen, turning them into a formidable fighting force.

It was July 15, 1987—six weeks, as it turned out, before the greatest bull market in history would peak and then begin its sickeningly swift downward descent, and precisely two years after Bob Rittereiser, in his moment of truth, had failed to seize Hutton from the mythmaker and turn it into a real corporation. But that all seemed distant in Washington's brand-new Grand Hyatt Hotel.

After two years of frustration, two unrelenting years of putting out financial fires, fighting off an imperious, obstructive old chairman, and wrestling with a slippery, vacillating board, this was Bob Rittereiser's coming-out.

For the first time in Hutton's history, the firm had assembled all of its branch office managers in one place—a symbol of the new unity Ritt wanted to forge at the by now hopelessly divided, crumbling organization.

On a personal level this unlikely gathering was a celebration of the crowning moment in Ritt's odyssey from poor inner-city kid, a truck driver's son, to chief executive of one of America's leading brokerage houses. That he was captain of a leaky tub, listing badly and under insufficient power, heading straight into a financial Bermuda Triangle, was ignored. His eyes were fixed on the stars.

Using the Roaring Twenties as the opening party's theme provided an eerie portent. But that was lost on most of those happily downing highballs and munching on Sterno-warmed canapés. Many were calling the event—which happened to be taking place on Rittereiser's forty-ninth birthday—a "coronation."

Even amid the alcohol-induced bonhomie of the opening cocktail party, it was hard to miss the perverse, Wonderland quality to the scene. Hutton's board, which had just given millions to the ousted chairman, refused to grant Ritt the contract he had been negotiating for six months. Hutton did not even have a chairman. The seat had been left vacant. Not only were Ritt's days at E. F. Hutton numbered, but the exasperated board had not given the slightest bit of thought to who would replace him.

Ritt had rebirth on his mind. With his million-dollar-a-year salary and his dreams, he was getting comfortable in his role. Just months earlier he had had the firm lease him a $60,000 Porsche to go alongside the BMW and Jaguar in his driveway. He had even spoken to Fred Wilpon, part owner of the New York Mets, about purchasing a small interest in the ball club, the sort of investment wealthy, sporting, and highly successful businessmen make.

Amid the banter at the Washington gala there were, however, some notably glum faces. Ken Wilson looked uncomfortable and depressed. Jerry Miller was shaking his head in disgust as he spoke with a group of his subordinates.

"I'm lobotomized," he was telling them. "I can't even think."

The focus of concern was a revelation at a casual meeting of

Hutton's management committee just a few hours earlier in Ritt's hotel suite. That was when Ritt had introduced the coloring book— or rather, when Jerry Welsh had unveiled "the Book."

Welsh had been appalled at the culture he found at Hutton, how remarkably out of touch it was with the firm's dire condition. More than that, he realized what an obstruction the culture was to his designs. How could he remake the retail brokerage operation if everyone in it still believed they were in fighting trim and second to none?

"You know, the ability of people with a vested interest in something to sincerely reject contrary views of reality is far greater than we imagine," he had explained. "People dying of cancer say they're healthy. People who smoke three packs a day say they aren't addicted.

"That's why I say I think many of these people are sincere. But it's a reflection of the fact that the culture is out of control at Hutton. I am referring to the fact that these people are allowed to have a sincere view about the state of the company that is demonstrably wrong. How can you run any enterprise when you have a view of reality that is palpably wrong? Here's the thing you got to understand. If a man is dying of cancer and doesn't even believe he has a hangnail, you can't get him to the therapy."

The coloring book was the first step in Welsh's therapy. The idea was to find an unorthodox means to deliver a harsh dose of reality. It was to become one of the most discussed marketing gimmicks developed in years—if not quite in the same manner Welsh had expected.

Welsh loved the notion of using such a wild approach to market his ideas—hey, it might win him another Harvard Business School case study. But sensing the potential for dissension, he clamped a tight lid on what became a secret guarded as closely as a formula for making nuclear weapons. Among Hutton's top executives, only Bob Rittereiser knew—until the management committee meeting in Washington.

Welsh explained to the executives in Ritt's suite that Wednesday afternoon that the Washington conference was historic. Warming to the subject, he worked himself up into an inspired monologue during which he mentioned an unusual book that had been prepared to deliver the message. Welsh averred that, while he was reluctant to show it yet, it was a real winner. But several of the executives, immediately sensing trouble, insisted. Welsh finally let them see. Shock spread through the room.

All of Hutton's branch managers would be greeted the next morning with a plastic bag hanging from their doorknobs, inside of which would be *The Hutton Neighborhood Coloring Book* and a six-pack of Binney & Smith crayons.

What stunned the executives was that this silly medium had been chosen to deliver an unremittingly bleak message—not the usual cheerleading heard at such gatherings, but a bucket of ice water thrown in the faces of Hutton's proud managers.

"We're no longer the nicest house on the block," the book said in its preadolescent imagery. "We're not even close. In fact, we're in big trouble."

It went on: "Last year we did a lot of business, but we lost a *bundle* on our lemonade. Even though everybody else in the neighborhood was *making* money on their lemonade.

"Let's face it, we've wasted a lot of time and money," the book added. "If we don't fix our problems *soon,* someone could even take away our home."

Welsh had chosen a coloring book introduced at a multimillion-dollar party to deliver the sobering message that, put plainly, Hutton was close to going out of business and needed a "small revolution," as the book put it, not to prosper, but just to survive.

Jerry Miller dropped the book, the color gone from his face for just a moment, the brief moment before it grew brilliantly red. The first question he asked was whether there was any way to stop the books from being distributed. The answer was no. In fact, selected media had already been given copies. The whole world was being told that Hutton had failed—and in what many thought was an insultingly juvenile manner.

The management committee members expected insanity from Welsh. What really angered them now was why Ritt, in whose hands Hutton's future rested, had kept this idiocy a secret, why he had not solicited the opinions of his top managers.

Ritt grew quiet, unwilling to defend himself or the book.

By the end of the next day the coloring book was all the managers discussed. That evening one group of drunken managers held a book-burning party at which dozens of the slim volumes were torched.

Some at Hutton tried to be sympathetic to the concept. Using a coloring book to deliver an unpopular message, they believed, would prove catchier than a dull speech. And, as many knew, Hutton's brokers had been coddled for too long. Painful as it was, the message was correct. But even backers expressed concern over its condescending tone.

"Morale is going up after all the shit we've been through, and now we're going to introduce a fucking coloring book? This is a disaster," Miller practically screamed to his equally disgruntled colleagues.

When asked by his branch managers and brokers how he could permit this to happen, Miller shook his head. "I know nothing about this," he said. "Talk to Ritt and Welsh. I'm sorry that you work for a firm that could do this to you. But you do."


The conference opened officially on Thursday morning, July 16. The preparations had been extraordinary. The Grand Hyatt's main ballroom was primed with a booming sound system and a curved screen behind the specially built dais. The backdrop was lit an azure blue, Hutton's corporate color. All the grand events were being recorded by Hutton Television.

Kicking things off was a lively, irreverent video on the firm's history prepared by Welsh's people. Set to rock music, the fast-paced production put a strange emphasis on scenes of war, a nice subliminal touch for the veterans in the audience, many of whom felt embattled that morning. In one particularly curious sequence, as the film showed an atomic bomb's deadly mushroom cloud filling the sky, the sound track had Jerry Lee Lewis belting out "Great Balls of Fire."

Wilson was depressed by the spectacle. The Las Vegas–style glitz that Hutton had splashed around the Grand Hyatt was humiliating to him. He felt like a carnival performer. But it was too late to turn back. "The Hutton Promise," as the meeting was called, was launched officially on Thursday morning at 8:15 A.M. with Bob Rittereiser's keynote address.

"Today we will take the first steps in a journey which will return E. F. Hutton to its former glory," Rittereiser began in his flat-footed manner, sounding like a high school senior running for class president. "E. F. Hutton is at a turning point, and the degree to which we, its managers, leave this meeting as a team, with common perceptions, goals, and values, will determine whether E. F. Hutton succeeds or fails."

Ritt bluntly addressed the weaknesses in Hutton's culture and operations even if he was, as usual, long on platitudes and short on specifics. He also addressed the growing rift between New York and the field.

"In a fundamental sense we in New York have analyzed the problem, and, to a degree, it is us. From now on New York headquarters will help solve problems rather than create them," Rittereiser said.

"In addition to the reverses caused by lapses in good management, we find ourselves in a total enterprise not coping very well with some fundamental changes in our business environment, changes that are transforming this industry into something quite different from what it was even five years ago. As we have drifted along, relying with too much confidence perhaps on the strengths of our past, external change has simply overtaken us.

"This meeting," he added, "marks the end of Hutton's period of frustration and drift and the beginning of a new period of focus, discipline, and cooperation."

Three charts, meticulously prepared in the sky-blue-and-gold color scheme selected for the conference, were flashed onto the screen to illustrate the extent of the firm's decline. One showed that expenses were growing faster than, and had outgrown, revenues.

"The continuing trend spells disaster," Ritt said. A second slide showed that the amount of revenues brought in on average for each employee had been declining.

"I'm convinced that we cannot now depend on an accounting study to tell us why we are slowly bleeding to death. We must stop the flow. Our current sales mix is, in itself, fundamentally unprofitable. Some products, some account executives, and some customers are not profitable."

Ritt also pleaded for understanding from his rebellious troops. "I would say it is about time that we climb out of the pit of confrontational rhetoric among different sectors of the firm and climbed up to a new plateau of common purpose," he declared.

Many listening to the speech could not but note the biting

irony in these words. Two weeks before the Washington meeting Norm Epstein, head of operations at Hutton for two decades, had quit in a feud with the CEO. In measured words that shocked, then frightened, then angered Ritt, Epstein explained that he would not go along with Ritt's plans and that he was leaving. Period.

It was well timed to embarrass Ritt, since Epstein had been scheduled to deliver an important address to the branch managers in Washington.

Although well regarded for his expertise, Epstein defended encroachments on his turf like a pit bull. Rittereiser had sought to narrow his territory by splitting operations into a retail group and a capital markets group. Under Ritt's plan Epstein would have run just the retail portion. Epstein quit in anger.

Friday evening was the gathering's crowning moment. The 450 branch managers and executives were shuttled in buses to Mt. Vernon, George Washington's handsome hilltop home overlooking the Potomac. A drum and fife corps in period dress greeted the guests, who sauntered toward a huge tent for cocktails and an official welcome.

It was a golden evening. The branch managers bathed in the dying glory of a once rich Wall Street powerhouse. Hutton's shareholders still knew how to throw an impressive party.

Dina Merrill, the movie actress and Hutton board member, delivered a brief but inspiring speech. "My name is Nedenia Hutton," she began. "My father often told me that he wanted E. F. Hutton to be the best source of brokerage advice in America. We're not there yet, but this meeting convinces me that we are on our way."

She lauded the firm's managers for upholding the tradition of service that, she said, had been so important to her father.

"I thank you," Merrill concluded soulfully, "from the bottom of my heart."

With that, glasses of champagne were raised, and the clear night sky sparkled as $50,000 worth of fireworks exploded over the Potomac.

"The essence of the message I bring you today," Ritt had said in his speech, "is that despite the monumental pressures we face from the marketplace, the most formidable barrier to our future success is within the firm."

# CHAPTER
# 20

THE BEAR
BEGINS TO GROWL

"I see money coming out of the woodwork but no heads. I'm telling you, this won't work without heads. Goddamn it, I need fifteen hundred fucking heads. Now!"

Rich Carbone, head of the NOVA project, bellowed his warnings. Once again he was the sentinel, describing the violent storm approaching. His tone, however, had grown shrill by this time, because nobody seemed to be listening. The man who knew more about Hutton's finances than anyone else at the firm was scared to death.

It was August, and Hutton was still not making any money. The risk was not that it would disappoint shareholders yet again, but that it would fail. Now, to top it all, NOVA, Hutton's last hope of slashing expenses to a sustainable level, was flopping. After four months and thousands of hours, NOVA had become just another illustrative anecdote, demonstrating anew that Rittereiser did not have the will to dismantle Hutton's self-destructive culture.

By late summer Carbone told Hutton's management that the $100 million NOVA was supposed to cut from Hutton's expenses—

an objective that had not been met—was not enough. He figured that, with the firm's continuing deterioration, $140 million was needed, maybe more.

What if Hutton collapsed? Which of Hutton's creditors might fail if Hutton went? What other weak securities firms would suffer a run by lenders in the panic that might follow Hutton's demise? These were no longer hypothetical concerns.

Never one to mince words, Carbone lashed out at Ritt and the other senior members of the NOVA committee.

"None of this bullshit is going to work. You're giving me telephones, taxis, other crap. I'm telling you, iiiitt wooooooonnn'tt wooooorkkk," Carbone whined. "You give me fifteen hundred heads now, or it's gonna be eight thousand heads in six months. And we have got to get out of this building. It is eating us up. We caaaaan't affoooooord it. You just don't fucking understand what you're up against."

"Rich," the mild-mannered, sad-eyed Ed Lill responded, flustered by Carbone's histrionics, "there's enough fat there to do the job without all the layoffs. Don't worry."

Hutton had entered the Twilight Zone. The coloring book had tainted the Washington meeting, the gala that was going to rally the troops. The branch managers departed more cynical than when they had arrived. Ritt looked increasingly ridiculous with his bright, but hollow, pronouncements.

The management committee, Ritt's democratic vehicle for running the firm, all but stopped functioning. Ritt grew uncommunicative, secretive, and insulated. Ritt's dance with the board over his contract continued to go nowhere. Where before he had loved meetings, now he avoided them. He spent hours in his office, poring over reports, exchanging a few words with his inner circle. He was paralyzed.

Hutton's board had accepted Ueberroth's two-faced stewardship. This was just the kind of situation for which he could avoid responsibility by having rejected the chairman's title. He was chairman when there were no risks.

August was the turning point for Carbone. He vowed after his outburst that, come bonus time in January—if Hutton lasted that long—he was going to bail out.

His soulmate was Ken Wilson. The two were bonded by their understanding that they were, as Wall Streeters like to say, shifting the deck chairs on the *Titanic*. They communicated through black quips, such as the photocopy of a newspaper ad that Carbone sent his friend one morning. It showed a dinosaur, over which was written, "Are you planning to remain competitive?"

For Wilson, the worries of August gave way to genuine fear in September. He was no longer an adviser, as he had been for so long at Salomon Brothers, detached and objective. This was his company. He was responsible for hundreds of people. He had a substantial financial stake in its future himself. And it was very clearly doing down the drain.

Ed Lill's confidential, two-page summary of Hutton's July performance for the board showed the firm breaking even for the month on an operating basis. In August, as the stock market hit its record high and trading volume soared, Hutton suffered a $9 million operating loss. There were no secrets being kept from the directors. They saw what was happening and did nothing.

Ken Wilson told Ritt about a new worry. More than one thousand layoffs were needed urgently. But such a restructuring, along with the other expense-reduction measures, would require that Hutton take another big write-off, perhaps $100 million, to cover special costs like severance. However, given the firm's pathetic finances, it was questionable that it could withstand such a hit.

Looming in the distance, Wilson added, was another downgrading by the credit rating agencies. Quietly officials from the rating agencies had been contacting Ed Lill and reminding him of Hutton's unfulfilled promises. How could Hutton survive both a downgrade and a write-off? Its lenders would flee. The patient would not survive the treatment for its maladies.

"Ken, there's no question that we have a real situation here," he said. "But just be patient. It'll work out."

Then came September. Memories of that month would later be blotted out by the maelstrom that followed, but it was a particularly bleak period on Wall Street. Interest rates began rising steeply, creating turmoil in the bond market. The stock market wobbled, then slanted downward.

Lill told Ritt and the board in his confidential monthly summary that Hutton had posted an operating loss of $33 million for September. It was devastating news, the final confirmation that Hutton was finished.

"Bob, this is not going to get any better," Wilson told a shell-shocked Ritt. "We're going to have to bite the bullet and make some decisions. You should just close the apartments down and get rid of a lot of this stuff. You've got to stop talking and do something. We've got to lay off a lot of people if we're going to make it."

"Ken, trust me," Ritt replied. "I have a plan that is going to take us to the next step."

Ritt had, indeed, made some contingency plans, modest though they might be. He had finally had enough of Jerry Miller's threats that the retail system would break apart if anything were changed. Ritt was sold on Welsh's plans for shrinking the retail operation and forming tiers of customers. If Miller would not implement it, Ritt would find someone who would.

In complete secrecy he turned to an old friend, Joe Grano. He contacted Grano, the head of Merrill Lynch's huge retail branch network, in early September. Ritt and Grano, a tough Vietnam veteran, were close from their Merrill days together; they owned a luxury condominium on Long Boat Key in Florida that they used on vacations.

Hutton's retail division, Ritt told his friend, was in desperate shape and needed a total overhaul. He explained that the current management of the division would not accept the changes. Someone had to come in and sweep things clean. Grano expressed some interest. He had been considering a career change and liked Ritt. This was a particularly enticing opportunity because Ritt indicated that he expected to be named chairman soon. He would then form, he said, a three-man office of the chairman, with two presidents. Grano would represent the retail division, and Wilson, the other president, would represent the capital markets division.

Ritt had also agreed to a plan for splitting the mutual fund operations away from Miller's control. The asset management business would be broken off as a separate subsidiary under Tom Stiles, the head of the equity division. Led by Stiles and Wilson, the move would have been a prelude to selling off part of the asset management business to the public or another institution. It was an effort to liberate this fast-growing operation from the dead hand of Hutton's executive suite and to generate some real value for Hutton's long-neglected shareholders. The spin-off of this profitable business was scheduled for November.

(Miller did not learn of Grano's role for another year. When he did, during an interview, he stammered in disbelief and anger. "That would have been it," he told an interviewer. "I can't believe he would do it. It would have destroyed the retail system. Everyone would have left. It would've been a disaster." A year later Grano was recruited by Paine Webber, where he launched a campaign to restructure and streamline its large retail branch system.)

While Ritt vacillated and tried to come to grips with Hutton's problems, Bob Fomon enjoyed his first free summer in more than thirty years in 1987. He took a few months off to relax, and then he formed Robert Fomon & Company, renting office space from his old friends at Kutak, Rock & Campbell on Park Avenue, in the same building as Peter Ueberroth and Jim Lopp.

His pace was unhurried. But soon he got on to the first order of business. Over lunch with Ace Greenberg, the chairman of Bear, Stearns & Company, he pitched the firm that had ousted him.

"Bob," Greenberg told his friend, "if Elizabeth Taylor was going public, I wouldn't merge with her, and I think she's pretty attractive. Our policy is to build the firm brick by brick. We won't do a merger."

Fomon contacted Peter Cohen. He already had enough on his plate, he told Fomon. Don Marron, the chairman of Paine Webber, agreed to come over to Fomon's apartment to chat. But he indicated that Hutton might be too big for Paine Webber to swallow, putting off the old chairman politely.

Fomon contacted Gerry Tsai, the head of Primerica, a onetime industrial concern that Tsai had transformed into a company devoted to the latest corporate fad, financial services. In May Primerica had acquired Smith Barney, the brokerage house. Tsai told Fomon he would pass on Hutton.

Over lunch at Bice, a chic Manhattan restaurant, Fomon surprised George Von der Linden, the CEO of Smith Barney and a longtime acquaintance, by offering Hutton up for sale.

"You should take a look at Hutton," Fomon said.

"To be honest, Bob, that's the last thing I'd like to do," came the reply. "I think it's too far gone. It's too late. You should talk to Jerry."

"I did," Fomon said. "He wasn't interested. I thought if I could get you interested, you might be able to talk to him."

Fomon lambasted Rittereiser, calling him weak and indecisive. "He was the worst mistake I ever made," he told Von der Linden. Von der Linden listened but told Fomon he was wasting his time.

Fomon was patient. Through his consulting agreement, contacts on the board, and lunch and dinner meetings with several Hutton executives, such as Jerry Miller, he knew what Ed Lill's depressing monthly earnings summaries were showing.

At the least, though, he had to think about what he would do with the roughly 230,000 shares of Hutton stock he had been given by a munificent board over the years. It was a tricky situation. Through his company contacts, Fomon knew that Hutton's financial condition was far more precarious than the public was being told. The stock price was, in fact, ridiculously inflated given the firm's condition. But if Fomon did sell using this information, he might be in violation of the insider trading laws which generally prohibit stock investors from profiting by using certain important, non-public information.

Still, Fomon decided to unload his shares, delicately, slowly, not in a panic, but at a steady pace. On August 27 he locked in the right to sell 60,000 shares through the options market, at an average price of $42.50 a share. Four days later he unloaded another 10,000 shares. He continued at an even more rapid clip throughout September, as Hutton's confidential results got worse. (Fomon admitted that he stayed in touch with people about Hutton's condition, but he denied he was trading on inside information. No charges have been filed against him.)


"Bob, just look at these numbers; I don't think we have the wherewithal to do it," Wilson complained to Ritt, sitting on one of the green leather and mahogany chairs in Ritt's new, light-filled office on the twenty-eighth floor of the World Headquarters. Soon after Fomon had left, Ritt had moved out of the comfortable but modest-size corner office Fomon had allocated him and had set up shop in a large conference room walled on three sides by floor-to-ceiling windows. It was a CEO-size aerie, from which Ritt could observe his firm's accelerating collapse.

"The management isn't there. We just don't have the financial resources to get us out of this, and we can't cut fast enough now to keep up with the problems. We just aren't going to make it."

"You may be right. We have to have a contingency plan," Ritt replied. "I'll think about it, but what do you have in mind?"

Wilson described his plan as finding "an investor," but that was a euphemism. Hutton was for sale. Wilson had an enormous task in front of him. Hutton's CEO could not be of much help in the effort because of his distance from the grim reality at the firm. The rating agencies could ditch the effort at any time by lowering Hutton's rating. Wilson was desperate but could not, at all costs, look desperate.

Toward the end of September Wilson sat down with Rich Carbone to prepare something that Hutton had never had before: a business plan. A buyer had to be convinced that the firm was not, despite all appearances, completely adrift. A business plan would create the appearance of direction, of control, of a future.

The plan had Hutton getting out of nearly all of the headquarters building and into cheaper space. It included more than one thousand layoffs and a major slimming down of the retail operation. The investment banking operation would be turned into a boutique, specializing in just a few areas. It was an idealized portrait to transform this overweight, scarred, headless matron into a ravishing bride.

Wilson also drew up a quick list of possible suitors, which he showed Ritt. It included U.S. West, Bell Atlantic, another of the so-called Baby Bells, and Sumitomo Life. There was some irony on the Japanese insurer making the list. Sumitomo had been trying, in its politely indirect, Japanese way, to acquire a substantial interest in Hutton to cement its ties. Ritt had not focused on the issue. It was becoming embarrassing for Sumitomo, as though it were now being rejected by the firm that had been so encouraging a year earlier. So frustrated had Sumitomo become that it had been forced to buy $30 million worth of Hutton's shares in the open market.

While naïfs like Sumitomo were buying, those in the know were bailing out—secretly. Bob Fomon's sales of Hutton stock picked up steam throughout September. He traded subtly, never selling more than 10,000 shares at a time, always using the options market. He locked in the right to sell the equivalent of 109,000 shares for slightly more than $40 a share on average.

Wilson, meanwhile, began subtle approaches to gauge the interest of potential buyers. He did not realize it at first, but he was under a spotlight. Word began to spread among key Hutton people, including some of the more important retail brokers, that Wilson was shopping the firm. Fully aware of Hutton's dire shape, they looked upon Wilson as an emissary of hope.

With Wilson functioning as the shadow CEO, Ritt went to Bermuda for his usual trip with his wife the first week of October. But he could not escape the news coming from Wall Street. By Tuesday, October 6, Hutton's trading desks were already in the red for the month. That day the Dow Jones Industrial Average plunged 91.55 points. A week later the firm was down $13 million from trading. On Wednesday, October 14, the Dow tumbled another 95.46 points.

The squalls Rich Carbone had spied were no longer on the horizon. They were on top of the firm. It was already clear that Hutton would turn in yet another losing month. Even more depressing was the latest NOVA progress report. A confidential summary issued on Thursday, October 15, showed Hutton coming up short of its goals by more than half. The project had failed.

As if mocking Ritt's paralysis, John Gutfreund did on October 12 what Ritt had long claimed he could not. Salomon Brothers announced the most sweeping, one-shot series of shutdowns and layoffs ever on Wall Street. Salomon laid off 12 percent of its workforce, or 800 of its 6,500 employees. It closed down two major departments, municipal bonds and commercial paper. The cutbacks were designed to save the firm $150 million a year. It was a humbling step for the once powerful and now deeply troubled Salomon and its baronial chairman. But at least the firm was doing something.

Shaken by NOVA's failure, Ritt finally decided to take action, months if not years late.

Through Dale Frey, the Denver-based regional vice-president, Wilson set up an appointment with Jack MacAllister, the chairman of U.S. West. Ostensibly the purpose was just to encourage him to give more investment banking business to Hutton. The subtext was that Hutton was looking for a buyer, which MacAllister picked up immediately. The date was set for Friday, October 23, in Denver.

The news from the market grew worse. On Thursday, October 15, banks raised their prime lending rate, and the market skidded another 57.61 points. The Dow had lost nearly 400 points from its peak on August 25.

Ritt pushed ahead with his plan. The next move began with a Hutton investment banker, Steve Kelleher, who had been brought over from Merrill Lynch to assess Hutton's hodgepodge of merchant banking investments. After doing some analysis, Kelleher decided Hutton would need help. He had recently heard that a new investment banking boutique, the Blackstone Group, had attracted investors for a $750 million merchant banking fund. He knew Peter G. Peterson, Blackstone's chairman, and decided the two firms might talk about working together.

Blackstone's founders were Peterson, a former secretary of commerce and former chairman of Lehman Brothers, and Stephen A. Schwarzman, a hot young merger expert with Lehman before its sale to Shearson. Kelleher contacted Peterson on October 13, and they agreed to set up the meeting for that Friday, October 16, at the Mayfair Regent Hotel on Park Avenue. At 7:45 A.M. Peterson shook hands with Ritt next to a conspicuously large table made up for eight, blocking the aisle slightly at the elegant restaurant. Ritt was joined by Kelleher and Ed Lill. Peterson was joined by his partner, Schwarzman.

After exchanging some small talk about the unsettled state of the financial system—Peterson had just written a magazine article warning that a major crash was imminent because of the federal government's reckless fiscal policies—Ritt began describing his grand plan for Hutton. The two CEOs hit it off.

Before long the discussion had gone far beyond merchant banking. It was as though Ritt had been laid on a psychiatrist's couch. In a cathartic outpouring, he went into Hutton's need for capital, the fact that it could no longer afford the medicine he was prescribing without a stronger financial base, and his problems with the board. He told Peterson that he felt the directors still had some loyalty to the deposed chairman and that they did not understand the securities business.

After one hour, the standard length of a power breakfast, Ritt was just warming to his theme. He was opening up as he never had to an outsider. It was slightly embarrassing to the Blackstone partners, but they were interested. By the time the group broke up at 10:00 A.M., Ritt had crossed an important line. The CEO of E. F.

Hutton had invited Blackstone to make a major investment in his firm—$250 million for a roughly 25 percent stake. He also indicated that he would offer Blackstone several board seats and would want its help in making a series of management changes.

It was potentially a shrewd offer by Rittereiser. First, through the newcomers he would obtain a more sympathetic ear on the board, a friend amid what had been an increasingly hostile group. Someone with the stature of Pete Peterson would influence the other directors. Second, Hutton would obtain the capital it needed to survive.

That was, the Blackstone partners felt, awfully far to get in a first meeting. Also, it was a lot more fun for Ritt to think of new possibilities than to confront the more depressing issues waiting for him at his office. And they would be depressing that day. The market plummeted another 108.35 points in the heaviest trading ever on the New York Stock Exchange up to that time. The plunge guaranteed that Hutton would suffer yet another losing month.

Before they left the breakfast, Peterson and his partners said they were willing to pursue the discussions. To assess the prospects, they asked for some internal financial data.

Ritt agreed to provide a packet right away—on Monday, October 19.

# 21

## ANATOMY
## OF A COLLAPSE

On this cool fall Monday morning, Tom Stiles got an early start from his weekend home in Spring Lake, New Jersey. Rising at 4:15 A.M., the head of Hutton's equity department and his wife, an investment banker at Salomon Brothers, hit the road before daylight, and Stiles arrived in his office just before 7:00 A.M. Normally the compactly built, tightly wound executive would have eased into the day with a relaxed preview of the week. Today a million things were racing through Stiles's mind before he had sipped his first cup of coffee. Monday, October 19, was going to be, he knew, a dark day.

The unparalleled adventure of E. F. Hutton began, appropriately, with some bad news. Stiles learned he would be operating largely on his own. Bob Rittereiser was in Palm Beach, where he had hosted with Dina Merrill and Ken Wilson a dinner for utility industry executives. Ritt would be taking a commercial flight home late that afternoon. Wilson was already on his way to Nashville for a corporate finance conference, which Stiles considered particularly bad news. Ritt was regarded as being dangerously out of touch with reality at times. His dithering response to the Washington fiasco and the collapse of NOVA—still a secret outside Hutton—had persuaded some senior executives at the firm that his mental state was fragile. Wilson was trusted by many officials as the only person at the top of Hutton who clearly grasped the depth of the firm's problems, and of the reality of the markets.

Stiles's first decision was to get right to the point and not try to pretend that anything other than a disaster was in store. He was determined to create the perception that the bad news was expected, understood, and manageable.

Hutton began each business day with a 7:45 A.M. research call. Stock analysts would speak over Profit Line, the internal communications system, touting their latest stock picks so that the brokers would have a new spiel.

Stiles altered the agenda. Forget the analysis of individual stocks, he told his researchers. Don't tell us that the third quarter earnings of such-and-such widget maker were disappointing. Today's call would be devoted to a general appraisal of the market's dire condition, based on the rout of the previous week, particularly the plunge on Friday and the worsening news over the weekend; incredibly, Treasury Secretary James Baker had rattled investors and market professionals with a threat to permit the value of the dollar to tumble as part of a dispute with the German government. However, a falling dollar could have forced the government to raise interest rates. Force up interest rates when the market was careering out of control? Baker's utterances guaranteed that the stock market was going to wobble dangerously.

Hutton's chief economist, Bob Barbera, led the way over Profit Line with a deeply gloomy assessment. He went over the familiar ground: rising interest rates, plummeting bond prices, a massacre of the prices of takeover stocks in the previous week, Baker's remarks. "Don't expect anything but the worst," he concluded. Stiles then joined the weekly meeting of the bond department, one floor below, something he rarely did. He was searching for some insight, some ray of hope, perhaps, into the forces churning the markets. The picture painted for him by the bond specialists was of a disorderly and unpredictable mass of dynamics that all indicated interest rates were still heading higher, which would push already depressed bond prices lower. The market, in short, was being guided by fear.

Even before the 9:30 A.M. bell on the New York Stock Exchange, there were reports from the floor of large sell orders flooding the exchange's laboring computer systems, creating a traffic jam. When the starting bell was struck, stock prices immediately went into free-fall—those stocks that could trade. Most could not even open for dealing. Nobody was willing to buy, and things just seized up, adding to the sense of panic.

With so many stocks unable to open, the indicator most traders were watching for some sign of where the market was heading was the stock index futures contract, traded in Chicago. Two minutes after the opening, that index contract was down the equivalent of nearly 90 points! By 11:00 A.M. the Dow was off more than 200 points. People at Hutton called buddies on the massive, massively expensive trading floor Fomon had installed to see if it was true; for the most part they couldn't get through. If they did, the answer was usually, "I can't talk, you can't believe what's happening."

The trading floor became a magnet for dozens of curious onlookers. Clerks, investment bankers, computer specialists, all found excuses to wander down to the fourth floor to witness the massacre. In truth there was little to see. The traders barked into their phones, and everyone said it was incredible. The numbers just got worse. There was no way to relate to them. The market had slipped its Newtonian fetters and was drifting in a vertiginous state.

One other problem began to show up. There was extraordinarily heavy selling of E. F. Hutton stock. The stocks of all the major brokerage houses were getting killed. What was different in Hutton's case was that much of the selling was coming from Hutton's own brokers and executives, which the traders on the floor of the stock exchange noticed. It was a worrying signal to be sending.


Bob Barbera sat in his fifth-floor office pondering the strange computer glow before him. It was a little past two P.M., and of all the anomalies he had witnessed on this extraordinary day, this was the first to trigger a spark of recognition.

The Dow was down nearly three hundred points, but he had been watching the movement of commodity prices, specifically copper and aluminum. All had been rising earlier that day, along with interest rates. But in the early afternoon the commodities markets started to reverse. They were falling.

Commodities, Barbera knew, were one of the surest trackers of inflation and economic growth rates. There was no flawless predictor of these trends, but commodity prices were one of the clearest ways traders expressed their expectations. Faster economic growth feeds inflationary forces, pushing interest rates and commodity prices higher. A slowing economy turns the trends around.

Barbera knew that the sudden downswing in commodity prices indicated a shift in the expectations of traders; they perceived the mayhem in the stock market as a forewarning of a recession—or depression. If that was so, interest rates would start to fall, too, causing bond prices to spurt upward.

That was the nut of the idea forming in Barbera's mind. The bond market was about to rally—stupendously. He raced to Fomon's granite-lined elevators and emerged at the third-floor bond trading room. He found Paul DeRosa, Mark Kessenich's savvy number two.

"Look at what's happening to commodities," Barbera exclaimed. "And look at the stock market. There's all this anxiety that this is going to lead to a depression. Bonds are going to move."

The conversation lasted less than ten seconds. DeRosa, glancing at the declining commodity prices he had quickly called up on his computer screen, grasped the point, spun around, and heard one of his traders say that a customer had called looking for a bid on $75 million worth of ten-year Treasury bonds.

"Buy 'em, as much as you can," DeRosa said. That was just the beginning. DeRosa would nearly double Hutton's position in the bond market—just as interest rates commenced one of their steepest drop in years. Hutton, in other words, could try to make up for its mounting stock market losses by putting more of its capital into bonds. The bond market's rally was a lifesaver.

By the end of Monday most on Wall Street stared in trancelike disbelief at what had happened. The Dow Jones Industrial Average had finished 508 points lower—nearly five times the largest previous decline, which took place on Friday. Trading volume on the New York Stock Exchange totaled 600 million shares, an astronomical figure that, days earlier, would have been unthinkable. It was like a pole vaulter suddenly clearing sixty feet, triple the old record.

Later that evening a Hutton clerk completed the firm's daily, handwritten, highly confidential profit and loss statement for its trading accounts. This 8½-by-14-inch grid of numbers was preliminary, and its figures would require adjustment later, but it told a fascinating tale. Hutton had, by comparison with many of its competitors, not done badly.

In Stiles's stock department, Hutton had lost $10 million from trading large blocks of stock for institutions, nearly $6 million from risk arbitrage, or trading in takeover stocks, and nearly $5 million from over-the-counter trading. (The OTC figure would rise much higher later.) Hutton made money in the stock options market, where it was primed for a drop. The net result was a loss of $16,083,400 from stock dealings.

Kessenich eked out a $5.4 million gain from bond trading. Adding in some other areas, Hutton racked up total losses of $19,013,700 from trading, not bad given the disastrous tumble—a total of more than $500 billion in value had been wiped out in the stock market.

Stiles ended the evening at close to 10:00 P.M. by taking anybody alert enough to drink to the nearby Bombay Palace restaurant, across the street from Fomon's sumptuous World Headquarters. The nearly twenty traders, analysts, and executives who made it over hoisted plenty of the Bombay's ample, relatively cheap drinks as they sought to unwind and preserve the suddenly warm team spirit that had, strangely, infused them.

Jerry Miller's jaw hung slack. "I think we're going to have to adjourn for a while," Miller said, suddenly very distracted. "I have to get to some things."

It was Tuesday, October 20, and Miller had just been given word on what was happening to Hutton's stock price.

Black Monday produced bigger headlines, but on Tuesday the vast financial structure that held the markets together started to become unhinged. It was no longer a matter of stock prices plummeting—in fact, they ended the day significantly higher after a series of wild oscillations. The more serious problem was concern that the credit system would buckle. Buyers began to lose confidence that they would receive their shares from panicky sellers. Sellers worried that buyers would not pay them or that the payment would get caught up in a paralyzed credit system. Both buyers and sellers had no idea what current prices were, with the market gyrating bizarrely.

And then there was a more basic worry. What if a major securities firm failed? What would happen to its customers' shares held for security? What would happen to the other firms to whom it owed money? What would happen to the $280 million in deferred compensation Hutton owed its executives?

Only a series of ad hoc measures held things together for the critical few hours mid-Tuesday when the systems teetered on the edge of chaos. Mystery remains over just what pulled things back from the brink, but at least one factor was the upswing in bond prices and the decline in interest rates. The Federal Reserve took a dramatic step on Tuesday that was key to sustaining this upswing. It began pouring cash into the banking system, pumping up the money supply. That forced interest rates lower and insured that commercial banks would have the capital needed to loan cash-starved securities firms.

But the Wall Street rumor mill was not easily assuaged by the Fed's moves. The rumors followed the weak, and there was no firm weaker than E. F. Hutton—in spite of the fact that its trading losses were significantly below those of its competitors. The concern was reflected in its plunging stock price.

Miller was sitting at the head of a regularly scheduled meeting of Hutton's regional vice-presidents on Tuesday when he got the note. From a price of $38 at the beginning of October, Hutton's shares had lost 20 percent of their value by the end of trading on Friday, October 16. By early Monday afternoon the price tumbled past $25 and bottomed at $20.50. But the stock had hurtled below $20 a share shortly after the opening on Tuesday, news of which shook up the assembled RVPs. Most of their personal wealth was tied up in Hutton stock.

Making matters worse, Hutton brokers were still among the heaviest sellers of Hutton stock. Most firms prohibited employees from borrowing against shares of their companies' stock, but not Hutton. Thus many Hutton brokers were forced into panicky dumping of the firm's shares to meet margin calls. And that frightened others on the exchange floor, who assumed that if Hutton brokers were selling the stock, they should be, too.

Later Tuesday afternoon Hutton's stock hit an air pocket; it tumbled to $11 a share. That was less than half of the firm's supposed cash, or book, value of $26 a share and just a third of its value only a week earlier. The market perceived the firm to be almost worthless.

Some shrewd traders, however, were able to take advantage of this dire news. Bob Fomon had been trading heavily in Hutton stock and by the end of October 19 had sold 40,000 shares for the month, all through options. All the sales were for more than $30 a share.

Then, on Tuesday, came the real coup. By having sold options in advance, Fomon was able to sell, or "put," 55,500 Hutton shares that day at a price set weeks earlier. His average selling price: about $37 a share. He knew through his contacts that a sale of the entire firm would bring in considerably less than $30 a share. He was thus earning nearly 40 percent more for his shares than Hutton's other shareholders would eventually get.

Indeed, Fomon's information about the crumbling level of confidence in Hutton was right. Hutton was not aware of it, but by Tuesday afternoon the New York Stock Exchange had formed a special group to monitor the firm in case a rescue was required. Word was spreading.

Fred Joseph, John Shad's one-time protégé at Hutton and now chief executive of Drexel Burnham Lambert, telephoned Bob Rittereiser when he saw what was happening to Hutton's stock price. Drexel was in a very solid financial position, Joseph said, and should Ritt need help, Drexel would be there. It was the first time another firm acknowledged that a lifeline might be necessary.

Shortly afterward Ritt received a call from Phil Purcell, chief executive of Dean Witter Reynolds, the big retail brokerage house owned by Sears.

"This may or may not be appropriate, but there are all kinds of rumors flying around today," Purcell said, trying to put the case delicately. "I don't know if they're true or not, but I just want you to know that if you do need to do something, we'd like to talk to you."

Ritt continued in the code. "I appreciate the call, Phil," he said. "If there's any reason for us to chat, we'll certainly get back to you. When the dust settles maybe we can get together."

• • •

"Now look, goddamn it, this is no fucking time for saying you'll think about it!" Kessenich bellowed into the phone. "I call it a renege. It's a fucking renege."

Kessenich slammed down the phone. He had been talking with a senior executive at the Bankers Trust Company about a disastrous problem that had cropped up Tuesday. It was the first sign that others were starting to treat Hutton as though it were already dead.

Bankers Trust, concerned about Hutton's viability, was refusing to honor a foreign exchange trade it had committed to doing with Hutton weeks earlier. It was not willing to take the risk that Hutton might not deliver on its end of the deal. The worst news was not that this one trade would fail, but that word of the fail would spread and encourage others to do the same. The blow could have knocked Hutton to its knees instantly.

That summer Hutton had created a desk for trading currencies—deutsche marks, French francs, Japanese yen, and the like. Despite Ritt's promise that he was shrinking the firm, he had authorized the hiring at huge cost of the head currency trader at the Irving Trust Company, Steve Peras. He was followed by a dozen of his colleagues. Irving Trust's currency trading operations were nearly shut down by the raid. Within a couple of months Peras had built a thirty-person desk at Hutton for engaging in the borderless, unregulated foreign exchange market.

Several weeks earlier Hutton had initiated a routine currency transaction with Bankers Trust, a major player in the market, in which it bought about $70 million worth of pounds, for delivery on October 20. This was known as a forward contract.

In normal times Bankers Trust would have paid the pounds into Hutton's account early in the day in London—currencies were usually paid at banks in their native countries. Bankers Trust would then have received the agreed-upon amount of dollars from Hutton several hours later, when New York banks were open.

Spooked by the tumult in the stock market and fearful of problems at Hutton, Bankers Trust decided it would not accept that risk. It would only complete the transaction if there was a simultaneous exchange of currencies, a complex maneuver because of the time lags.

Only with the intervention of the First National Bank of Chicago did Hutton squirm its way out of the spot—at an extra cost of more than $50,000. Bankers Trust did something similar with several contracts to sell deutsche marks to Hutton. (Hutton had company. Over the next few days a number of senior executives at Wall Street firms would complain bitterly about how they were treated during the crisis by Bankers Trust.)

It was ironic that, in one of the few instances in which Hutton was performing better than most of its competitors, the market still perceived the perennial laggard to be failing. On Tuesday Hutton enjoyed a net trading profit of $1.3 million. On Wednesday the company would earn $20,947,200 from its trading, according to the secret daily trading reports. But it did not matter. Nobody had confidence in a firm with such basic structural weaknesses.

The problems with commercial banks were getting more critical. Every day Hutton had to borrow well over $1 billion from banks on an overnight basis to meet its regular operating needs, like any large securities firm. In normal times finding this capital was not difficult. But during the crash—when the need for cash was even greater—some of Hutton's lenders pulled back.

Several regional banks simply cut Hutton off. The First Interstate Bank and the PNC Financial Group both slammed the credit door. Hutton officials spent hours trying to persuade banks to stick by the firm, but the outflow grew. The banks slashed Hutton's borrowings by about $500 million.

Then several major institutions ceased their stock dealings with Hutton. "If you are being told by anybody that they have orders not to do business with you, I want to know that now," Stiles barked to his stock traders and salesmen.

And indeed Stiles spent much of the day ringing up executives trying to explain in the calmest voice he could muster that Hutton was doing just fine.

"I am certainly understanding of the concerns you have," he said over and over. "I just wanted to call to bring you up-to-date."

With one exception, Stiles's precautions worked. Fidelity, the huge mutual funds company based in Boston, pulled back and resisted the firm's entreaties.

The last credit problem to pop up was the worst. Hutton's commercial paper started drying up. Commercial paper is a short-term IOU issued by corporations. It matures in anywhere from a few weeks to a few months. A range of institutions, such as insurance companies and some corporations, buy commercial paper when they have surplus cash to invest. Of Hutton's daily cash needs of several billion dollars, $1.3 billion came from selling commerical paper.

By midweek some key buyers of Hutton's commercial paper wanted their cash back and refused to renew their loans when their existing holdings matured. Hutton's outstanding commercial paper shrank to $900 million, a loss of slightly over a fourth of this precious financing. By itself the decline in capital was not critical, but the trend was.

Bit by bit the gossamer threads that had replaced the bricks in Hutton's financial foundation were pulling apart. If anything further happened, if rumors of major losses stuck, if word of the liquidity squeeze leaked, if there were a downgrading of the credit rating of Hutton's commercial paper, Hutton would disappear in a matter of hours.

# 22

---

# A TASTE OF REVENGE

Jack MacAllister was game. Ken Wilson sat in the Denver office of the chairman of U.S. West with Dale Frey, Hutton's regional vice-president. His prayers were being answered. U.S. West, MacAllister was explaining, still saw a great opportunity in the brokerage business.

It was Friday morning, October 23. Despite the crash Wilson had flown out to Denver late Thursday for the scheduled meeting. Wilson began the session by sounding like an investment banker trying to drum up business. After a few minutes of bantering, though, MacAllister took over and talked for an hour about U.S. West's powerful interest in buying Hutton. Showing no sign of his anxiety over Hutton's worsening condition, Wilson agreed to meet MacAllister again soon, this time with Rittereiser.

Back in New York, Blackstone had also been giving a lot of thought to Hutton's situation. Hutton was a big retail brokerage firm, a type of business that Pete Peterson and Steve Schwarzman did not know nearly as well as investment banking. They decided that it would make sense to consult someone who was more familiar with the retail trade before jumping into any deals. The obvious choice was Sanford I. Weill.

After building up the firm that came to be known as Shearson Lehman Brothers, Sandy Weill sold it to American Express. The huskily built, well-tanned, curly-haired, cigar-chomping executive had then become president of American Express under Jim Robinson. After a couple years the aggressive, restless Weill made his move for the top job. Gracefully he left when Robinson repelled his charge.

Weill had then spent a year shopping for opportunities. In his first move he'd tried to take control of the faltering Bank of America, once the country's largest bank. He had sought to interest the bank's board in a deal in which he would help raise $1 billion of fresh capital and become chief executive. The proposal eventually was brushed aside. So Weill ended up accepting the job as chief executive of the Commercial Credit Company, a medium-size, Baltimore-based insurance and financing concern.

It was clearly an interim step. Commercial Credit was not a big-league player. But Weill saw it as a base for expansion. He had spent months surveying acquisition possibilities when he got the call from Pete Peterson. Without mentioning any names, Peterson said that he had discussed an investment prospect with a Wall Street firm in which Weill might be able to help. Was he interested?

Within seconds Weill was sure that E. F. Hutton was the unnamed firm. Yes, he told Peterson, he would be happy to discuss the issue. Peterson contacted Rittereiser to see if he approved of Weill's becoming involved, and Ritt gave the go-ahead. On Friday, October 23, while Ken Wilson was working on U.S. West, Weill visited Blackstone's offices in New York.

The proposal was clear: Commercial Credit would put up about $100 million of the $250 million investment Blackstone was considering. Weill would join the Hutton board along with a Blackstone representative. In effect, he would take control without having to buy the firm outright. To Weill, the talks were getting interesting.

During a break, Weill phoned his secretary. He was startled and amused by one of the messages she relayed. Bob Fomon had called and had said he wanted to hear from Weill as soon as possible. Weill pushed the meeting with Blackstone to a close, hurried back to his office, and phoned the former chairman of E. F. Hutton. Fomon proposed a face-to-face meeting, and Weill invited him to his office after lunch that same day.

Fomon got right down to business and proposed that Commercial Credit acquire E. F. Hutton. He said plainly that he had contacted Shearson, the obvious candidate, and that there was evidently no interest there.

Weill insisted that he would not get involved in a competition or allow an expression of interest on his part to be used as a negotiating tool by Fomon to extract a higher price from someone else. Fomon went on to express his bitter resentment of Rittereiser and described Hutton as weak and failing under the usurper. The board, he added, was fed up with Ritt's platitudes and lack of results. Fomon also boasted of his continuing influence over the Hutton directors.

From Weill's perspective, the situation was tantalizing. With so much turmoil, chances were good that Commercial Credit could march off with the prize at a rock-bottom price. Were there an open competition for Hutton, Commercial Credit would not stand a chance against a better-capitalized Wall Street behemoth such as Merrill Lynch or Shearson. But if he were first to go after a rapidly deteriorating company, Weill thought, he might scare Hutton into a hasty transaction.

"If the board is so disillusioned, I want to hear it from them, not you," Weill told Fomon, challenging him to deliver the directors.

"When can we meet?" Fomon replied. Weill suggested the next day, Saturday, at his home in Greenwich, Connecticut.

It was a delicious moment for Fomon. He was already tasting the sweetness of revenge.

Fomon knew Ed Cazier was in London and would not be back for a few days. Peter Ueberroth was on his way to Minnesota for the sixth game of the World Series. So Fomon called Warren Law, the easiest target. Law had always been cowed by Fomon's commanding manner.

As expected, Law accepted the offer. He flew down from Boston Saturday morning, at Fomon's expense. Fomon met him at the airport with his limousine, and the two chatted about Hutton's weakening condition along the way to Greenwich, the handsome, leafy, wealthy community. So disillusioned was Law with Rittereiser's long-winded fumblings, and so weak was he in his resolve about what to do, that he agreed to open the door wide to the ousted king's proclaimed ambition of seeking revenge.

The lunch was straightforward. It hardly mattered what Law said because the main point was that Fomon had, as promised, delivered a director. Weill discussed his views on the retail brokerage business and the tough environment that was developing. He also made clear that, since Commercial Credit did not already own a brokerage operation, it would not have to lay off many Hutton employees.

Law said the board had run out of patience with Ritt and his management team, with their failure to meet any of their own projections. Yet they had no one else to turn to. "There's so much turmoil inside the firm that there would be tremendous enthusiasm if you got rid of Rittereiser and put someone in there who could lead," Fomon said. "People would be enthusiastic about Sandy Weill."

Weill explained that he had a merger in mind, not an acquisition. In an acquisition Commercial Credit would have to shell out cash, or cash and some debt securities, to buy Hutton's stock from the shareholders. It would be a tremendous strain on his modest-size company.

But in a merger Commercial Credit could just issue more stock and swap it for Hutton's existing shares. The result would be the same: Weill would be in charge. But it would be far less costly for Commercial Credit. And Hutton's shareholders would not receive the premium cash value a takeover would provide.

Law was noncommittal. But it was another instance where not rejecting the proposal meant the talks could progress. Fomon had scored.

The pace quickened. Fomon contacted his friend Cazier and, with little prodding, persuaded him to stop in New York on his way back to Los Angeles from London. Dina Merrill also agreed to meet with the other directors at the home of the man she had once bitterly denounced. It was almost too easy. But then that had always been Bob Fomon's forte, getting others to intercede on his behalf. He had spent thirty-six years at E. F. Hutton, and that method had always served him well. Those thirty-six years now came down to this, Fomon's use of his friends to destroy the man who pretended to occupy his throne.

A dinner in Fomon's apartment was set up to complete the grand double cross. The climax was surprisingly businesslike and ordinary. The directors fell into place. The minute they sipped the first-growth Bordeaux Fomon served for the delicious occasion, his success was complete. A ruby red toast sealed Ritt's humiliation and completed Fomon's acid finale. The board had abandoned Ritt and was following Fomon's lead again.

The directors received Sandy Weill warmly. Unschooled in Wall Street's deal-making hardball, they were stepping happily into the trap. They were going behind their CEO's back to engage in serious discussions about the sale of the company. Weill went through his views of the business and the bright future Hutton would have in the right hands. He knew how to play to his audience.

The cautious Law wanted to avoid being sued, wanted to avoid catastrophes, and wanted to remain a director for the supplement it provided to his income. Dina Merrill wanted the Hutton name carried on. Ed Cazier wanted to help his old friend achieve the vengeance that was his due. And Cazier saw some financial incentives as well. He encouraged Fomon to ask Weill for an investment banking fee—in which Cazier expected to share.

"What do you consider a fair fee?" Weill had asked when the subject came up in a private conversation.

"Three million dollars," Fomon replied.

"Fine."

In articulating his vision of the brokerage business that evening, Weill made it clear that he would not be paying top dollar but intended to do a share swap on something like a one-for-one basis. Hutton's shareholders would receive no premium at all on their badly depressed stock.

Law indicated that he found that a trifle cheap and suggested Weill consider buying a large minority stake, say 25 percent, for cash and perhaps become chairman. Weill indicated politely that this shark was not interested in one bite.

Having supped wonderfully, the three directors excused themselves and went to Fomon's living room to discuss the proposal. It was not a rich bid. But they agreed that nobody had any better ideas. Weill might be their escape hatch.

"We can't say anything definitive," Warren Law told Weill. "But it's not out of reason."

The three said they would take the issue up at the upcoming board meeting, on November 10. Then they descended, well taken care of by their gracious host, to their cars, waiting downstairs.

The pursuit of U.S. West was picking up steam. Ritt and Wilson met with Jack MacAllister, the company's chairman, in New York. He was interested enough to ask them to come out to Denver again. Early on Halloween morning, a Saturday, Ritt, Ed Lill, and Wilson gathered at the small airport in Teterboro, New Jersey, and took off in the Hutton jet at 7:00 A.M. for Denver.

Once they arrived and gathered with MacAllister, Ritt did most of the talking. It was one of Hutton's most serious opportunities to bring in a buyer to ease its growing crisis. The session, however, was a disaster. Ritt launched into a rambling discussion of the future of financial services, the nature of marketing on Wall Street, and the theory behind a retail distribution system.

For his part, MacAllister grew weary of the dialogue. By the time the three executives took off for New York that afternoon at 3:00 P.M., much of U.S. West's excitement had been extinguished.

Ritt also had promised to get together with Phil Purcell of Dean Witter. They had breakfast at the Hotel Dorset, where the two probed each other's financial condition in the wake of the crash. As usual, there was a subtext: Dean Witter was still willing to tango with Hutton.

Ritt prepared several presentations for the November 10 board meeting. First on his list was an update on the firm's financial condition. Ed Lill completed the monthly earnings statement, showing that Hutton had lost $31 million in October. The majority of the loss was accounted for by one problem: a plunge in the value of Vista Chemical's shares. Ironically that investment had been one of Hutton's few bright spots earlier in the year, a crutch that Hutton had leaned on because of its lack of earnings from its main businesses.

The second item was a presentation on what was euphemisti-

cally called "alternative capital choices." The code words meant
that the firm was being shopped.

Finally, Ritt wanted to provide his business plan for the next
year, a familiar litany of layoffs, cutbacks, and expense reductions—
and his contract. One last time he wanted to ask the board to
conclude the negotiations on his own golden parachute.

Sitting in his sunny office, working over the documents, thinking of the future, that was when Ritt got the news. Andre Backar,
an unctuous broker with an unparalleled capacity for claiming
acquaintanceship with nearly every human on earth and a habit of
expressing the deepest affection for everyone he talked to, called
Ritt.

Backar was one of Fomon's old carousing buddies and was
legendary for his ability to procure attractive women for customers
or friends. But he was angry at the former chairman for denying
him the title he had sought for years—executive vice-president.
Now Backar had found his little way of getting even. He told Ritt
about the dinner at Fomon's home with the directors and a potential buyer, which he had learned about through one of the evening's waiters. Backar did not know who the suitor was, but it
hardly mattered. Fomon had won. Ritt took in the information
with his mind in almost total disarray. It was impossible. He didn't
want to believe it. But Backar was insistent. The dinner had taken
place.

Rittereiser fumed. Fomon had done it. That son of a bitch had
gotten those lightweight directors to take his bait, Ritt thought. His
heavy eyebrows sagged as he took on the familiar pained look. The
directors had allowed the old king to stab his successor in the back.

# BURNING

"Bob, as you know, Sandy Weill has an interest in doing something with the company, and some of the directors have met with him," Ed Cazier began.

Forty-one floors above Park Avenue in the Board Room Club, on Monday night, November 9, at a dinner regularly held before board meetings, Bob Rittereiser had barely started into his long-planned agenda when Cazier broke in and destroyed the last shreds of self-denial that Ritt had been clinging to.

"What do you mean, 'as I know'? Because I do not know, and what are you talking about?" Ritt shot back, his temperature rising, his reedy voice getting husky. "What contacts have been made, because I have to tell you there are already rumors out there. I heard them on Friday.

"Peter," Ritt asked pointedly of Ueberroth, "what do you know about this?"

Several of the directors exchanged uncomfortable glances; they had expected Ed Cazier to speak with Ritt before the meeting to let him know about Weill, but Cazier had not had the nerve to face the CEO, just as none of the others had, either. Ueberroth, his face expressionless, said he knew nothing of the contacts. He hated confrontations that might expose his real position.

The directors had lost interest in Ritt's plans, his presentations, and his contract. Just that afternoon Ritt had spent an hour and a half explaining a new compensation system he had worked on for weeks, and now he realized none of the directors had cared or listened. They had not had the courtesy to tell him he was wasting his breath, making a fool of himself by playacting CEO.

Over the uneasy dinner that followed, the board instructed Ritt to contact Sandy Weill to discuss plans for a merger. Hutton made no public disclosure, but there it was. Almost a year to the day since the failed talks with Shearson, the board had decided to sell again.

Early Tuesday morning Ritt walked down to Ken Wilson's office for a talk. Wilson was slightly frightened by Ritt's state. Dark clouds seemed to have gathered in his agitated mind. It seemed as though he were losing his grip. He would suddenly start to babble incoherently on an unrelated subject, then snap back.

Ritt explained the humiliation of the previous evening and eventually agreed with Wilson that, uncomfortable as he might be, he had to grit his teeth and handle himself professionally or risk a disaster far vaster than either of them could imagine. They had to get the firm sold. Ritt took the first step by placing a phone call.

"Sandy, this is Bob Rittereiser," he began.

He told Weill he would like to set up a meeting in a few weeks to discuss the merger proposal. Weill said they had to meet sooner—in fact, immediately. They spoke in Weill's Manhattan apartment that afternoon, held a long session on Friday, and then met at Weill's Connecticut home, with Wilson, on Saturday.

Ritt worked hard at trying to make the process smooth and intelligent, but he could not purge from his deeply usettled mind just why he was speaking to Weill.

"I wish you'd have come to me any way but through Fomon," he kept repeating to Weill. "I think I would have liked you. But with Fomon . . . I just can't get around that."

Ed Lill received an unnerving piece of information on Thursday, November 12. A Standard & Poor's official had called to demand a meeting to review Hutton's financial status. Lill proposed mid-December, when Hutton's plans for 1988 would be nearly completed. The official agreed. However, the next day, Friday the thirteenth, he called again. While Ritt was meeting with Sandy Weill, the S&P official told Lill that the agency's executive committee would not wait. They had to meet on Tuesday. It was obvious that Hutton was about to have its rating cut, and it was equally obvious that the blow could cause the firm's collapse. Hutton had until Tuesday, November 17, to come up with a buyer.

Lill turned to Paul Beehler, head of Hutton's treasury department, and asked him to determine how Hutton would finance itself when the inevitable downgrading came. Beehler did not need to call on his depth of experience to answer. Hutton's crucial commercial paper borrowings would shrink to a maximum of $400 million from the $1.3 billion level prior to the crash, he said. (Salomon Brothers, when it was called in shortly afterward, figured Hutton would be lucky to sell $200 million of commercial paper.) The brokerage house would lose almost all of its short-term financing. Everything would just implode.


Ueberroth had been insistent: Ritt should meet with no one other than Weill, and no investment bankers should be engaged.

By late Saturday, when Ritt concluded the day's conversations with Commercial Credit, he realized that Weill was trying to push a deal through hurriedly with the acquiescence of Hutton's panicky board.

What if Hutton did blow up? If the liquidity squeeze did blossom into a full-fledged emergency, how strongly would his board stand behind him then? Clearly they would run for cover and point their fingers at the CEO. Ritt saw what was coming. If a sale went through, the board would take credit. If the firm collapsed, Ritt would take the fall. It had never been clearer why Ueberroth had refused the chairmanship.

For a change, Ritt made up his mind quickly. Hutton desperately needed the best professional help, no matter what Ueberroth had said. Sunday morning Ritt called John Gutfreund and retained Salomon Brothers. He also called Blackstone and set up a breakfast for Monday morning at the Links Club, an exclusive midtown club, to retain them, too.

• • •

"The company is very liquid," Ed Lill said, explaining Hutton's financial status to Peter Ueberroth and some of the other directors on Monday morning, November 16, the day before the meeting with Standard & Poor's would take place. He added, though, that Hutton was going to have to reduce costs.

The directors wrestled with the meaning of the figures being run past them. Dina Merrill, chatting at one point with Ed Lill and some of his accountants in a conference room, suggested her own solution.

"If it really is such a burden," she wondered, "why don't we just sell the building?"

Lill stifled a smirk and then explained that, even with all the hundreds of millions of dollars Fomon had sunk into the structure, the firm did not own it and thus could not sell it.

Ken Wilson could no longer watch this charade. Hutton was collapsing—the largest collapse of a brokerage firm in Wall Street history—and its chief financial officer was still talking as though the firm needed no more than some fine-tuning.

"Uh, Ed, maybe you should tell them about your discussion with S and P," Wilson said.

"Well," Lill replied, "they did move up their review from January to tomorrow."

"Ed, what do you think that is likely to mean for our rating?" Wilson continued.

"Well, a downgrade is likely."

"What is that going to mean for the firm?" Ueberroth asked, finally catching on.

"Peter, it means you're out of business," Wilson blurted out.

"Ed, is that right?" asked Ueberroth.

"Uh, well, I guess it would make the financing very difficult."

Ueberroth stood up. "We never heard this before. I'm very surprised. Ken, Ed, I think you should leave the room so that we can meet in executive session."

A few minutes later the Hutton executives, along with Ritt, were called back by Ueberroth and the other directors.

"Bob, we're going to be making the decisions now," Ueberroth said.

The de facto chairman of the board had just relieved the CEO of his duties.

It was the grimmest day in Bob Rittereiser's career, perhaps his life. The only thing it lacked was comic relief—but not for long.

That Monday night the Denver Broncos took to the field against the Chicago Bears. Jerry Welsh had chosen that game as the venue for the next big step after Washington, the "relaunch of E. F. Hutton in the marketplace," as he put it. It was so important an occasion that Welsh had a video made and sent to every Hutton branch office beforehand simply to explain to the firm's battered brokers that they were about to rise, Lazarus-like, with his new multimillion-dollar television commercial campaign.

Set to the melodious, chanted tones of the theme song from the movie *The Mission,* the commercial unfolded with its handsomely filmed, snappy visual pacing. It showed Hutton officials getting out of bed, dressing, going to work, talking on the phone. They looked intense, sincere.

It would have been banal were it not for the spiritual strains of music, crisp editing—and finale. Not a word was spoken during the ad, and the Hutton name appeared only fleetingly. As the ad closed, with a rising sun just edging clear of the Empire State Building, some white type flashed starkly against a black background.

"A New Day Has Begun."

"E. F. Hutton. We listen."

It was unorthodox, inspired, farcical. It was the last television ad Hutton ran.

Unbeknownst to the *Monday Night Football* fans, Ed Lill had pulled together a few more relevant bits of information for the board. He was projecting Hutton would lose $100 million in the fourth quarter and, because of the steady collapse of the brokerage house's businesses, another $50 million in January and February, at least.

Hutton had at that time $300 million of capital in excess of the minimum required by the regulators. So those losses would halve the excess to $150 million.

Then there was the deferred compensation. Of the nearly $280 million to be paid out to Hutton's employees in 1988, $180

million would go in early February. That alone would have put
Hutton $30 million below the regulatory capital minimum. The
New York Stock Exchange would have blocked Hutton from pay-
ing out the deferred compensation, triggering a panic.

There was also a tax disaster in store. Connected with the
payment of the deferred compensation was a $140 million tax
credit Hutton had already booked. However, the firm could only
claim the break if it had taxable income—if it made money. That
was now impossible. The result: Hutton would have had to reverse
the $140 million benefit. It would have turned into a $140 million
bite out of the remaining capital.

Ueberroth met shortly afterward with the Salomon and Blackstone investment bankers and made clear that he, not Hutton's
CEO, was calling the shots. He instructed them to contact only
non–brokerage industry buyers, such as insurance companies, industrial companies with financial arms, or foreign firms. A nonin-
dustry buyer would be less likely to initiate massive layoffs and just
might keep Hutton's board more or less intact.

It was not difficult for the advisers to draw up the list of candidates, which they then split up. Jack Welsh, General Electric's
chief executive, gave his visitors precisely fifteen minutes, during
which he listened politely, thanked them for coming, and whisked
them out again. The Hutton officials did not know it, but GE was
trying to unload Kidder; efforts to sell a large minority stake to
Nomura Securities of Japan had fallen apart after the crash, to GE's
great disappointment.

Equitable Life was also more of a seller of its own brokerage
unit, Donaldson, Lufkin & Jenrette, than a buyer. General Motors,
Ford, and Chrysler, all of whom had large financial subsidiaries,
expressed no interest. Japan's so-called Big Four securities firms
said they would pass. Sumitomo Life, which had spent the past year
trying to make a large strategic investment in Hutton, said that it
could not move as fast as the situation required. Xerox, which also
had a growing financial services arm, did not nibble.

While the investment bankers made a serious effort to interest
these potential buyers, it was clear to them that this was a side-
show. It was just a matter of time, perhaps days, before Hutton's
board faced up to the obvious: the only real buyer was Shearson
Lehman.

Shearson was the only firm with the experience to conclude a deal quickly enough to save Hutton. Shearson would lay off thousands of Hutton's employees, but by doing so it would generate enormous cost savings. That would allow it to pay a higher price than most others. Also, Peter Cohen was known to be hungry for the deal. It was a unique opportunity for Shearson to challenge Merrill Lynch as the largest retail brokerage house.

Two of Peter Cohen's best friends were Tom Strauss, Salomon Brothers' president, and Lee Kimmell, head of Salomon's financial institutions group and a key Hutton adviser. Thus it was no surprise that Cohen knew precisely what was happening. He waited patiently, secure in the knowledge that his phone would ring soon with the expected news.

There was more depressing news in store for Hutton's advisers, though. Throughout that week they had their analysts combing through the firm's financial records and balance sheet. Before long they began locating the horrors tucked into every nook and cranny.

Blackstone and Salomon Brothers figured that, with the deferred compensation and tax problems, the bulging load of litigation over the tax shelters, the albatross of a headquarters, the overvaluation of numerous Hutton investments, and other problems, Hutton's net worth was about half of its stated value of $26 a share, probably less. And the figure was deteriorating by the day.

The first job was to buy some time to doll up the corpse. They had to stop the rating agencies from hitting the alarm button. Salomon handled that task, informing Standard & Poor's just before the Tuesday deadline that an extraordinary transaction was in store that would benefit Hutton's rating. It was a clear signal that a sale was under way. S&P agreed to a postponement.

Sandy Weill, who had retained Morgan Stanley as his investment banker, had continued his conversations with Hutton's directors and executives. But it was clear that his chances of stealing the company at a bargain price were diminishing with some clearheaded advisers involved.

The investment bankers wanted to bring the discussions with Weill to a head so that he would have to put up a real bid or drop out. But they could take no steps without Ueberroth. The commissioner of baseball was in Ann Arbor, Michigan, on Saturday, watching Ohio State eke out a come-from-behind victory over Michigan in an annual college football ritual. He returned on Sunday, November 22, to meet with Weill.

Ueberroth was optimistic. He told the investment bankers that there just might be a signed agreement by the time they went to bed Sunday. Weill came in with his team early Sunday evening and was immediately pressed by Ueberroth to name his price. Weill refused to be pinned down. He wanted to enter a negotiation process in which he would lock Hutton up but could still leave his bid contingent on what he found Hutton's real worth to be. This was a tough negotiating tango with neither side willing to budge.

Weill and his team were then allowed to sit down with several of Hutton's accountants and review the firm's balance sheet. It was the first time that Weill was given a real peek at Hutton's mountain of problems.

"What kind of bid will you make?" Ueberroth asked Weill.

"I've just had one hour," Weill said plaintively. "I don't have a bid."

But he went on to outline a very tentative deal, with lots of contingencies, that would involve an exchange of securities. Ueberroth then excused Weill and sat down with Hutton's investment bankers. They flatly rejected the offer as worth only about $18 a share.

Cazier exploded in anger. He characterized the investment bankers as unduly negative and insisted the contingencies in Weill's proposals did not necessarily mean his price would drop. The investment bankers resisted rolling their eyes at what they considered Cazier's self-interest and naïveté.

The advisers stood their ground. Weill was out.

"Okay," Ueberroth asked his advisers just before midnight Sunday. "What's the next step?"


Starting at 8:00 P.M. Monday morning, a week after Jerry Welsh's "New Day" had begun, it ended. Bob Rittereiser began making the calls. First was Peter Cohen at Shearson. Next he phoned Dan Tully, his former rival and now president of Merrill Lynch, Phil Purcell of Dean Witter, and Fred Joseph of Drexel.

When word got out that the firm was on the block, the real crisis would begin. People would stop working. Brokers would jump ship to avoid the uncertainty. If a deal were not completed in a matter of days, there would be nothing left to sell. The move was risky but unavoidable. One way or another Hutton's independence would end.

Following Ueberroth's instructions, Ritt made a straightforward pitch. He informed the other brokerage houses that E. F. Hutton would be sold in a kind of auction. Those interested in bidding would receive a packet of information about Hutton's finances and would be given access to all of Hutton's records. Bids would be due at noon the following Tuesday, December 1.

Shortly afterward Quadrex Securities, a financial concern involved principally in the foreign exchange business, expressed some interest in bidding. Quadrex took one look and fled.

Later Monday morning, Hutton's public relations department issued one of its last releases. In an effort to save face, the statement said that Hutton had been contacted by several buyers and that it had instructed its financial advisers to pursue discussions for a capital injection or a sale. It was a transparent notice of sale. Fomon heard the news with a combination of satisfaction and frustration. The $3 million fee had just slipped through his fingers, but he had realized his first aim.

As expected, Hutton completely seized up. Brokers stopped working, updated their résumés, and swapped rumors about who would buy Hutton. The firm was dead in the water.

Shearson's acquisition machine instantly snapped into gear. Peter Cohen mobilized dozens of professionals to examine everything from Hutton's mounting legal liabilities and the expense of its headquarters to the value of its investments and the productivity of its brokers. He also had his firm issue an announcement of Shearson's keen interest in Hutton. It was a preemptive shot to let any competitors know that Shearson wanted this one badly. The battle of perceptions had begun.

There were two unalterable facts that Hutton's advisers had to face. The first was that Shearson was going to win the bidding. The second was that if Shearson knew that from the start, and did not feel the spur of competition, it would underpay.

The whole point now was to get top dollar for Hutton's shareholders, by whatever ruse or stratagem the advisers could muster. Somehow they had to manufacture the appearance of a horse race.

CHAPTER

# 24

## A SIXTEEN

Disaster struck at 11:30 A.M., Saturday morning, November 28.

Ken Wilson and Rich Carbone had spent the morning preparing for a crucial meeting with Dean Witter's executives. Dean Witter, like the other prospective bidders, had been scouring Hutton's internal records to determine what it was willing to pay. But Hutton's headquarters tower was eerily quiet. The bankers were not showing up.

Wilson nervously tried to track down a Dean Witter investment banker.

"Bill, what's going on? Where are your people? We've got everything together," Wilson said after finding him at home.

"Haven't you talked to Ueberroth?"

"No. What's the story?"

"I shouldn't talk about it. I really think you should speak with Ueberroth."

"Hey, come on," Wilson pleaded. "What is going on? Don't just leave me swinging here."

The investment banker then told him what Ueberroth had not. Phil Purcell had been in touch with the executives at Sears, Dean Witter's owner, and they had decided that Dean Witter would not participate in an auction. Auctions are usually held for hard assets, not for something as intangible as a services business. In addition, the Sears officials were concerned about the haste. If there were deeper problems locked away at Hutton, there would not be enough time to root them out and reduce their bid accordingly.

Wilson was stunned. Shearson had also expressed some misgivings over the auction idea. Suddenly there was a prospect that nobody would show up on Tuesday. Merrill Lynch was technically a bidder, but it too had made its lack of enthusiasm clear. The whole process was collapsing.

Wilson phoned Ueberroth at his Manhattan home.

"Peter, we're in deep trouble."

"What do you mean?"

"This thing may not work," Wilson said. "I heard about Dean Witter."

Ueberroth described, unemotionally, his conversation with Purcell the previous evening—probably the most important exchange in the sale process. It was a depressing shock for Wilson. Wilson insisted that Ueberroth had to get Dean Witter to at least appear to be a bidder. Otherwise Cohen would sit back, wait until Hutton was screaming for help, and walk away with the prize for nothing.

"Phil, we may not have the auction," Ueberroth told Purcell later that day. He suggested that if a quiet negotiation was what Purcell wanted, Hutton might agree because it liked Dean Witter's style.

Ritt pumped Purcell also. He insisted that Hutton's brokers and executives seemed much more compatible with Dean Witter's officials. Ritt also argued that Hutton's sale represented Dean Witter's last chance to buy its way into the top echelon of the brokerage business. There were no other Huttons out there to be acquired.

There was one other point that Ritt hinted at: if Dean Witter just appeared to be stepping up to the plate, it would make the acquisition a lot more expensive for Shearson. True, Dean Witter would lose the prize, but Shearson, a major competitor, would pay dearly. It might even be crippled. Purcell caught on immediately. He called back later to say that Dean Witter would not submit a formal bid by the Tuesday noon deadline, but it would stand ready to enter an exclusive negotiation if Hutton decided to drop the auction ruse. More important, the Hutton officials managed to set up a meeting on Monday, for lunch, between Hutton's management committee and Dean Witter's. It would be a big lunch at Hutton's offices, where lots of people—including Shearson's spies—would be able to see that Dean Witter was still in the game.

Hutton's advisers were convinced by that time that one of Hutton's top executives was a mole for Shearson. (Several Hutton advisers insisted it had been Jerry Miller, but Miller denied it.) So they decided to use this channel to deliver the message to Shearson that the race was still on. It worked like a charm.

That was just one of several forms of espionage employed in the attempt to convince Shearson that it could not steal Hutton. Separate "data rooms," for instance, had been set up at Hutton's headquarters for prospective bidders to peruse Hutton's confidential records. The rooms were set up within sight of each other so that each bidder would be able to see its rivals.

Shearson's investment bankers employed their own cloak-and-dagger techniques. They probed sources all across Wall Street to assess how serious Dean Witter and Merrill Lynch were. Shearson's people secretly rifled through the Hutton building's sign-in book over the Thanksgiving break to see who was entering and leaving.

"There's potential here for a helluva bluff," Cohen told his team.

He was right. Merrill had no interest in buying Hutton's problems. Joe Grano, head of Merrill's retail sales force, took a look at the liabilities and figured Hutton was worth half its stated book value, or about $400 million. That came to approximately $12 a share.

Even after Dean Witter had been persuaded to keep its hat in the ring, there was little cheer at Hutton or among its advisers. The field consisted of one real bidder, which knew it had little competition, and two decoys.

(Not unexpectedly, Dan Tully of Merrill Lynch called Ritt on Monday evening and told him Merrill would not be sending over an envelope on Tuesday.)

Peter Cohen had spent Thanksgiving at Greenbrier, the exclusive West Virginia resort, where he had rented two bungalows for a large family gathering. He spent much of the time racing from floor to floor, room to room, to field calls on the half-dozen telephones there from his staff in New York. Cohen flew back early Sunday and found crowds of staffers awaiting him. They all tried to look busy, but many of them were there just to witness firsthand the triumph. There was an expectant, excited air at Shearson's lower Manhattan headquarters.

Cohen was brimming with self-confidence. Shearson knew more about the collapsing firm, he was convinced, than either Hutton's inept board of directors or the firm's advisers. After spending the afternoon pulling together the results from each of his separate teams, Peter Cohen spoke to Lee Kimmell, the Salomon investment banker, and tried to muscle him to end the competition. Cohen was still trying to angle for every possible advantage in the contest.

"You're making a big mistake with this auction," Cohen told his friend. "There are big problems at that company you don't even know about.

"Your real nightmare is that nobody shows up," Cohen concluded, trying to drive in his psychological knife a little deeper. He then proposed that Ueberroth sit down and simply hammer out a deal with Shearson and forget the auction. Despite its professed love of free markets, Wall Street hates nothing more than genuine competition. Cohen, like Weill and Purcell, was trying to eliminate it now.

Kimmell called back and proposed that Cohen meet with Ueberroth that evening. Cohen said it could not be done Sunday: it was his anniversary, and he and his wife planned to take their kids to a Japanese restaurant for dinner. The meeting was set for Monday morning, 7:30 A.M., at the office of Shearson's outside law firm, Willkie, Farr & Gallagher.

When the two sides gathered, several of Hutton's advisers complained bitterly. They were sure that Cohen was laying some sort of trap for Ueberroth that would compromise Hutton's already weak negotiating position. Ueberroth prided himself on his great negotiating skills. But, the advisers knew, he had never faced a room full of investment bankers. They insisted that Ueberroth keep his advisers at his side, but Ueberroth infuriated them by saying he would handle Cohen alone.

Even before the meeting with Cohen began, Ueberroth shocked his advisers; he kicked off the discussion by offering Shearson a $45 million break.

He said that the board had already decided that it would not declare the sale a legal "change of control" for the purposes of Hutton's employee stock award plan. Thus, 1.6 million shares held by Hutton officials under the plan, but not yet distributed, would not become effective. Those awards had been made to keep edgy Hutton brokers and executives at the firm when its problems began to surface in 1985. Now that the plan had served its purpose, Ueberroth was pulling the plug. It was, from Shearson's perspective, an auspicious beginning.

Cohen still angled for all the leverage he could get. Again he ran through the lengthy list of problems Shearson had found. He ended by saying Shearson would pay $18 in cash per share and some securities that would raise the consideration to about $21 or $22 a share. Ueberroth did not seem enthusiastic.

As the discussion continued, Cohen indicated that, if Hutton were willing to sign an agreement quickly, the price would go to $25 a share in cash, or a total of $825 million for Hutton's approximately 33 million shares.

Purcell had already indicated privately to Ueberroth that Dean Witter would offer less than that—way less. Purcell believed the firm was so damaged that Dean Witter's offer would come to less than $15 per share.

"They have totally lost their way," Purcell told the other members of his team, somewhat incredulous at what he'd found at Hutton. "This company is profit-proof."

After Cohen put his proposal on the table, Ueberroth huddled with his advisers, came back, and said the bid was not preemptive. The mating dance was in full swing.


At a quarter to twelve on Tuesday, December 1, Cohen told his assistant, Andrea Furace, to make the delivery and get a receipt. Furace had been sitting in a car parked in front of the soaring columns of Hutton's headquarters, chatting on a cellular telephone.

Minutes later Cohen received a call from Kimmell and Pete Peterson. They proposed that Cohen make another preemptive offer for the company.

"You haven't even looked at our envelope yet," Cohen complained.

"We didn't know you delivered one," came the reply.

"Get it, read it, and then call me," Cohen said, bursting with confidence.

A few minutes later Kimmell called Cohen again. "Okay, Peter, what do you want to do?"

"Let's finish this thing," Cohen said.

For the rest of the afternoon Hutton dangled before Cohen the prospect of a signed agreement without going back to Dean Witter. That was the last inducement Hutton could apply. It was out of tricks.

Cohen, still nervously looking over his shoulder, nudged the $25 figure up to $28 and then, finally, to $29.25 a share, a total of $965 million. Of that amount, $25 would be paid in cash and the remainder in Shearson preferred stock. Shearson did not know it yet, but it was offering more than twice the price of the number-two bidder. Cohen had been bluffed, to the tune of nearly $500 million. The prospect of being chairman of the firm that was about to overtake Merrill Lynch was too juicy to pass up.

Hammering out the final details was a slow and nerve-racking process, since things could still collapse at any moment. But there was one light, if strange, moment. Around midday Tuesday Ueberroth was informed that there was another bidder urgently trying to reach him. In fact, the bidder was in the lobby of the building. Ueberroth thought someone was playing a practical joke when he was given the bidder's identity.

It was John Latshaw, the former head of Hutton's central region, whose branches were heavily implicated in the overdrafting scandal. Ueberroth agreed to speak to him and was told that Latshaw and Perry Bacon, author of the "smoking gun" memo on the overdrafting, wanted to buy Hutton with an investment group. The two of them were running a small regional brokerage house, B. C. Christopher, in Kansas City. They had bought a large amount of Hutton stock when its price plummeted after the crash and had, they claimed, lined up financing to buy a lot more. And they had an idea of how they would manage the firm: they had invited John Shad, Fomon's old nemesis, former SEC chairman and now ambassador to the Netherlands, to become chief executive.

Ueberroth could hardly believe what he was hearing. The irony was so painfully obvious that he continued to think it a hoax. Latshaw and Bacon insisted they were serious. The proposal, however, was considered far too tentative to be pursued.

The incident leavened an otherwise tense day. At one point Cohen threatened to leave the talks if Hutton's advisers continued to push for more cash in Shearson's offer. At another point Cohen proposed lifting his offer if Hutton's directors would forgo their own golden parachutes. A Hutton lawyer exploded in anger at the suggestion, and it was dropped.

Finally, at 8:00 P.M., the two sides shook hands. They walked up the grand staircase to the empty executive dining room, where they toasted the deal with glasses of New York State champagne. Phil Purcell received a courtesy call at 9:10 P.M. with the news.

It would be another twenty-four hours before the lawyers completed the documents, and there would be more disputes over technical details. But that clinking of glasses in Fomon's palace sealed Hutton's sale. Bob Rittereiser watched in uncharacteristic silence as the throne was snatched away from him for good. Bob Fomon was absent, but in a way he was still in charge. A satisfied Fomon received congratulatory calls from a few friends.

Peter Cohen and Jeff Lane arrived on Wednesday afternoon to speak to the Hutton board. Not knowing by how much they had overpaid, they were ebullient. Cohen had won, and that meant a great deal to him—especially since he had bested his old mentor, Sandy Weill. Cohen expressed his pride in the deal and told Hutton's directors about Shearson's history of growth and success. Only two directors had much to say.

Dina Merrill asked whether the Hutton name would be preserved. Cohen refused to make a commitment, saying that he would only decide after a series of marketing surveys had been completed.

Ed Cazier also spoke up, but in private. He buttonholed Cohen after the meeting and pressed him about giving board seats to himself and some of the others. Cohen did not beat around the bush. He said only one person would move to Shearson's board, Dina Merrill. She would be the link to the glorious Hutton tradition, something Cohen was eager to preserve and pass on to his own brokers. He also refused to make any special payments to

Cazier beyond those he was entitled to under the board's retirement plan.

The next day Ritt spoke over Profit Line to provide details on the deal, which had already been reported in the papers. It was a combination farewell speech and question-and-answer session over the two-way communications system.

For a change, Ritt was brief. He ached inside, but he struggled to maintain his solid facade for just a few more days. He thanked everyone for their professionalism, in spite of the fact that more than a hundred Hutton brokers had bailed out already and that those who remained had done nothing for the past two weeks. He told them that this was a good deal for them, pointing out that the deferred compensation had been saved.

Ritt spoke of how difficult the process had been on himself and Hutton's other senior executives. He also admitted his disappointment that the firm had not been able to push on independently. But, he insisted, Hutton had gotten the best it could under the circumstances.

"How do you think you performed, you yourself?" one broker asked over the system.

"On a scale of one to ten," Ritt replied, "I'd give myself a sixteen. There's no question this was an incredibly difficult process, and we got a good deal for the firm and the employees."

That was all Hutton's proud, shattered, vengeful troops needed to hear. They refused to believe they had anything to do with this finale. Now they had found their scapegoat. Fomon, more responsible than anyone for Hutton's humiliating demise, had deftly stepped out of harm's way. He was in Palm Beach, planning construction of a new home. He had left Rittereiser as the focus for the brokers' anger.

"You asshole!" one broker screamed. "You sold us out."

"I hope you're golden parachute doesn't open," bellowed another.

"Great job, real great job, you fucking lightweight."

Ritt's eyebrows sagged, and his face blanched. His watery eyes filled. Profound, shattering pain was etched into his jowly, round, ashen face. Ken Wilson, sitting next to him, could not bear to look at this image of ruin.

"It was one of the most humiliating experiences of my life," said Wilson. "There was such a sense that you had failed."

# EPILOGUE

The sale was completed. Hutton was gone. But the Hutton spirit was not vanquished so easily, at least among its top brokers. Convinced that their old tactics of wresting big payouts by threatening to walk out would work on the new owners, they tried to secure favored positions at the new brokerage house. Cohen had already decided he would not give the Directors Advisory Council members anything special, but he tried to be diplomatic. A dinner was set up for December 14 at Shearson's headquarters to create the impression that the firm was willing to listen.

The air crackled with tension before the group even sat down with Cohen, Jeff Lane, and a handful of other top Shearson executives. Jerry Miller, who dreaded the confrontation that was building, was drinking heavily. He knew there was likely to be an embarrassing scene as the old Hutton confronted the real world.

As the evening unfolded and the drinks were followed by plenty of good food and wine, several of the brokers spoke and made it clear they wanted better financial deals to stay. Then Bruce Tuthill, a Boston-based broker who was a leader of the group, stood to speak.

"I want to thank you," he began, shocking his colleagues, who expected him to take an aggressive stand. "You saved the jobs of two-thirds of the people with the firm, you saved my customers, and you saved Wall Street the embarrassment of a major firm going under.

"And thank you," he added, "for helping me have dinner with the presidents of four Wall Street firms in the past week, because the recruiting is really heavy." It was Tuthill's way of letting them know that he would not play the game. He was leaving and would not bluff his way into a better deal.

When another DAC member reacted angrily afterward, Tuthill shot back, "Dammit, it's over. Don't you fucking get it? O-V-E-R."


Any lingering doubts that things had indeed changed ended the next day at 2 P.M. Tom Stiles, head of Hutton's equity department, received a fax from Shearson's headquarters. It was a list of about 400 names with instructions that the people were to be dismissed and cleared from the building—immediately.

Mark Kessenich had gotten a similar fax. He was to lay off more than 200 people. Ken Wilson's investment banking staff had all been classified, like camp prisoners. "A" meant they had jobs, "B" meant they could remain temporarily, and "C" meant they were out. There were lots of C's. A total of nearly 1,500 people were laid off summarily that day. People who had spent their careers being told they were the best were now being handled with undisguised contempt.

Stiles had not taken any time off since the trauma of the crash and was physically and emotionally drained. But he had to hold on a while longer. He gathered the 400 people in an auditorium and explained the situation as calmly as he could. He said he would do everything possible to help them find new jobs and encouraged them to work on their resumes rather than wallow in bitterness. He spoke to an audience that barely understood what was happening.

Hutton's headquarters was like a morgue where the well-dressed corpses walked. Many greeted the news with blank stares; it was just not conceivable that they could be dismissed summarily, less than two weeks before Christmas, and then thrown out of the building. There was no appeal, nowhere to turn.

Men in their natty navy blue suits and yellow foulard ties and women in high heels and silky blouses with flouncy bows cried openly at their desks as they threw their belongings into the cardboard boxes hastily made available, little coffins into which the remains of their careers were to be stuffed.

Some had gotten drunk and tried in vain to incite their traumatized colleagues to acts of collective vandalism. People felt and looked ridiculous. E.F. Hutton was dying with a humiliating whimper, its death throes an unattractive blend of self-pity, intoxication, and denial. Beneath the glimmering gold mosaic ceiling of the lobby, several dozen uniformed Shearson guards rushed to the building, inspected every box going in or out, and confiscated company property. Heated arguments sprang up as outraged former staff members struggled, with no success, to leave the building with their dignity. It was as though the guards were confiscating that, too.

The next day Tom Stiles came in, still in a daze, and surveyed the rows of emptied desks. He hurt physically and emotionally. In fact, by noon he felt terrible pangs in his chest. His arms tingled. He pushed on before it dawned on him that he might be dying from a heart attack. He had all the classic symptoms. He raced to the hospital and found that his blood pressure had soared to an almost deadly level. It turned out to be stress, just stress.


Peter Ueberroth and his fellow directors had some pressing final work to do.

As promised, they voted that the sale to Shearson was not a legal "change of control" for the purposes of the employee stock plan, depriving several hundred Hutton officials, top brokers and executives of about $45 million in stock they had been promised.

The directors were determined not to leave empty-handed themselves, however. As agreed on privately beforehand, they deemed that the takeover was a change of control for just 480,000 shares in the plan, shares belonging to a coterie of senior executives. Among them, Ritt held 50,000 shares, Jerry Miller 40,000 shares, Dick Locke 20,000 shares, Steve Friedman 20,000 shares, Ed Lill 20,000 shares, and Jerry Welsh 30,000 shares. Lawsuits soon followed from disgruntled shareholders and employees, but this was within the board's rights.

There was more. The board voted that the sale was a change of control for their own retirement plan. That assured they would be paid handsomely for their stewardship of the good name of E.F. Hutton.

Cazier received $420,000; Ueberroth $420,000; Law $370,-000; Merrill $307,500; Milliken $295,000; Yasuda $245,000; and Talbot, who had been on the board less than six months, $135,000. Ueberroth had placed a special call to Ed Lill to make sure that Talbot was not left out.

Peter Ueberroth also persuaded the other directors that he ought to receive an extra payment for his extraordinary service. The compliant directors voted to provide him with another $1 million. Shearson balked, so the figure was held to $500,000. The board met and passed the measure on Tuesday, January 19. Bob Rittereiser, although still a director, was not told of or invited to the meeting.

Blackstone and Salomon Brothers were paid $3.35 million each for advising Hutton's board.

Hutton's last press release was issued on January 15, 1988. It reported that the firm had lost a total of $112.7 million in October and November.


Delighted with his victory, Peter Cohen and the other top Shearson managers tried to look ahead, to getting their retail machine humming and surpassing Merrill Lynch once and for all. Eager to tap the principal asset of their acquisition, they quickly appropriated its name. The new firm was to be called Shearson Lehman Hutton. Not surprisingly, more than a third of Hutton's brokers had quit for higher paying jobs elsewhere, many of them at Dean Witter and George Ball's deeply troubled Prudential-Bache. A total of about 8,000 of Hutton's 18,000 employees were dismissed. But that was only slightly worse than expected.

Slowly, however, some bugs began to pop up in Shearson's money machine. First there were unanticipated legal problems. Two brokers in Hutton's Providence, Rhode Island, office had earlier been charged with laundering money for organized crime figures. Now one pleaded guilty and was handed a 3-month sentence. During the investigation, the government discovered a Hutton connection to a notorious call-girl ring in Providence that had involved several Brown University coeds. Two Hutton brokers had entertained their customers by setting them up with the women, the investigators found.

In May 1988, Shearson was forced to pay a $1 million fine and plead guilty to three felonies related to the money laundering. That meant more negative headlines. Shearson also disclosed that the United States Attorney in Manhattan was investigating what appeared to be widespread money laundering in a number of Hutton's New York branch offices.

The lawsuits surrounding the Famco and George Aubin matters and the tax shelter disasters also droned on, and on. Shearson poured more than $10 million each into the Aubin and Famco cases, while recovering nothing. Don Sanders and his partner, John Mundy, pressed a suit against Shearson, claiming they were owed some $4 million in commissions on Aubin's account. Through arbitration, they received several million dollars. The acquisition was turning into a financial black hole. Hutton's top executives were slowly shunted aside. All that seemed to remain of Hutton was its curse.

Within two years of the completion of the deal, Shearson was suffering from a massive capital shortage. A major part of the problem was the total write-off of Hutton; Shearson, in fact, had taken $1.4 billion of charges and write-offs for the Hutton mess, significantly more than what it had paid. In 1989, a year after the acquisition, Shearson reported another $165 million in charges due to the Hutton acquisition. In the first quarter of 1990 the hemorrhaging grew worse, as Shearson reported an unprecedented $915 million loss and was forced into a hasty and drastic reorganization to stay afloat.

In a replay of Hutton's collapse, Shearson started getting nervous calls from the rating agencies. Frantically, it first announced a plan to raise $900 million to bolster its weakened balance sheet. In the documents for the recapitalization, Shearson also disclosed tens of millions of dollars of losses it was suffering from Hutton's and its own failed tax shelter programs.

Then the recapitalization fell apart as it became clear that Shearson would not be able to sell the securities at reasonable prices. American Express had to step in and do something it dreaded, acquire all of Shearson Lehman. It was forced to pump in $1.15 billion to keep Shearson from sinking. Finally, Peter Cohen lost his job in a bitter row with Jim Robinson, once one of his greatest fans. The Hutton disaster, along with the public relations debacle of Shearson's failed effort to participate in the leveraged buyout of R.J.R. Nabisco, had ended his career there. Cohen was eventually granted a severance package worth about $10 million. Shearson was quickly broken apart into an investment bank, to be called Lehman Brothers, and a retail brokerage, which would keep the Shearson name. No one even questioned the conspicuous omission—the Hutton name was killed for good.

"In hindsight," said Jim Robinson, the American Express chairman, "knowing what we know, we probably wouldn't have done the Hutton deal."


Ritt, Lill, and a few others remained in their 28th floor offices after the sale, working with Shearson on the transition. Lill's golden parachute opened, as did those of Wilson, Welsh, Friedman, and Kessenich. They walked away with millions of dollars, as did the several dozen people they had hired in Hutton's final year. Lill went back to his old job at Deloitte Haskins & Sells, the accounting firm, richer by far. Ken Wilson bought a big new house in Westchester County and formed Ranieri, Wilson & Co. with Lew Ranieri, the former vice-chairman of Salomon Brothers, to buy thrift institutions and advise financial institutions. A year later they had split, and Wilson joined Lazard Frères & Co., largely to advise financial institutions in trouble. Jerry Welsh formed a marketing consulting firm and hired Pam O'Neill, Fomon's old girlfriend and the secretary who discovered the incriminating overdrafting memos. Steve Friedman became general counsel at Equitable Life, still far from his ambition to run a major financial institution. Mark Kessenich split off with the same group he had brought to Hutton from Citibank and formed Eastbridge Capital, an old-fashioned bond-trading firm funded by a Japanese bank.

Jim Lopp, Fomon's old crony, continued to run Financial Security Assurance, the bond insurance firm Hutton had formed for him in 1985. In 1989 it was acquired for $345 million by U.S. West, still eager to gain a toehold in the financial services business. Scott

Pierce found a senior-level job at a unit of Prudential Insurance, with some help from George Ball. After a hiatus, John Shad reappeared on Wall Street. He left the Securities and Exchange Commission in mid-1987 to become ambassador to the Netherlands, and then surprised many when he accepted the job as chairman of the embattled Drexel Burnham Lambert in April 1989. Drexel had just settled landmark charges of serious securities law violations. The move reunited Shad with his old protégé, Fred Joseph, Drexel's chief executive, and a number of investment bankers who had left Hutton for Drexel in 1984. But Shad's tenure was brief: Drexel departed with a bang, filing for bankruptcy on February 13, 1990, as its financing dried up.

Peter Ueberroth collected his checks from Hutton's new owner, left the Baseball Commissioner's office, and looked for new heights to scale.

Shortly afterward Ueberroth showed up with his friend Tom Talbot, as participants in a group bidding for Eastern Airlines. They eventually lost the takeover battle, but returned later in 1989 to acquire troubled Hawaiian Airlines, bringing Ueberroth back to his travel industry roots.

Unlike those he had hired, Ritt had no contract and thus no guarantee of anything. Even so, Shearson agreed to pay him his 1987 salary during 1988 and 1989, $1.2 million a year.

It was ghostly quiet, but there were a few new occupants on the opulent 28th floor of Hutton's headquarters. As soon as the sale was announced Ritt received a number of death threats and Shearson provided him with a 24-hour guard. While Ritt spent Christmas with his family at home in New Jersey, trying to create some seasonal cheer, three beefy bodyguards sat in his driveway, sipping coffee in their cars, trying to stay warm and watching out for the furious former brokers who swore they would kill the firm's last CEO.

One look at Ritt might have discouraged any would-be assassin, however. His fragile emotional state frightened many of those who still worked with him. Many were convinced he had suffered some sort of breakdown.

On a bitterly cold day in early January 1988, I met Ritt for the first time since the takeover to discuss what had happened. I had waited in the empty 28th floor lobby on a peach-hued couch for fifteen minutes. The walls had been stripped of art and some of the hooks held battered 8 by 10 photos of Ritt that some employees had slashed. After twenty minutes, a shell of a man greeted me. Ritt's face was an unearthly flat white. His fleshy jowls hung loose. His gray-flecked hair looked as though it had been dusted with ashes. His slate gray eyes, rimmed with red, flashed wildly.

From his handsome, spacious office Ritt looked out on a world of snow and frozen steel. All around, Hutton's overwrought headquarters tower was eerily still. Sunlight spilled into empty offices, throwing highlights on the shiny tufted green leather chairs and mahogany desks. The hundreds of brand-new telephones were silent. There was no sound except for the tale Ritt was relating, for the first time, of how E.F. Hutton was destroyed.

Ritt's sentences flowed out in a rush, then grew less and less coherent. He twisted on his chair and eventually jumped to his feet, pacing around the office. He stared into space at times, his mouth hanging open; then he grew violent recalling how he had failed to overcome the evil.

Ritt did not speak; he howled into the storm that raged inside him. Unspeakable things were tearing at him in that sad setting, which he would occupy in his loneliness for more than a year, returning week after week to rule over nothing, as though he still had not digested just who had won the elemental battle.

He would accept his checks from Shearson and burn over the past. Slowly, however, he began to look ahead and, eventually, with his brother, Fred, and another investor, he bought a small chemical company near his home in New Jersey. Called Hancock Research and Development, its principal product was a fire-resistant fabric that, when burned, produced no poisonous smoke.

"There's a chance I'll go back into the securities business," he said. "I still think I know what needs to be done in the long run. What I'm not going to do is go into the wrong situation."


Fomon's tan deepened after the sale, as he spent most of his time looking after the construction of a new house in Palm Beach. He spoke with the ease of a man fulfilled. Shearson struggled to find a loophole in his golden parachute. There were none, and the money was eventually sent. In addition, Fomon's timely sales of

Hutton stock and his options trading netted him close to $1 million more for his stock than he would have earned had he waited for Shearson's $29.25 a share. He never received the $3 million fee Sandy Weill had promised, but then he won ample psychic compensation, the kind of reward money cannot buy.

He entertained me at his New York apartment and spoke for hours about anything and everything. With the noise of the city just a dim, organlike note in the background, Fomon stopped at a window to admire the magnolia trees in the garden of the Frick mansion across the street and wondered out loud why he could not find the same type for his new Palm Beach home.

On another day, he sauntered into his Park Avenue office—rented from Kutak Rock & Campbell, a couple of floors from both Jim Lopp and Peter Ueberroth—and stopped at his secretary's desk, demanding a clip from a morning tabloid.

"I don't care about these damn things," Fomon said as he perused the gossip column hungrily and then pressed it on me.

The article described Fomon as one of the "most noticeable romantics" at a party in Bridgehampton thrown by David Mahoney, well known on Wall Street as recipient of one of the corporate world's largest-ever golden parachutes, about $18 million, when he forced the sale of the company he'd once run, Norton Simon. Fomon's affections were being lavished on a woman who, the columnist reminded his readers, had won a social Oscar just months earlier for Best Divorce. They were married—Fomon's third time—a year later.

Fomon also bragged about the quality investments his new firm, Robert M. Fomon & Company, was making. He had always insisted he had a special knack for two things: picking people and making deals. He now admitted with some enthusiasm that he had blown it in picking Ritt, but he maintained that his nose for a good investment was as sharp as ever. In its first big foray into the deal-making arena, Fomon's little firm did a leveraged buyout of Cuisinarts Inc., the manufacturer of home food-processing machines. A little over a year later, on August 2, 1989, Cuisinarts filed for bankruptcy.

Fomon kept almost no personal mementos from his Hutton days. One of the few items in his New York apartment recalling his tenure at the brokerage house was the framed photo taken of him and Rittereiser in Houston in early 1986, Fomon sitting atop the bull and Ritt, smiling, standing alongside.

Fomon did, however, try to save one meaningful item. After the sale, he called Ritt and asked if he would arrange to have an oil portrait of Edward F. Hutton in the firm's offices sent to Fomon's apartment. Ritt passed the request to Shearson. When Fomon was asked if he had proof that the painting was his, Fomon said that Marjorie Merriweather Post, Ed Hutton's second wife, had offered it to him. Fomon was pressed to provide some documentation of the transfer. Shearson never heard from him again on the matter.

Instead, Shearson chose to give Dina Merrill the painting at her first Shearson board meeting, a symbolic gesture honoring the firm's pedigree. A year later Shearson was struggling for its life. In fact, Merrill Lynch, whom Hutton and then Shearson had been chasing, would also be sinking into the expense mire. Merrill announced a $470 million write-off at the end of 1989 to cover the costs of a reorganization. Prudential-Bache was struggling and losing executives. Kidder Peabody had to be saved by its owner, General Electric. Drexel Burnham Lambert sold off its retail business, then went bankrupt after years of pressure from the insider-trading scandal. The economics that had helped kill off Hutton were taking their toll on the other major retail firms.

In the spring of 1989, a group of former Hutton officials threw a big reunion party. They rented the *Intrepid,* a vintage aircraft carrier turned into a museum, for the evening.

Fomon got up to speak briefly at the bash, to which Ritt had not been invited, and was met with a few catcalls and hisses. But they died down quickly as the former chairman, his back straight and his gaze piercing, recalled the days they had all enjoyed at E.F. Hutton & Company, the best firm on Wall Street.

# INDEX